Globalization and Human Rights, Social Justice and Political Challenges

ABOUT THE AUTHOR

Prof. Andy.Therborn, is an Ecologist and Social Justice Specialist with more than 20 years of academic and consulting experience. He holds a Ph.D in Human Rights from the Univeristy of Birmingham,UK and wrote the Ph.D and Master Academic Programs of Environmental Sciences for the Universidad de Guayana, Venezuela.

ABOUT THE BOOK

Globalization (or globalisation) describes a process by which regional economies, societies, and cultures have become integrated through a globe-spanning network of communication and trade. The term is sometimes used to refer specifically to economic globalization: the integration of national economies into the international economy through trade, foreign direct investment, capital flows, migration, and the spread of technology. Human rights are thus conceived in a universalist and egalitarian fashion. Such entitlements can exist as shared norms of actual human moralities, as justified moral norms or natural rights supported by strong reasons, or as legal rights either at a national level or within international law. However, there is no consensus as to precise nature of what in particular should or should not be regarded as a human right in any of the preceding senses, and the abstract concept of human rights has been a subject of intense philosophical debate and criticism. The ideology of human rights is one of the most powerful forces today largely at the level of rhetoric, but also as justification for action, particularly the collective interventions by the international community in oppressive states. The ideology of rights and the acceptance that the international community has the overriding responsibility for their protection has been invoked to justify limits on state sovereignty, a cornerstone of the international system. This book, which we hope will lay the foundations for the next generation of this subject.

Globalization and Human Rights, Social Justice and Political Challenges

Prof. Andy. Therborn

AMIGA PRESS. INC
Delhi -110051

AMIGA PRESS. INC
H.O :- 28-A, Indra Park, Chander Nagar
Delhi :- 110051 (India)
Tel :- 011-22504028, +91-98736-57000
Email :- info@amigapress.co.in
amigapub@gmail.com
Website :- www.amigapress@co.in

This edition is published by Amiga Press.Inc

ISBN : 978-93-87295-15-5

First Published 2019

Printed and bound in India by Replika Press Pvt. Ltd.

Preface

The effects of globalization enable us to gain fresh insights into the nature of rights. Certain kinds of rights are important for globalization property, association, independent judiciary and the rule of law. But globalization does not conceive of social and economic rights it thinks in terms of social and economic benefits as outcomes of markets, not as any kind of preconditions. It points to various weaknesses of the regime of rights: in an age of mass migrations many rights are restricted to citizens; the human rights regime provides no redress against the violation of rights by non-state institutions, despite the overwhelming power of transnational corporations to determine our life chances; and the basic framework for the protection and enforcement of rights is still the state, while the obligations to protect human rights are international. The international system is vigourous in elaborating norms, but lacks the jurisdictional basis and often the political will to enforce them. However, most states lack resources to protect human rights, especially economic and social rights. Globalization has sharpened the distinction between civil and political rights, which it needs, and economic, social and cultural rights, which threaten its dominance. Clearly, rhetoric is less powerful than material forces.

Human Rights are those minimum rights which are compulsorily obtainable by every individual as he/she is a member of human family. The concept of human rights is related to the concept of human dignity. In this way all such rights which are essential for the maintenance of human dignity can be put in the category of human rights. (2) Human Rights can be divided on the basis of their nature into two categories as (i) civil and political rights and (ii) economic and social rights. Human Rights mean to provide all the rights and dignities to human being as human viz. right to life with dignity, right to liberty, right to equality, right to social security etc. Liberalism believes in the unity of mankind, therefore, the rights of men and women are the same but because of certain situational factors it is imperative to discuss the women's human rights separately.

Arguments about social justice were shunned when the then Secretary of State for Education and Science, Kenneth Baker, proposed a radical restructuring of the school system. Introducing the Education Reform Bill at the 1987 Conservative Party Conference he declared 'the pursuit of egalitarianism is over'. The national goal was quality. The National Curriculum would deliver it 'for all our children, over all our country'. Effective opposition was contained by the language of access and entitlement but the idea of a common 'entitlement' curriculum was not new. HMI had been arguing for it since at least 1977.

Human rights advocates acknowledge that the state, the market and civil society are complex, interacting entities. In today's world, focusing on the state as the only human rights duty-bearer does not reflect the increased influence of the market and its primary actors, corporations. However, the human rights responsibilities of companies are not the same as the obligations of states. Our view is that businesses must comply with national and international law, including human rights law, and that this is best understood as a requirement to respect human rights, not to benefit from violations of human rights, and not to be complicit in human rights abuses. In fact, the Universal Declaration of Human Rights states in its opening preamble that "every organ of society" must respect human rights and secure their observance.

By introducing the dimension of an international legal obligation, the human rights perspective adds legitimacy to the demand for making poverty reduction the primary goal of policy-making. The last decade has witnessed a move towards poverty reduction as the focus of international cooperation as well as of national policy-making. The human rights perspective adds strength to this movement by drawing attention to the fact that poverty signifies non-realization of human rights so that the adoption of a poverty reduction strategy is therefore not just desirable but obligatory on the part of States that have ratified international human rights instruments.

Recognition of the principles of equality and non-discrimination, which is a central premise of the human rights approach, helps to highlight the fact that a great deal of poverty originates from discriminatory practices – both overt and covert – at the international, national and local levels. This recognition calls for the reorientation of poverty reduction strategies from a tendency to focus on narrow economic issues towards a broader strategy that also addresses socio-cultural and political-legal institutions that sustain the structures of discrimination.

This is a reference book. All the matter is just compiled and edited in nature, taken from the various sources which are in public domain.

This book, which we hope will lay the foundations for the next generation of this subject.

—Editor

Contents

1

Introduction

GLOBALIZATION AND HUMAN RIGHTS

The effects of globalization enable us to gain fresh insights into the nature of rights. Certain kinds of rights are important for globalization property, association, independent judiciary and the rule of law. But globalization does not conceive of social and economic rights it thinks in terms of social and economic benefits as outcomes of markets, not as any kind of preconditions. It points to various weaknesses of the regime of rights: in an age of mass migrations many rights are restricted to citizens; the human rights regime provides no redress against the violation of rights by non-state institutions, despite the overwhelming power of transnational corporations to determine our life chances; and the basic framework for the protection and enforcement of rights is still the state, while the obligations to protect human rights are international. The international system is vigourous in elaborating norms, but lacks the jurisdictional basis and often the political will to enforce them. However, most states lack resources to protect human rights, especially economic and social rights. Globalization has sharpened the distinction between civil and political rights, which it needs, and economic, social and cultural rights, which threaten its dominance. Clearly, rhetoric is less powerful than material forces.

PHILOSOPHY OF HUMAN RIGHTS

The philosophy of human rights attempts to examine the underlying basis of the concept of human rights and critically looks at its content and justification. Several theoretical approaches have been advanced to explain how and why the concept of human rights developed.

One of the oldest Western philosophies on human rights is that they are a product of a natural law, stemming from different philosophical or religious grounds. Other theories hold that human rights codify moral behavior which is a human social product developed by a process of biological and social evolution (associated with Hume). Human rights are also described as a sociological pattern of rule setting (as in the sociological theory of law and the work of Weber). These approaches include the notion that individuals in a society accept rules from legitimate authority in exchange for security and economic advantage (as in Rawls) – a social contract. The two theories that dominate contemporary human rights discussion are the interest theory and the will theory. Interest theory argues that the that the principal function of human rights is to protect and promote certain essential human interests, while will theory attempts to establish the validity of human rights based on the unique human capacity for freedom.

Natural Rights

Natural law theories base human rights on a "natural" moral, religious or even biological order that is independent of transitory human laws or traditions. Socrates and his philosophic heirs, Plato and Aristotle, posited the existence of natural justice or natural right (*dikaion physikon*, Latin *ius naturale*). Of these, Aristotle is often said to be the father of natural law, although evidence for this is due largely to the interpretations of his work by Thomas Aquinas.

The development of this tradition of natural justice into one of natural law is usually attributed to the Stoics. Some of the early Church Fathers sought to incorporate the until then pagan concept of natural law into Christianity. Natural law theories have featured greatly in the philosophies of Thomas Aquinas, Francisco Suárez, Richard Hooker, Thomas Hobbes, Hugo Grotius, Samuel von Pufendorf, and John Locke.

In the 17th century Thomas Hobbes founded a contractualist theory of legal positivism beginning from the principal that man in the state of nature, which is to say without a "commonwealth" (a state) is in a state of constant war one with the other and thus in fear of his life and possessions (there being no property nor right without a sovereign to define it). Hobbes asserted natural law as was how a rational human, seeking to survive and prosper, would act; the first principle of natural law being to seek peace, in which is self-preservation. Natural law (which Hobbes accepted was a misnomer, there being no law without a commonwealth) was discovered by considering humankind's natural interests, whereas previous philosophers had said that natural rights were discovered by considering the natural law. In Hobbes' opinion, the only way natural law could prevail was for men to agree to create a commonwealth by submitting to the command of a sovereign, whether a man or an assembly of men. In this lay the foundations of the theory of a social contract between the governed and the governor. Hugo Grotius based his philosophy of international law on natural law. He wrote that "even the will of an omnipotent being cannot change or abrogate" natural law, which "would maintain its objective validity even if we should assume the impossible, that there is no God or that he does not care for human affairs." (*De iure belli ac pacis*, Prolegomeni XI). This is the famous argument *etiamsi daremus* (*non esse Deum*), that made natural law no longer dependent on theology.

John Locke incorporated natural law into many of his theories and philosophy, especially in *Two Treatises of Government*. Locke turned Hobbes' prescription around, saying that if the ruler went against natural law and failed to protect "life, liberty, and property," people could justifiably overthrow the existing state and create a new one.

The Belgian philosopher of law Frank Van Dun is one among those who are elaborating a secular conception of natural law in the liberal tradition. There are also emerging and secular forms of natural law theory that define human rights as derivative of the notion of universal human dignity.

The term "human rights" has replaced the term "natural rights" in popularity, because the rights are less and less frequently seen as requiring natural law for their existence. But in actual fact, the campaigning for the legal recognition of new "human rights" (such as a right to practise a homosexual lifestyle, or euthanasia) must necessarily be based on the assumption that some kind of "Natural Law" commands the recognition of those "rights". The debate on human rights remains thus a debate around the correct interpretation of Natural Law, and human rights themselves a positive, but reductionist, expression thereof

SOCIAL CONTRACT

The English philosopher Thomas Hobbes suggested the existence of a hypothetical *social contract* where a group of free individuals agree for the sake of preservation to form institutions to govern them. They give up their natural complete liberty in exchange for protection from the Sovereign. This led to John Locke's theory that a failure of the government to secure rights is a failure which justifies the removal of the government, and was mirrored in later postulation by Jean-Jacques Rousseau in his "Du Contrat Social" (The Social Contract).

International equity expert Paul Finn has echoed this view: "the most fundamental fiduciary relationship in our society is manifestly that which exists between the community (the people) and the state, its agencies and officials."
—Paul Finn

The relationship between government and the governed in countries which follow the English law tradition is a fiduciary one. In equity law, a politician's fiduciary obligations are not only the duties of good faith and loyalty, but also include duties of skill and competence in managing a country and its people. Originating from within the Courts of Equity, the fiduciary concept exists to prevent those holding positions of power from abusing their authority. The fiduciary relationship between government and the governed arises from the governments ability to control people with the exercise of its power. In effect, if a government has the power to abolish any rights, it is equally burdened with the fiduciary duty to protect such an interest because it would benefit from the exercise of its own discretion to extinguish rights which it alone had the power to dispose of.

Reciprocity

The Golden Rule, or the *ethic of reciprocity* states that one must do unto others as one would be treated themselves; the principle being that reciprocal recognition and respect of rights ensures that one's own rights will be protected. This principle can be found in all the world's major religions in only slightly differing forms, and was enshrined in the "Declaration Toward a Global Ethic" by the Parliament of the World's Religions in 1993.

HUMAN RIGHTS, JUSTICE AND THEOLOGY

A difference between cultures marks the starting point of Jon Sobrino's analysis where he contrasts "European Theology" and "Latin American Theology." On the basic question, "Why do theology"? both "European" and "Latin American" theology would agree that theology is concerned with mediating between people's faith and their culture. The word "faith" can mean both the personal commitment of believers—the act of faith—and the beliefs to which they are committed—doctrines expressed in particular theological languages. The language in which the beliefs are expressed is, of course, related to culture. From the "European" perspective the problem is that the accepted beliefs may come under attack to such a degree that many no longer may find them credible and reject the belief system. The critical issue to be addressed is this threatened, or actual, fracturing of the belief system and consequent unbelief. The task of theology is to sustain the belief system, for example by showing that Christian beliefs, although not reducible to reason, are supremely reasonable. Further, if the belief system is discarded, it cannot provide a coherent pattern giving meaning to people's lives. Hence, theology's task includes providing such a coherent meaning for life.

For "Latin American" theology, the problem is different. In this case the basic threat is not the fracturing of meaning patterns, but the real and actual fracturing of human persons and communities by hunger, oppression and captivity. This theology has its starting point, not in the threat to meaning, but in the actual destruction brought about by the structures of the society which are condemned as "sinful." The question which theology must ask is not how this interpretation of sin can be aligned with the interpretations of sin provided by the Scriptures and Church doctrine, and thus integrated in a coherent system of meaning. Rather, the task of theology is to identify the presence of sin and to ask how to be rid of it, that is, how to contribute to changing the situation. As Sobrino expresses it, the task of theology is "... to transform this real world and at the same time recover the meaning of faith."

Ethical concern has a key place in this conception of theology. In the first place, an ethical judgment is involved in interpreting a given situation as sinful. A further ethical question is to be asked in inquiring why one does theology and what happens when theology is conducted in a particular way? If the motive for doing theology is basically to provide a coherent pattern of meaning for human persons and communities living in a certain situation, the status quo of that situation remains unchanged and, at least indirectly, justified. Theology of the "European" type would be prone to do precisely this.

Whatever view one takes as to the role of theology, it is clear that it involves a mediation between faith and interpretations of the existing cultural and historical realities. In this discussion, I propose to focus on some of the interpretations of the situation of Central America which have been presented in the preceding chapters. In particular, I will focus upon the following: distorted power relationships, distorted communication, and the corrosive attack on persons and society. As we have seen in Chapters VI and VII, literature interprets the response to this "wasteland" situation by asking how to regain one's country and oneself by processing through language what one has been suffering. The goals formulated are: to improve reality by shaping it through *justice* to liberate people from economic and political oppression. The task is that of a prophet carrying on a critique of society and of a soothsayer pointing to the future and initiating change. The criterion for a good interpretation (in literature) is the opening of possibilities for freedom, responsibility and a fuller living. A bad interpretation, in turn, is one which deadens and diminishes these possibilities.

There is a moral element in these proposals which theology must seek to grasp and interpret within its own perspective. For example, it should focus on distorted power relationships and formulate goals in terms of justice and/ or liberation, taking as criteria the possibilities for more complete freedom and richer living revealed in the Christian message. Specifically, in its moral perspective, theology would focus upon violence in its structural and actual forms, the abuse of human rights, the deaths, and the external ideological, economic and military pressures which threaten to destroy effective resolution of the problems. Given these realities, how are we to go about formulating a theological response?

CIVIL RIGHTS MOVEMENT

When civil and political rights are not guaranteed to all as part of equal protection of laws, or when such guarantees exist on paper but are not respected in practice, opposition and even social unrest may ensue. The civil rights movement was a worldwide political movement for equality before the law occurring between approximately 1950 and 1980. The movement had a legal and constitutional aspect, and resulting in much law-making at both national and international levels. It also had an activist side, particularly in situations where violations of rights were widespread. Movements with the proclaimed aim of securing observance of civil and political rights included:

- the US civil rights struggle in the 1960s in the southern United States, where rights of black citizens had been violated;
- the Northern Ireland Civil Rights Association, formed in 1967 following failures in this province of the United Kingdom to respect the Catholic minority's rights; and
- movements in many Communist countries, such as Charter 77 in Czechoslovakia.

Most civil rights movements relied on the technique of civil resistance, using nonviolent methods of struggle, to achieve their aims. In some countries, struggles for civil rights were accompanied, or followed, by civil unrest and even armed rebellion. While civil rights movements over the last 60 years have resulted in an extension of civil and political rights, the process was long and tenuous in many countries, and many of these movements did not achieve or fully achieve their objectives.

Problems and Analysis

Questions about civil and political rights have frequently emerged. For example, to what extent should the government intervene to protect individuals from infringement on their rights by other individuals, or from corporations — e.g., in what way should employment discrimination in the private sector be dealt with?

Political theory deals with civil and political rights. Robert Nozick and John Rawls expressed competing visions in Nozick's *Anarchy, State, and Utopia* and Rawls' *A Theory of Justice*. Other influential authors in the area include Wesley Newcomb Hohfeld and Jean Edward Smith.

CIVIL AND POLITICAL RIGHTS

Civil and political rights are a class of rights that protect individuals' freedom from unwarranted infringement by governments and private organizations, and ensure one's ability to participate in the civil and political life of the state without discrimination or repression. Civil rights include the ensuring of peoples' physical integrity and safety; protection from discrimination on grounds such as physical or mental disability, gender, religion, race, national origin, age, sexual orientation, or gender identity; and individual rights such as the freedoms of thought and conscience, speech and expression, religion, the press, and movement.

Political rights include natural justice (procedural fairness) in law, such as the rights of the accused, including the right to a fair trial; due process; the right to seek redress or a legal remedy; and rights of participation in civil society and politics such as freedom of association, the right to assemble, the right to petition, and the right to vote. Civil and political rights form the original and main part of international human rights. They comprise the first portion of the 1948 Universal Declaration of Human Rights (with economic, social and cultural rights comprising the second portion). The theory of three generations of human rights considers this group of rights to be "first-generation rights", and the theory of negative and positive rights considers them to be generally negative rights.

The phrase "civil rights" is a translation of Latin *ius civis* (rights of citizens). Roman citizens could be either free (*libertas*) or servile (*servitus*), but they all had rights in law. After the Edict of the Milan in 313, these rights included the freedom of religion. Roman legal doctrine was lost during the Middle Ages, but claims of universal rights could still be made based on religious doctrine. According to the leaders of Kett's Rebellion (1549), "all bond men may be made free, for God made all free with his precious blood-shedding."

In the 17th century, English common law judge Sir Edward Coke revived the idea of rights based on citizenship by arguing that Englishman had historically enjoyed such rights The English Bill of Rights was adopted in 1689. The Virginia Declaration of Rights, by George Mason and James Madison, was adopted in 1776. The Virginia declaration is the direct ancestor and model for the U.S. Bill of Rights (1789). In early 19th century Britain, the phrase "civil rights" most commonly referred to the problem of legal discrimination against Catholics. In the House of Commons support for the British civil rights movement was divided, many more largely known politicians supported the discrimination towards Catholics. Independent MPs (such as Lewis Eves and Matthew Mountford) applied pressure on the larger parties to pass the civil rights act of the 1920s. In the 1860s, Americans adapted this usage to newly freed blacks. Congress enacted civil rights acts in 1866, 1871, 1875, 1957, 1960, 1964, 1968, and 1991.

GUARANTEES OF RIGHTS

T.H. Marshall Notes that civil rights were among the first to be recognized and codified, followed later by political rights and still later by social rights. In many countries, they are constitutional rights and are included in a bill of rights or similar document. They are also defined in international human rights instruments, such as the 1948 Universal Declaration of Human Rights and the 1966 International Covenant on Civil and Political Rights. Civil and political rights need not be codified to be protected, although most democracies worldwide do have formal written guarantees of civil and political rights. Civil rights are often considered to be natural rights. Thomas Jefferson wrote in his 1774 *A Summary View of the Rights of British America* that "a free people [claim] their rights as derived from the laws of nature, and not as the gift of their chief magistrate."

Custom also plays a role. Implied or unenumerated rights are rights that courts may find to exist even though not expressly guaranteed by written law or custom; one example is the right to privacy in the United States. The question of to whom civil and political rights apply is a subject of controversy. In many countries, citizens have greater protections against infringement of rights than non-citizens; at the same time, civil and political rights are considered to be universal rights that apply to all persons.

SOCIAL JUSTICE: ECONOMIC, SOCIAL AND CULTURAL RIGHTS

The Legal Foundations

In adopting the framework of human rights, the Copenhagen Declaration, in conformity with United Nations orthodoxy, places equal importance on all human rights. But realistically, it is economic and social rights that are essential to the Copenhagen agenda. Civil and political rights are undoubtedly important in organizing demands for greater equity, and in themselves for facilitating an open and accountable society.

But the evidence that these rights also lead to economic and social development is not conclusive. So economic and social rights that directly provide housing, food, education and clothing are crucial. Unfortunately, economic and social rights are so far the Cinderella of rights; they are attacked, conceptually, for lacking the qualifications to be called rights, as the beneficiaries and providers are not easily identified, and even when identified the legal process cannot enforce rights.

They are also attacked politically, as increasing state power, and interfering with the autonomy, and assets, of individuals. Thus in so far as economic and social rights are central to the achievement of the Copenhagen agenda, considerable research and lobbying will be necessary to transform these rights into clear and enforceable targets and standards. This will require some intellectual ingenuity and political will, but that it can be done is clear from countries, such as Sri Lanka, that have been able to provide many of these rights despite a relatively poor economy.

The United Nations Charter committed its members to promote higher standards of living, full employment, and conditions of economic and social progress and development and solutions of international economic, social, health and related problems, and international cultural and educational cooperation.

The Universal Declaration of Human Rights contains a number of economic, social and cultural rights: the right to social security, and economic, social and cultural rights indispensable for the individual's dignity and the free development of the individual's personality; the right to work, free choice of employment, just and favourable conditions of work and protection against unemployment, including the right to join trade unions; the right to rest and leisure; the right to a standard of living adequate for family health and well-being, including food, clothing, housing, medical care and necessary social services; the right to education; and the right to participate in the cultural life of the community, to enjoy the arts and to share in scientific advancement and its benefits.

These rights formed the core of the ICESCR, but the formulation is too broad to provide sufficient guidance on implementation and the machinery for implementation and supervision is much weaker than for the ICCPR, typified by the omission of any complaints procedure. These rights also find their way into conventions for the protection of women, children, indigenous peoples and migrant workers, and form one of the core components of the Declaration on the Right to Development in the following expression:

- States should undertake, at the national level, all necessary measures for the realization of the right to development and shall ensure, inter alia, equality of opportunity for all in their access to basic resources, education, health services, food, housing, employment and the fair

> distribution of income. Effective measures should be undertaken to ensure that women have an active role in the development process. Appropriate economic and social reforms shall be carried out with a view to eradicating all social injustices.

Several national constitutions require or urge the state to provide similar services, although for the most part they are mandatory only for disadvantaged groups. India and South Africa are two outstanding examples, where the obligations on the state are based on the moral and political recognition of past injustices to particular ethnic or social groups. The recent Fiji Constitution imposes a legal obligation on the government to institute schemes for preferential policies for poorer communities and groups. Several other countries such as Australia, Canada, Malaysia and the United States, as well as Northern Ireland, also have preferential policies. However, these policies have not always helped the really disadvantaged the resources having been appropriated by the better-off in the various communities, and used for political and patronage purposes. In any case, the resources allocated for these policies are too limited to make a major impact on poverty.

The Record

These provisions have not been used to provide assistance for economic, social and cultural rights in the post-Cold War era in the way political rights in the ICCPR were seized on to promote democracy. A 1998 UNDP report notes that fifty years after the adoption of the Universal Declaration of Human Rights, one third of the developing world's people are enslaved by a poverty so complete that it denies them fundamental human rights... Nearly 12 million children die each year before their fifth birthday. More than 800 million people go hungry.. It also notes that 30 per cent of all children under five are malnourished and that 38 per cent of all adult women are illiterate. Another report observes that nearly 100 million people are homeless, and the number of those without adequate housing exceeds one billion.

It is often claimed that economic, social and cultural rights are different from other rights in that they are not justiciable and cannot be enforced in courts. State obligations under the ICESCR or national constitutions are not enforceable rights of the people. Moreover, because the ICESCR commits member states to take steps, individually and through international assistance and cooperation, especially economic and technical, to the maximum of its available resources, with a view to achieving progressively the full realization of the rights recognised in the present Covenant by all appropriate means, some national courts have taken the view that the Covenant is not directly applicable in their states but requires national legislation. However, the United

Nations Committee on Economic, Social and Cultural Rights has declared that at least some rights in the Covenant were intended for and are capable of immediate and direct application.

Most arguments advanced about the difficulties of making social and economic rights enforceable are not persuasive, nor is it productive to think of rights only in terms of judicial enforcement. It is more valuable to focus on the obligations of states; as has been pointed out, a state's obligation in relation to all categories of rights may be seen as involving different types of obligations that can be fulfilled variously by positive action, by refraining from acting, or by creating an environment in which rights can be achieved. There is no reason why the beneficiaries of these rights should not be involved in the planning and implementing of programmes for achieving the rights, or why their access to the appropriate institutions responsible for implementing rights should not be guaranteed.

The fact is that the non-enforceability of economic and social rights springs from the low regard in which these rights are held by dominant national and international groups. Philip Alston has pointed to the low priority given to these rights and the limited resources devoted to their implementation. He says that denials of the most fundamental economic and social rights continue on a massive scale that affects hundreds of millions of people and offers various explanations for the neglect of economic, social and cultural rights:

- Preeminent among them was the impact of the Cold War and of the ideological struggles between communism and capitalism. This factor changed what was a rational and balanced debate between 1944 and 1947 into a struggle that encouraged the taking of extreme positions and prevented objective consideration of the key issues raised by the concept of economic and social rights.

Another reason is that the implementation of these rights requires skills and expertise that are alien to what has been termed the normative-judicial model of human rights implementation. The result is that the human rights lawyers, the diplomatic representatives, the secretariat officials and the NGO representatives who have come to dominate human rights discussions will feel distinctively ill at ease and ill-equipped to deal with many of the most pressing issues arising from a concern wiTheconomic, social and cultural rights. Finally, the proposition that minimum core economic and social rights ought to be accorded to every individual is still automatically made subject by decision makers to an economic calculus that will often culminate in various economically compelling reasons as to why such rights simply cannot be recognised. Little attempt has been made to establish criteria for measuring the success of the progressive implementation of these rights.

However, in recent years increasing attention has been paid to economic and social rights as a result of a series of world conferences such as those on women, children and social development. The 1973 Human Rights Conference endorsed the right to development. The current United Nations Secretary-General, KofiAnnan, has tried to make human rights a core concern of the United Nations and its agencies, which has stimulated thinking about the means of mainstreaming human rights into development.

The High Commissioner for Human Rights has entered into agreements with UNDP and other agencies to promote human rights in their work. The World Food Summit of 1996, convened by the Food and Agriculture Organization of the United Nations, noted the appealingly low standards of nutrition of millions of people, particularly children and women, and the terrible consequences of malnutrition and hunger, observing that the problem was not so much the lack of food as the access to it. The governments of the world pledged themselves to achieving food security for all and as an immediate objective to reducing the number of undernourished people to half the 1996 level by 2015. The OECD has a commitment, together with member states, to reduce the level of poverty by half by 2015.

HUMAN RIGHTS – THE MODERN INVENTION

The term "*human rights*" is a relatively modern invention.

It covers under its umbrella three different types of rights:

1. The fundamental freedoms or classical civil liberties,
2. Ethnic and religious rights
3. Socio-economic rights.

Some constitutions have enumerated the first or the first and the second and attempted to set up judicial enforcement of such rights. The third category has not been stated in a constitution in an enforceable form, but some constitutions refer to them as directive principles of state policy.

The more important rights may be said to include the right of each individual to:

- Freedom of speech and expression,
- Freedom from arrest or detention except under authority of law,
- Freedom from cruel, inhumane or degrading punishments and the right to a fair trial by a competent and independent court,
- Freedom to enjoy lawfully acquired property,
- Equality of persons before the law,
- Freedom of assembly and association (including public meeting and withdrawal of labour),
- Freedom of thought, conscience and religion,

- Freedom to contract,
- freedom to engage in a trade, profession or occupation,
- Freedom of movement within a nation and across national borders.

The idea of these rights has arisen in multi-linguistic, multi-cultural, multi-racial and multi-religious populations. The notion of equality before the law and equal protection of the law underlies the rights and is generally included in constitutions which have bills of rights, though in a particular situation it may be available in conjunction with some other right. The idea of equality before the law implies that persons or groups must not be discriminated against without justification. The words *"without justification"* are relevant. Discrimination is both inevitable and proper in human affairs because of the differences between human beings, accidents (both natural and man induced) and many factors which affect the nurture and development of individuals. These by their nature are not justiciable in the courts.

Alleged duties of the states

In this category are alleged duties of the state: to secure full employment for all people of working age, to provide adequate standards of living and education to all citizens, to rapidly develop the country, to distribute the social product equitably, to eliminate economic and social privilege and disparity, to ensure social security and welfare, to develop the culture and languages of ethnic groups, to protect the environment, to safeguard the independence, sovereignty, unity and territorial integrity of the, country and to promote international peace and co-operation.

Past History of Human rights in Different Countries

The analysis refers to three types of rights:

1. The traditional rights primarily involving protection of individuals from government,
2. Ethnic and religious rights and
3. Social welfare rights.

It is important to distinguish between the different historical and conceptual bases of these three categories of rights which are loosely termed *"human rights"*. Such differences between them are often blurred or ignored, with serious consequences for the operation of fundamental freedoms.

Since the second world war, there has been a great emphasis on human rights other than the classical civil liberties: on socio-economic rights, and on the rights of groups or classes or nations. The recognition that the promotion of socio-economic rights, as rights to benefit from the state, stand in great tension with civil liberties may be often deliberately obscured, but it is nevertheless widespread and it is, of course, a correct recognition. The traditional civil liberties, many have correctly recognised, require institutional settings, historical traditions, a sense of community.

The socio-economic rights can, in principle, be granted by the state, even by a state which suppresses all non-state organisations and institutions. Very different kinds of societies may be involved.... The attempt to elevate human rights, in any particular formulation, uncritically, as urgent, unhistorical, abstract demands is not only based on intellectual error but is like most propaganda and moral indoctrination inherently unstable and unable to cope with genuine criticism.

Human rights can only be understood, and therefore must be taught, in the concrete contexts in which they arise and have to be implemented. This is the social context of concrete history and real politics.

There is also, in an important sense, a concrete human context. This is best portrayed by world literature, or at least by the great literature of the world, and not by shallow declarations and proclamations. The third category commonly included within the term *"human rights"*, namely *"socio-economic rights"*, raises basic questions regarding the meaning and operation of human rights.

The recognition of this category as rights has created certain contradictions within the concept, leading to the weakening of civil liberties. The consequences of such recognition and the conflict that arises between civil liberties and socio-economic *"rights"* creates many problems.

There are human needs. Yet where a need exists, however compelling, a right cannot be said to automatically spring into existence.

Restrictions on Rights

In countries which have bills of rights there is a basic statement of freedoms subject to permitted abridgment of such freedoms. Freedoms are restricted in the public interest on grounds of national security, to preserve public order, to protect public health, to maintain moral standards, to secure due recognition and respect for the rights and freedoms of others or to meet the just requirements of the general welfare of a democratic society. The United States Supreme Court has over the years qualified the rights in the constitution. Any statement of rights is not absolute and must of necessity be subject to limitations on the Above lines. The right of free speech and expression does not extend to sedition, slander, defamation and obscenity.

The principle of equality before the law cannot deny a legislature the power to classify persons for legislative purposes and to legislate affecting them, provided that the classification is not arbitrary and is based on a real and substantial distinction bearing a reasonable and just relation to the objects sought to be achieved.

Thus the legislature could enact legislation regulating the activities of money lenders. This would amount to a singling out of money lenders and would be prima facie in conflict with the principle of equality before the law.

But provided the classification is reasonable and there is a legitimate object to be achieved the legislation would nonetheless be valid. The instances of legitimate restrictions of rights. They are intended to illustrate that no right available to an individual or group is or can be absolute. This seems obvious but is often not appreciated.

The Clash of Rights

The reality that human rights are not absolute, and are subject to reasonable restrictions, does not mean that the rights can be arbitrarily curtailed just as to legislative or bureaucratic discretion. The manner in which restrictions are to be determined and imposed and the criteria which apply to the formulation of restrictions are crucial. If human rights are to be meaningful they cannot be subject to crude majoritarian dictates.

What distinguishes a human right from any other right is that a human right is available to and enforceable by a minority, however small, even against the wishes of a majority. If human rights were to become subject to ordinary parliamentary control they would be no different from any other statutory right which parliament is free to confer and withdraw at its pleasure. The restriction of human rights is therefore a crucial and delicate question. They cannot be based on ideological perceptions of parliamentarians, bureaucrats or the Human Rights Commission but must be grounded on objectively ascertained and comprehended criteria.

The *National Times*, week ending 25 August, 1979, referred to "*the right to march demonstrations*" and by way of example: "*Senator George Georges was gaoled yet again for upholding the principle of the right to democratic protest in Brisbane streets*". What are these rights? There is no absolute right to democratic protest or to march.

There are rights of speech and expression and assembly. But these rights are subject to limitations. The right to freedom of association must be exercised so as not to interfere with the rights of others to move about the streets or go about their business. Where there is a clash of rights, methods must be devised through rational analysis, political avenues and the courts so that the rights of all parties could be exercised so as not to inconvenience each other. If this is not possible (as it often is not) there must be a compromise or one must be restricted and give way to the other.

The clash of rights is a factor which the United States courts and citizens are very familiar with. An example of a conflict of rights is where the right of free expression of the press to coverage of news stories may clash with the right of an accused in a criminal case not to be prejudiced by adverse publicity of allegations made against him prior to trial or in a pre-trial hearing. American journalists generally would not show such an obvious lack of understanding of the basic principles underlying fundamental rights as is demonstrated by the quotation. The is just one of numerous examples in contemporary Australia where so called rights are claimed without reference to conflicting rights and basic common sense.

Exaltation of Particular Rights

One of the real problems in the human rights arena today is the failure by the Human Rights Commission and many who profess to be concerned about human rights to appreciate that human rights are complementary to each other. The pursuit of one particular right without regard to others is self defeating and destructive of the overall framework of rights which is essential to the operation of specific rights.

Human rights activists overlook this dimension. Some rights such as the right to equality of persons before the law, freedom of speech and freedom of person and property are more important than other rights. If one right must prevail over another a rational basis must be provided. This involves an examination of the two rights, an evaluation of the importance of each and the context within which they operate.

THE INTERNATIONAL COVENANT ON CIVIL AND POLITICAL RIGHTS

The International Covenant on Civil and Political Rights addresses the State's traditional responsibilities for administering justice and maintaining the rule of law. Many of the provisions in the Covenant address the relationship between the individual and the State. In discharging these responsibilities, States must ensure that human rights are respected, not only those of the victim but also those of the accused. The civil and political rights defined in the Covenant include, inter alia, the right to self-determination; the right to life, liberty and security; freedom of movement, including freedom to choose a place of residence and the right to leave the country; freedom of thought, conscience, religion, peaceful assembly and association; freedom from torture and other cruel and degrading treatment or punishment; freedom from slavery, forced labour, and arbitrary arrest or detention; the right to a fair and prompt trial; and the right to privacy.

There are also other provisions which protect members of ethnic, religious or linguistic minorities. Under Article 2, all States Parties undertake to respect and take the necessary steps to ensure the rights recognized in the Covenant without distinction of any kind, such as race, colour, sex, language, religion, political or other opinion, national or social origin, property, birth or other status. The Covenant has two Optional Protocols. The first establishes the procedure for dealing with communications (or complaints) from individuals claiming to be victims of violations of any of the rights set out in the Covenant. The second envisages the abolition of the death penalty.

Unlike the Universal Declaration and the Covenant on Economic, Social and Cultural Rights, the Covenant on Civil and Political Rights authorizes a State to derogate from, or in other words restrict, the enjoyment of certain rights in times of an official public emergency which threatens the life of a nation. Such limitations are permitted only to the extent strictly required under the circumstances and must be reported to the United Nations. Even so, some provisions such as the right to life and freedom from torture and slavery may never e suspended.

The Covenant provides for the establishment of a Human Rights Committee to monitor implementation of the Covenant's provisions by States parties. As at March 2000, 144 States were parties to the Covenant, 95 States were parties to the Optional Protocol and 39 States were parties to the Second Optional Protocol.

International Convention on the Elimination of all Forms of Racial Discrimination

The phenomenon of racial discrimination was one of the concerns behind the establishment of the United Nations and has therefore been one of its major areas of attention. The International Convention on the Elimination of All Forms of Racial Discrimination was adopted by the General Assembly in 1965 and entered into force in 1969. Article 1 of the Convention defines the terms.racial discrimination. as: any distinction, exclusion, restriction or preference based on race, colour, descent, national or ethnic origin with the purpose or effect of nullifying or impairing the recognition, enjoyment or exercise, on an equal footing, of human rights in any field of public life, including political, economic, social or cultural life"

It is notable that this definition encompasses a much wider range of grounds on which discrimination can take place than that commonly referred to as "race". It is also significant that the definition includes the language "purpose or effect.. As a consequence, the definition covers not only intentional discrimination, but also laws, norms and practices which appear neutral, but result in discrimination in their impact Parties to the Convention agree to eliminate discrimination in the enjoyment of civil, political, economic, social and cultural rights and to provide effective remedies against any acts of racial discrimination through national tribunals and State institutions.

States parties undertake not to engage in acts or practices of racial discrimination against individuals, groups of persons or institutions and to ensure that public authorities and institutions do likewise; not to sponsor, defend or support racial discrimination by persons or organizations; to review government, national and local policies and to amend or repeal laws and regulations which create or perpetuate racial discrimination; to prohibit and put a stop to racial discrimination by persons, groups and organizations; and to encourage integration or multiracial organizations, movements and other means of eliminating barriers between races, as well as to discourage anything which tends to strengthen racial divisiveness. The Committee on the Elimination of Racial Discrimination was established by the Convention to ensure that States parties ful fil their obligations. As at March 2000, 155 States were parties to the Convention.

2

Globalization

Globalization (or globalisation) describes a process by which regional economies, societies, and cultures have become integrated through a globe-spanning network of communication and trade. The term is sometimes used to refer specifically to economic globalization: the integration of national economies into the international economy through trade, foreign direct investment, capital flows, migration, and the spread of technology. However, globalization is usually recognized as being driven by a combination of economic, technological, sociocultural, political, and biological factors. The term can also refer to the transnational circulation of ideas, languages, or popular culture through acculturation.

DEFINITIONS

An early description of globalization was penned by the American entrepreneur-turned-minister Charles Taze Russell who coined the term 'corporate giants' in 1897, although it was not until the 1960s that the term began to be widely used by economists and other social scientists. The term has since then achieved widespread use in the mainstream press by the later half of the 1980s. Since its inception, the concept of globalization has inspired numerous competing definitions and interpretations..

The United Nations ESCWA has written that globalization "is a widely-used term that can be defined in a number of different ways. When used in an economic context, it refers to the reduction and removal of barriers between national borders in order to facilitate the flow of goods, capital, services and labour... although considerable barriers remain to the flow of labour... Globalization is not a new phenomenon. It began in the late nineteenth century, but it slowed down during the period from the start of the First World War until the third quarter of the twentieth century. This slowdown can be attributed to the inward-looking policies pursued by a number of countries in order to protect their respective industries... however, the pace of globalization picked up rapidly during the fourth quarter of the twentieth century..."

Saskia Sassen writes that "a good part of globalization consists of an enormous variety of micro-processes that begin to denationalize what had been constructed as national — whether policies, capital, political subjectivity, urban spaces, temporal frames, or any other of a variety of dynamics and domains."

Tom J. Palmer of the Cato Institute defines globalization as "the diminution or elimination of state-enforced restrictions on exchanges across borders and the increasingly integrated and complex global system of production and exchange that has emerged as a result."

Thomas L. Friedman has examined the impact of the "flattening" of the world, and argues that globalized trade, outsourcing, supply-chaining, and political forces have changed the world permanently, for both better and worse. He also argues that the pace of globalization is quickening and will continue to have a growing impact on business organization and practice.

Noam Chomsky argues that the word globalization is also used, in a doctrinal sense, to describe the neoliberal form of economic globalization.

Herman E. Daly argues that sometimes the terms internationalization and globalization are used interchangeably but there is a significant formal difference. The term "internationalization" (or internationalisation) refers to the importance of international trade, relations, treaties etc. owing to the (hypothetical) immobility of labour and capital between or among nations.

Finally, Takis Fotopoulos argues that globalization is the result of systemic trends manifesting the market economy's grow-or-die dynamic, following the rapid expansion of transnational corporations. Because these trends have not been offset effectively by counter-tendencies that could have emanated from trade-union action and other forms of political activity, the outcome has been globalisation. This is a multi-faceted and irreversible phenomenon within the system of the market economy and it is expressed as: economic globalisation, namely, the opening and deregulation of commodity, capital and labour markets which led to the present form of neoliberal globalisation; political globalisation, i.e., the emergence of a transnational elite and the phasing out of the all powerful-nation state of the statist period; cultural globalisation, i.e., the worldwide homogenisation of culture; ideological globalisation; technological globalisation; social globalisation.

GLOBALIZATION AND ITS MEANING

Broadly speaking, the term 'globalization' means integration of economies and societies through cross country flows of information, ideas, technologies, goods, services, capital, finance and people. Cross border integration can have several dimensions – cultural, social, political and economic. In fact, some people fear cultural and social integration even more than economic integration. The fear of "cultural hegemony" haunts many. Limiting ourselves to economic integration, one can see this happen through the three channels of (a) trade in goods and services, (b) movement of capital and (c) flow of finance. Besides, there is also the channel through movement of people.

Historical Development

Globalization has been a historical process with ebbs and flows. During the Pre-World War I period of 1870 to 1914, there was rapid integration of the economies in terms of trade flows, movement of capital and migration of people. The growth of globalization was mainly led by the technological forces in the fields of transport and communication. There were less barriers to flow of trade and people across the geographical boundaries. Indeed there were no passports and visa requirements and very few non-tariff barriers and restrictions on fund flows. The pace of globalization, however, decelerated between the First and the Second World War.

The inter-war period witnessed the erection of various barriers to restrict free movement of goods and services. Most economies thought that they could thrive better under high protective walls. After World War II, all the leading countries resolved not to repeat the mistakes they had committed previously by opting for isolation. Although after 1945, there was a drive to increased integration, it took a long time to reach the Pre-World War I level.

In terms of percentage of exports and imports to total output, the US could reach the pre-World War level of 11 per cent only around 1970. Most of the developing countries which gained Independence from the colonial rule in the immediate Post-World War II period followed an import substitution industrialization regime.

The Soviet bloc countries were also shielded from the process of global economic integration. However, times have changed. In the last two decades, the process of globalization has proceeded with greater vigour. The former Soviet bloc countries are getting integrated with the global economy. More and more developing countries are turning towards outward oriented policy of growth. Yet, studies point out that trade and capital markets are no more globalized today than they were at the end of the 19th century. Nevertheless, there are more concerns about globalization now than before because of the nature and speed of transformation. What is striking in the current episode is not only the rapid pace but also the enormous impact of new information technologies on market integration, efficiency and industrial organization.

Globalization of financial markets has far outpaced the integration of product markets.

Gains from Globalization

The gains from globalization can be analyzed in the context of the three types of channels of economic globalization identified earlier.

Trade in Goods and Services

According to the standard theory, international trade leads to allocation of resources that is consistent with comparative advantage. This results in specialization which enhances productivity. It is accepted that international trade, in general, is beneficial and that restrictive trade practices impede growth. That is the reason why many of the emerging economies, which originally depended on a growth model of import substitution, have moved over to a policy of outward orientation.

However, in relation to trade in goods and services, there is one major concern. Emerging economies will reap the benefits of international trade only if they reach the full potential of their resource availability. This will probably require time. That is why international trade agreements make exceptions by allowing longer time to developing economies in terms of reduction in tariff and non-tariff barriers. "Special and differentiated treatment", as it is very often called has become an accepted principle.

Movement of Capital

Capital flows across countries have played an important role in enhancing the production base. This was very much true in 19th and 20th centuries. Capital mobility enables the total savings of the world to be distributed among countries which have the highest investment potential. Under these circumstances, one country's growth is not constrained by its own domestic savings. The inflow of foreign capital has played a significant role in the development in the recent period of the East Asian countries.

The current account deficit of some of these countries had exceeded 5 per cent of the GDP in most of the period when growth was rapid. Capital flows can take either the form of foreign direct investment or portfolio investment. For developing countries the preferred alternative is foreign direct investment. Portfolio investment does not directly lead to expansion of productive capacity. It may do so, however, at one step removed. Portfolio investment can be volatile particularly in times of loss of confidence. That is why countries want to put restrictions on portfolio investment. However, in an open system such restrictions cannot work easily.

Financial Flows

The rapid development of the capital market has been one of the important features of the current process of globalization. While the growth in capital and foreign exchange markets have facilitated the transfer of resources across borders, the gross turnover in foreign exchange markets has been extremely large. It is estimated that the gross turnover is around $ 1.5 trillion per day worldwide (Frankel, 2000). This is of the order of hundred times greater than the volume of trade in goods and services. Currency trade has become an end in itself. The expansion in foreign exchange markets and capital markets is a necessary pre-requisite for international transfer of capital. However, the volatility in the foreign exchange market and the ease with which funds can be withdrawn from countries have created often times panic situations. The most recent example of this was the East Asian crisis. Contagion of financial crises is a worrying phenomenon. When one country faces a crisis, it affects others. It is not as if financial crises are solely caused by foreign exchange traders. What the financial markets tend to do is to exaggerate weaknesses. Herd instinct is not uncommon in financial markets. When an economy becomes more open to capital and financial flows, there is even greater compulsion to ensure that factors relating to macro-economic stability are not ignored. This is a lesson all developing countries have to learn from East Asian crisis. As one commentator aptly said "The trigger was sentiment, but vulnerability was due to fundamentals".

Concerns and Fears

On the impact of globalization, there are two major concerns. These may be described as even fears. Under each major concern there are many related anxieties. The first major concern is that globalization leads to a more iniquitous distribution of income among countries and within countries. The second fear is that globalization leads to loss of national sovereignty and that countries are finding it increasingly difficult to follow independent domestic policies. These two issues have to be addressed both theoretically and empirically. The argument that globalization leads to inequality is based on the premise that since globalization emphasizes efficiency, gains will accrue to countries which are favourably endowed with natural and human resources. Advanced countries have had a head start over the other countries by at least three centuries. The technological base of these countries is not only wide but highly sophisticated. While trade benefits all countries, greater gains accrue to the industrially advanced countries. This is the reason why even in the present trade agreements, a case has been built up for special and differential treatment in relation to developing countries. By and large, this treatment provides for longer transition periods in relation to adjustment. However, there are two changes with respect to international trade which may work to the advantage of the developing countries. First, for a variety of reasons, the industrially advanced countries are vacating certain areas of production. These can be filled in by developing countries. A good example of this is what the East Asian countries did in the 1970s and 1980s. Second, international trade is no longer determined by the distribution of natural resources. With the advent of information technology, the role of human resources has emerged as more important. Specialized human skills will become the determining factor in the coming decades. Productive activities are becoming "knowledge intensive" rather than "resource intensive". While there is a divide between developing and the advanced countries even in this area – some people call it the digital divide-it is a gap which can be bridged. A globalized economy with increased specialization can lead to improved productivity and faster growth. What will be required is a balancing mechanism to ensure that the handicaps of the developing countries are overcome.

Apart from the possible iniquitous distribution of income among countries, it has also been argued that globalization leads to widening income gaps within the countries as well. This can happen both in the developed and developing economies. The argument is the same as was advanced in relation to iniquitous distribution among countries. Globalization may benefit even within a country those who have the skills and the technology. The higher growth rate achieved by an economy can be at the expense of declining incomes of people who may be rendered redundant. In this context, it has to be noted that while globalization may accelerate the process of technology substitution in developing economies, these countries even without globalization will face the problem associated with moving from lower to higher technology. If the growth rate of the economy accelerates sufficiently, then part of the resources can be diverted by the state to modernize and re-equip people who may be affected by the process of technology up gradation.

The second concern relates to the loss of autonomy in the pursuit of economic policies. In a highly integrated world economy, it is true that one country cannot pursue policies which are not in consonance with the worldwide trends. Capital and technology are fluid and they will move where the benefits are greater. As the nations come together whether it be in the political, social or economic arena, some sacrifice of sovereignty is inevitable. The constraints of a globalised economic system on the pursuit of domestic policies have to be recognised. However, it need not result in the abdication of domestic objectives.

Another fear associated with globalization is insecurity and volatility. When countries are inter-related strongly, a small spark can start a large conflagration. Panic and fear spread fast. The downside to globalization essentially emphasizes the need to create countervailing forces in the form of institutions and policies at the international level. Global governance cannot be pushed to the periphery, as integration gathers speed.

Empirical evidence on the impact of globalization on inequality is not very clear. The share in aggregate world exports and in world output of the developing countries has been increasing. In aggregate world exports, the share of developing countries increased from 20.6 per cent in 1988-90 to 29.9 per cent in 2000. Similarly the share in aggregate world output of developing countries has increased from 17.9 per cent in 1988-90 to 40.4 per cent in 2000.

The growth rate of the developing countries both in terms of GDP and per capita GDP has been higher than those of the industrial countries. These growth rates have been in fact higher in the 1990s than in the 1980s. All these data do not indicate that the developing countries as a group have suffered in the process of globalization. In fact, there have been substantial gains.

But within developing countries, Africa has not done well and some of the South Asian countries have done better only in the 1990s. While the growth rate in per capita income of the developing countries in the 1990s is nearly two times higher than that of industrialized countries, in absolute terms the gap in per capita income has widened. As for income distribution within the countries, it is difficult to judge whether globalization is the primary factor responsible for any deterioration in the distribution of income. We have had considerable controversies in our country on what happened to the poverty ratio in the second half of 1990s. Most analysts even for India would agree that the poverty ratio has declined in the 1990s. Differences may exist as to what rate at which this has fallen. Nevertheless, whether it is in India or any other country, it is very difficult to trace the changes in the distribution of income within the countries directly to globalization.

GLOBALIZATION AND DECENTRALIZATION IN INDIA

The surprising policy reversal of 1981 was one of the earliest manifestations of the impact of globalization on India's economic policy. India's balance of payments position deteriorated after the second oil shock. At the same time, India's worst drought since independence sliced agricultural production by 15 percent and contributed to high inflation ? 17 percent in 1979-80 and 18 percent in 1980-81 ? and growing fiscal deficits — 8.1 percent of GDP in 1980-81. In contrast, to previous economic crises when India responded with import controls and fiscal conservatism, India responded to its problems of 1979-81 with a strategy of ?expansionary adjustment? which included increased investment in domestic oil production and infrastructure along with incentives to increase exports. The considerable growth in foreign remittances, that in large measure came from Indian workers in the Middle East following the hikes in oil prices demonstrated that the international economy could be a source of valuable capital. India's expansionary adjustment also depended on a $5.8 billion loan from the IMF.

As the 1980's progressed, the government increasingly took advantage of India's high credit rating to borrow from private commercial sources. Long-term debt to private creditors rose from $1.7 billion in 1980 to $22.8 billion in 1990. Short-term debt rose $1.3 billion to $8.5 billion. India's total debt jumped from $21 billion to $84 billion in 1990, later peaking at $103 billion in 1994 The Indian government's resort to foreign finance during the 1980s, not only funded its current account deficits, but facilitated unprecedented fiscal deficits. Central government deficits grew from an average of 4.9 percent of GDP for the last five years of the 1970s to an average of 8.6 percent of GDP for the last half of the 1980s.

India's resort to foreign borrowing should be understood in the context of the evolution of its political competition. Since 1967, Indian politics at both the national and state levels have become increasingly competitive. By the 1980's, the Congress had developed into an office-seeking party that attracted most of its supporters by dispensing government largesse. During the 1960's, subsidies accounted for less than ten percent of central government expenditures. Subsidies increased to almost a fourth (24.1 percent) of all government expenditures by 1989. In the 1980's, Congress leaders also turned to foreign investors and contractors for illicit contributions to fill the party coffers. India's opening to foreign credit and capital was in no small measure driven by the Congress party leaders desire to build support by distributing state patronage.

Like China, India attempted to exploit globalization to bolster its previous economic regime before deciding to reform it. Although Rajiv Gandhi initiated some modest reform measures in the 1980s, India's reform program began in earnest only after its balance of payment's crisis in 1991. The 1991 crisis made it clear that if India was to continue to take advantage of the opportunities offered by expanding world markets and increased international capital flows, it would have to implement major changes in the Nehruvian economic regime.

Many of India's reforms following the 1991 crises were responses to the changes brought about by globalization. Some of these reforms, for instance the decline in the average tariff rate from more than 120 percent in 1991 to 35 percent in 1997 did not produce much decentralization. Two categories of reform, however, have introduced important measures of administrative decentralization: 1) India has attempted to attract foreign capital in financial and infrastructural sectors by creating independent regulatory agencies which limit central government intervention and curtail its arbitrariness, and 2) India virtually abolished its industrial licensing regime thereby increasing the autonomy of its states to compete for foreign and domestic investment.

The creation of independent regulatory agencies can be understood as movement from distributive to procedural regulation. Prior to the reforms, central government agencies used various forms of regulation to intervene in the market to alter distributive outcomes. Reforms, to a greater or lesser degree, curtailed these interventions and established independent regulatory agencies that regulated, not market outcomes, but the procedures by which the market operated. For instance, prior to 1992, India's stock exchanges were regulated by the Controller of Capital Issues, (CCI) an agency within the central government's Finance Ministry. The CCI regulated what firms could access the country's stock markets and the prices for their initial public offerings. In 1992, the CCI was abolished and the Securities and Exchange Bureau of India (SEBI) was given legal sanction. SEBI's objective has been to develop general procedures and norms for accessing and trading on India's stock exchanges in a manner that increases domestic and foreign investment by curtailing arbitrary interventions and enhancing predictability and calculability. (Shah 1999; Echeverri-Gent 1999) Similiarly, the Telecom Regulatory Authority was established to regulate the bidding of firms for contracts to provide telecom services in India. Its creation has curtailed the power of the Government of India's Ministry of Telecommunications which prior to the reforms served as the major provider of telecommunication equipment and services and the primary regulator of the sector. Other independent regulatory authorities recently have been set up in power and insurance sectors. While each of these agencies has been established in sectors where the state has attempted to accelerate investment and enhance the efficiency of its allocation, the effectiveness of these agencies varies and is rapidly evolving.

While the transition from distributive to procedural regulation curtails central government effort to dictate market outcomes in the short run, in the long-run it is likely to enhance the autonomy of subnational governments by contributing to the development of India's market for the bonds of state and local governments. Currently, state governments and parastatal organizations issue a limited number of bonds. Ahmedabad bond issue in 1996 is the first instance of a municipality issuing bonds in recent memory. Reform in the financial sector and greater fiscal responsibility by central and state governments are essential for bond market development in India. More effective regulation of capital markets by SEBI has already made modest contributions to developing the debt market and India's mutual fund industry. Proper regulation of the insurance industry will increase the country's investment pool, and improved regulation of various infrastructural sectors will enhance their attractiveness for domestic and foreign investors. By developing India's bond market, these reforms could make a major contribution to helping subnational governments meet India's infrastructural needs.

The rollback of India's system of industrial licensing beginning with the modest measures under Rajiv Gandhi and the reforms that followed the 1991 crisis ? has greatly enhanced the role of subnational governments in attracting foreign and domestic investment. Ever since the Industries (Development and Regulation) Act of 1951, capitalists had to secure a licence from the central government before it could invest in new undertakings or expand existing ones. The virtual elimination of industrial licensing by 1991, greatly reduced central government control over the location of new investment. Rather than competing for the favour of the central government politicians and bureaucrats to win new investments, state governments now compete for investments by providing an attractive investment climate. Virtually all Indian states have established industrial development corporations to encourage private investment. Regardless, of their ideology, the leaders of India's states travel abroad and meet with domestic business leaders to solicit their investment. They have engaged in bidding wars to win investment projects. As central government reforms begin to transform state governments' traditionally soft budget constraints, the state's quest for capital has begun to transform of state level politics. State-level political leaders like Chandrababu Naidu in Andhra Pradesh and Digvijay Singh have taken steps away from the populism that has predominated the politics of most Indian states to a more developmentalist approach whereby state governments attract private investment by providing efficient infrastructure and a well educated labour force. The economic and political success of Chandrababu Naidu in particular, may provide a model that encourages state-level leaders to discard populism and pursue a developmentalist political strategy.

INDIA'S STANCE

What should be India's attitude in this environment of growing globalization? At the outset it must be mentioned that opting out of globalization is not a viable choice. There are at present 149 members in the World Trade Organisation (WTO). Some 25 countries are waiting to join the WTO. China has recently been admitted as a member. What is needed is to evolve an appropriate framework to wrest maximum benefits out of international trade and investment. This framework should include (a) making explicit the list of demands that India would like to make on the multilateral trade system, and (b) steps that India should take to realize the full potential from globalization.

Demands on the Trading System

Without being exhaustive, the demands of the developing countries on the multilateral trading system should include (1) establishing symmetry as between the movement of capital and natural persons, (2) delinking environmental standards and labour related considerations from trade negotiations, (3) zero tariffs in industrialized countries on labour intensive exports of developing countries, (4) adequate protection to genetic or biological material and traditional knowledge of developing countries, (5) prohibition of unilateral trade action and extra territorial application of national laws and regulations, and (6) effective restraint on industrialized countries in initiating anti-dumping and countervailing action against exports from developing countries.

The purpose of the new trading system must be to ensure "free and fair" trade among countries. The emphasis so far has been on "free" rather than "fair" trade. It is in this context that the rich industrially advanced countries have an obligation. They have often indulged in "double speak". While requiring developing countries to dismantle barriers and join the main stream of international trade, they have been raising significant tariff and non-tariff barriers on trade from developing countries. Very often, this has been the consequence of heavy lobbying in the advanced countries to protect 'labour'. Although average tariffs in the United States, Canada, European Union and Japan – the so called Quad countries – range from only 4.3 per cent in Japan to 8.3 per cent in Canada, their tariff and trade barriers remain much higher on many products exported by developing countries. Major agricultural food products such as meat, sugar and dairy products attract tariff rates exceeding 100 per cent. Fruits and vegetables such as bananas are hit with a 180 per cent tariff by the European Union, once they exceed quotas.

The tariffs collected by the US on $ 2 billion worth of imports from Bangladesh are higher than those imposed on imports worth $ 30 billion from France. In fact, these trade barriers impose a serious burden on the developing countries. It is important that if the rich countries want a trading system that is truly fair, they should come forward to reduce the trade barriers and subsidies that prevent the products of developing countries from reaching their markets. Otherwise the pleas of these countries for a competitive system will sound hollow. To some extent, conflicts among countries on trade matters are endemic. Until recently, agriculture was a major bone of contention between U.S. and

E.U. countries. Frictions are also bound to arise among developing countries as well. When import tariffs on edible oil were increased in India, the most severe protest came from Malaysia which was a major exporter of Palm Oil. Entrepreneurs in India complain of cheaper imports from China. In the export of rice, a major competitor of India is Thailand. If development is accepted as the major objective of trade as the Doha declaration proclaimed, it should be possible to work out a trading arrangement that is beneficial to all countries.

There have been protracted negotiations at WTO in reforming the trade system. Admittedly, the tariff and non-tariff barriers are coming down. However, there are apprehensions that the concerns of developing countries are not being addressed adequately. Looked at from this angle, the recent Hong Kong Ministerial is a modest success. Despite reservations, we must acknowledge that it is a step forward. Domestic support to agriculture by developed countries constitutes a major stumbling block to third world trade expansion. However, India's stand in relation to agriculture has been 'defensive'. We are not a major player in the world agricultural market. The impact of what has been accepted in relation to Non-Agricultural Market Access and services will vary from country to country. Despite some contrarian opinion, the gain to India from services can be significant. However, the Hong Kong Ministerial is only a broad statement of intentions. Much will depend upon how these ideas are translated into concrete actions.

Actions by India

The second set of measures that should form part of the action plan must relate to strengthening India's position in international trade. India has many strengths, which several developing countries lack. In that sense, India is different and is in a stronger position to gain from international trade and investment. India's rise to the top of the IT industry in the world is a reflection of the abundance of skilled manpower in our country. It is, therefore, in India's interest to ensure that there is a greater freedom of movement of skilled manpower.

At the same time, we should attempt to take all efforts to ensure that we continue to remain a frontline country in the area of skilled manpower. India can attract greater foreign investment, if we can accelerate our growth with stability. Stability, in this context, means reasonable balance on the fiscal and external accounts. We must maintain a competitive environment domestically so that we can take full advantage of wider market access. We must make good use of the extended time given to developing countries to dismantle trade barriers. Wherever legislations are required to protect sectors like agriculture, they need to be enacted quickly. In fact, we had taken a long time to pass the

Protection of Plant Varieties and Farmers' Rights Act. We must also be active in ensuring that our firms make effective use of the new patent rights. South Korea has been able to file in recent years as many as 5000 patent applications in the United States whereas in 1986, the country filed only 162. China has also been very active in this area. We need a truly active agency in India to encourage Indian firms to file patent applications. In effect, we must build the complementary institutions necessary for maximizing the benefits from international trade and investment.

Changes in the foreign trade and foreign investment policies have altered the environment in which Indian industries have to operate. The path of transition is, no doubt, difficult. A greater integration of the Indian economy with the rest of the world is unavoidable. It is important that Indian industry be forward looking and get organized to compete with the rest of the world at levels of tariff comparable to those of other developing countries. Obviously, the Indian Government should be alert to ensure that Indian industries are not the victims of unfair trade practices. The safeguards available in the WTO agreement must be fully utilized to protect the interests of Indian industries.

Indian industry has a right to demand that the macro economic policy environment should be conducive to rapid economic growth. The configuration of policy decisions in the recent period has been attempting to do that. It is, however, time for Indian industrial units to recognize that the challenges of the new century demand greater action at the enterprise level.

They have to learn to swim in the tempestuous waters of competition and away from the protected waters of the swimming pools. India is no longer a country producing goods and services for the domestic market alone. Indian firms are becoming and have to become global players.

At the minimum, they must be able to meet global competition. The search for identifying new competitive advantages must begin earnestly. India's ascendancy in Information Technology (IT) is only partly by design. However, it must be said to the credit of policy makers that once the potential in this area was discovered, the policy environment became strongly industry friendly. Over a wide spectrum of activities, India's advantage, actual and that which can be realized in a short span of time must be drawn up. Of course, in a number of cases, it will require building plants on a global scale.

But, this need not necessarily be so in all cases. In fact the advent of IT is modifying the industrial structure. The revolution in telecommunications and IT is simultaneously creating a huge single market economy, while making the parts smaller and more powerful. What we need today is a road map for the Indian industry. It must delineate the path different industries must take to achieve productivity and efficiency levels comparable to the best in the world. Globalization, in a fundamental sense, is not a new phenomenon. Its roots extend farther and deeper than the visible part of the plant. It is as old as history, starting with the great migrations of people across the great landmasses. Only recent developments in computer and communication technologies have accelerated the process of integration, with geographic distances becoming less of a factor.

Is this 'end of geography' a boon or a bane? Borders have become porous and the sky is open. With modern technologies which do not recognize geography, it is not possible to hold back ideas either in the political, economic or cultural spheres. Each country must prepare itself to meet the new challenges so that it is not being bypassed by this huge wave of technological and institutional changes.

Nothing is an unmixed blessing. Globalization in its present form though spurred by far reaching technological changes is not a pure technological phenomenon. It has many dimensions including ideological. To deal with this phenomenon, we must understand the gains and losses, the benefits as well as dangers. To be forewarned, as the saying goes, is to be forearmed. But we should not throw the baby with bath water. We should also resist the temptation to blame globalization for all our failures. Most often, as the poet said, the fault is in ourselves.

Risks of an open economy are well known. We must not, nevertheless, miss the opportunities that the global system can offer. As an eminent critic put it, the world cannot marginalize India. But India, if it chooses, can marginalize itself. We must guard ourselves against this danger. More than many other developing countries, India is in a position to wrest significant gains from globalization.

However, we must voice our concerns and in cooperation with other developing countries modify the international trading arrangements to take care of the special needs of such countries. At the same time, we must identify and strengthen our comparative advantages. It is this two-fold approach which will enable us to meet the challenges of globalization which may be the defining characteristic of the new millennium.

WHAT GLOBALIZATION STRATEGY FOR INDIA?

All eyes are focused on the Reserve Bank of India (RBI) as it makes key decisions on liquidity and interest rates. These decisions, which will aim to head off the very real threat of overheating while maintaining reasonable growth, will define more broadly the exit strategy from the substantial policy support provided in the aftermath of the global financial crisis. Very senior government policymakers have been generous in offering public (and unsolicited) advice to RBI to the extent that markets have lurched between Delhi and Mumbai to read the tea leaves on the future course of monetary policy.

Comparative advantage, let alone bureaucratic propriety, would dictate that cyclical monetary management be left to RBI. Coordination between Delhi and Mumbai should focus instead on other more strategic and long-term issues. One such issue is India's future globalization strategy and in particular the liberalization of the financial sector and the capital account. What lessons have policymakers drawn from the experience of the financial crisis? How much and what kind of globalization should India aim for?

The crisis served as a useful natural experiment to test two extreme models of globalization that countries had adopted going into the crisis. These models of globalization reflected choices about openness to foreign capital and to exports. The first can be described as the "foreign finance fetish" model, which relied on importing a lot of foreign capital, especially financial capital. This strategy was exemplified by many Eastern European emerging market economies that ran current account deficits well in excess of 10 percent of GDP.

The second model can be described as the "export fetish" or the mercantilist model, which entailed a reliance on exports as development strategy assisted by government intervention, for example through an undervalued exchange rate, and combined with a curtailment of some forms of foreign financial capital. China, of course, was the exemplar par excellence of the export fetish model.

India fell somewhere in the middle, pursuing—or rather lapsing into—what I have called the Goldilocks globalization model. India was neither overly reliant on exports for its growth nor, despite the surge in foreign capital, did it become overly reliant, in some absolute sense, on foreign finance.

The Goldilocks model meant that India escaped the whiplash from the crisis that would have been felt either because of the sudden withdrawal of foreign capital or the precipitous collapse of export demand. Going forward, the question is whether India should persist with this model. Policymakers will respond in the affirmative. Its appeal is not just its moderation. Its appeal is also that its preservation seems to require no new policy decisions. The thinking would run as follows: we followed the middle path, avoiding the extremes. It served us reasonably well. Let us continue with it, especially because inertia and inaction will guarantee continuation.

But here's the key point that policymakers must internalize: indecision will not preserve the Goldilocks globalization strategy. Indecision will instead lead India surely and steadily to the foreign finance fetish model, to a situation where inflows of foreign capital rise continuously over time. Two factors explain this prediction.

The first relates to the natural forces of economic convergence. As India grows more rapidly than the rest of the world, and with policy barriers already attenuated, India, for the foreseeable future, will be a haven for footloose foreign capital seeking the highest returns. That is inevitable.

The second factor is more subtle, and relates to domestic political economy, which will continue to favor further opening up to capital. The parallel with trade protection is instructive. Societies are predisposed toward protectionism because of the imbalance in its impact. The costs of import restrictions—higher prices—are diffused over many consumers while their benefits are concentrated in the hands of a few producers. Concentrated interests have more at stake and are, therefore, able to mobilize easily whereas collective action is more difficult for the consumers.

Something similar applies to foreign capital. The benefits of foreign capital often accrue to domestic firms and producers in the form of lower borrowing costs. And where domestic financial systems are inefficient, as they are in India, access to foreign capital is particularly valuable. So the benefits are concentrated. Moreover, these benefits are frontloaded: firms see immediately the lowering of the costs of borrowing. The potential costs, on the other hand, happen in some distant future because financial crises—one of the costs of excessive foreign borrowing—occur, if they do, only after a certain period of overreliance on foreign capital.

The other cost of foreign borrowing is its tendency to drive up the exchange rate and make a country's exports less competitive. In principle, therefore, if exporting interests are strong and a country follows a flexible exchange rate, this political economy imbalance in favor of opening up to foreign capital can be rectified. Flexibility leads foreign capital flows to put upward pressure on the currency, jeopardizing the profit margins of exporters, who can mobilize to complain about the outcome.

In practice, the mobilization of exporting interests will be impeded by the fact that RBI will not follow a pure float. By dampening and smoothing upward pressures on the currency, RBI will reduce the incentives for exporters to lobby against capital opening. The experience of the years leading up to the crisis, when capital flows surged, suggests that the finance lobby will tend to prevail over the export lobby.

It is possible that embracing foreign capital—and in copious amounts—is what policymakers really want or believe is in India's interest. If that is so, they should make that clear. However, they cannot claim that they are for the current middle path on globalization and believe that policy inertia will keep India on this path: they will have to resist the natural forces of economic convergence and battle against domestic political forces that will inevitably take India toward the foreign finance fetish strategy. Policy activism, especially in relation to the capital account, will be required to maintain the status quo of Goldilocks globalization.

BEST OF TIMES UNDER GLOBALIZATION

THE rate of growth of the Gross Domestic Product of India has been on the increase from 5.6 per cent during 1980-90 to seven per cent in the 1993-2001 period. In the last four years, the annual growth rate of the GDP was impressive at 7.5 per cent (2003-04), 8.5 per cent (2004-05), nine per cent (2005-06) and 9.2 per cent (2006-07). Prime Minister Manmohan Singh is confident of having a 10 per cent growth in the GDP in the Eleventh Five Year Plan period. The foreign exchange reserves (as at the end of the financial year) were $ 39 billion (2000-01), $ 107 billion (2003-04), $ 145 billion (2005-06) and $ 180 billion (in February 2007). It is expected that India will cross the $ 200 billion mark soon.

The cumulative FDI inflows from 1991 to September 2006 were Rs 1,81,566 crores (US $ 43.29 billion). The sectors attracting highest FDI inflows are electrical equipments including computer software and electronics (18 per cent), service sector (13 per cent), telecommunications (10 per cent), transportation industry (nine per cent), etc. In the inflow of FDI, India has surpassed South Korea to become the fourth largest recipient. India controls at the present 45 per cent of the global outsourcing market with an estimated income of $ 50 billion.

In respect of market capitalisation (which takes into account the market value of a quoted company by multiplying its current share price by the number of shares in issue), India is in the fourth position with $ 894 billion after the US ($ 17,000 billion), Japan ($ 4800 billion) and China ($ 1000). India is expected to soon cross the trillion dollar mark.

As per the Forbes list for 2007, the number of billionaires of India has risen to 40 (from 36 last year)—more than those of Japan (24), China (17), France (14) and Italy (14) this year. A press report was jubilant: "This is the richest year for India." The combined wealth of the Indian billionaires marked an increase of 60 per cent from $ 106 billion in 2006 to $ 170 billion in 2007. The 40 Indian billionaires have assets worth about Rs 7.50 lakh crores whereas the cumulative investment in the 91 Public Sector Undertakings by the Central Government of India is Rs 3.93 lakh crores only.

Worst of Times

ON the other side of the medal, there is a long list of the 'worst of the times', the foremost casualty being the agriculture sector. Agriculture has been and still remains the backbone of the Indian economy. It plays a vital role not only in providing food and nutrition to the people, but also in the supply of raw material to industries and to export trade. In 1951, agriculture provided employment to 72 per cent of the population and contributed 59 per cent of the gross domestic product. However, by 2001 the population depending upon agriculture came to 58 per cent whereas the share of agriculture in the GDP went down drastically to 24 per cent and further to 22 per cent in 2006-07. This has resulted in a lowering the per capita income of the farmers and increasing the rural indebtedness. The agricultural growth of 3.2 per cent observed from 1980 to 1997 decelerated to two per cent subsequently. The Approach to the Eleventh Five Year Plan released in December 2006 stated that "the growth rate of agricultural GDP including forestry and fishing is likely to be below two per cent in the Tenth Plan period".

The reasons for the deceleration of the growth of agriculture are given in the Economic Survey 2006-07: "Low investment, imbalance in fertiliser use, low seeds replacement rate, a distorted incentive system and lo post-harvest value addition continued to be a drag on the sector's performance. With more than half the population directly depending on this sector, low agricultural growth has serious implications for the 'inclusiveness' of growth." The number of rural landless families increased from 35 per cent in 1987 to 45 per cent in 1999, further to 55 per cent in 2005. The farmers are destined to die of starvation or suicide. Replying to the Short Duration Discussion on 'Import of Wheat and Agrarian Distress' on May 18, 2006, Agriculture Minister Sharad Pawar informed the Rajya Sabha that roughly 1,00,000 farmers committed suicide during the period 1993-2003 mainly due to indebtedness.

In his interview to The Indian Express on November 15, 2005, Sharad Pawar said: "The farming community has been ignored in this country and especially so over the last eight to ten years. The total investment in the agriculture sector is going down... In the last few years, the average budgetary provision from the Indian Government for irrigation is less than 0.35 percent."

During the post-reform period, India has been shining brilliantly with a growing number of billionaires. Nobody has taken note of the sufferings of the family members of those unfortunate hundred thousand farmers.

Further, the proportion of people depending in India on agriculture is about 60 per cent whereas the same for the UK is two per cent, USA two per cent and Japan three per cent. The developed countries, having a low proportion of population in agriculture, have readily adopted globalization which favours more the growth of the manufacturing and service sectors.

About the plight of agriculture in developing countries, Nobel Prize-winning economist Joseph Stiglitz said: "Trade agreements now forbid most subsidies—except for agricultural goods. This depresses incomes of those farmers in the developing countries who do not get subsidies. And since 70 per cent of those in the developing countries depend directly or indirectly on agriculture, this means that the incomes of the developing countries are depressed. But by whatever standard one uses, today's international trading regime is unfair to developing countries." (Making Globalization Work, pp. 73-74) He also pointed out: "The average European cow gets a subsidy of $ 2 a day (the World Bank measure of poverty); more than half the people in the developing world live on less than that. It appears that it is better to be a cow in Europe than to be a poor person in a developing country."

Demoting Agriculture

THE Economic Survey reports released till 1991 contained the Chapters in the following order: (1) Introduction, (2) Agricultural Production, (3) Industrial Performance and Policies, (4) Infrastructure, (5) Human Resources, (6) Prices, Price Policy and Public Distribution System, (7) Fiscal Policy and Government Budget, (8) Monetary and Credit Developments, (9) The External Sector and (10) Problems and Prospects.

In the Economic Survey 1991-92, Finance Minister Manmohan Singh recast the Chapters in the following order: (1) Introduction, (2) Public Finance, (3) Money and Credit, (4) Prices and Distribution, (5) Balance of Payments, (6) Industry, (7) Agriculture, (8) Infrastructure and (9) Social Sectors.

It is not known as to why the Finance Minister demoted the importance of agriculture that has about 90 per cent population from the second place to the seventh in the annual Economic Survey of the country. In a way does it symbolise the low importance deliberately given to the growth of the agriculture sector in the scheme of globalization?

Strategy of Globalization

IN the Report (2006) 'East Asian Renaissance', World Bank Advisor Dr Indermit Gill stated: "Cities are at the core of a development strategy based on international integration, investment and innovation. East Asia is witnessing the largest rural-to-urban shift of population in history. Two million new urban dwellers are expected in East Asian cities every month for the next 20 years. This will mean planning for and building dynamic, connected cities that are linked both domestically and to the outside world so that economic growth continues and social cohesion is strengthened." The market economy seems to be more concerned with the growth of consumerism to attract the high income groups who are mostly in the cities in the developing countries. Rural economy and the agricultural sector were out of focus in the strategy of globalization.

Growth of Unemployment—Poverty

THE proportion of the unemployed to the total labour force has been increasing from 2.62 per cent (1993-94) to 2.78 per cent (1999-2000) and 3.06 per cent (2004-05). In absolute figures, the number of unemployed had been in those years 9.02 million, 10.51 million and 13.10 million respectively.

In reply to a question, the Minister for Labour and Employment informed the Lok Sabha on March 19, 2007, that the enrolment of the unemployed in the Employment Exchanges in 2006-07 was 79 lakhs against the average of 58 lakhs in the past ten years.

About the impact of globalization, in particular on the development of India, the ILO Report (2004) stated: "In India, there had been winners and losers. The lives of the educated and the rich had been enriched by globalization. The information technology (IT) sector was a particular beneficiary. But the benefits had not yet reached the majority, and new risks had cropped up for the losers—the socially deprived and the rural poor. Significant numbers of 'non-perennial' poor, who had worked hard to escape poverty, were finding their gains reversed. Power was shifting from elected local institutions to unaccountable trans-national bodies. Western perceptions, which dominated the globe media, were not aligned with local perspectives; they encouraged consumerism in the midst of extreme poverty and posed a threat to cultural and linguistic diversity."

Social Services

ABOUT the quality of education given to children, the Approach to the Eleventh Five Year Plan stated: "A recent study has found that 38 per cent of the children who have completed four years of schooling cannot read a small paragraph with short sentences meant to be read by a student of Class II. About 55 per cent of such children cannot divide a three digit number by a one digit number. These are indicators of serious learning problems which must be addressed." The Approach paper added further: "Universalisation of education will not suffice in the knowledge economy. A person with a mere eight years of schooling will be as disadvantaged in a knowledge economy by ICT as an illiterate person in modern industry an services."

The less said about the achievements in health the better. The Approach to the Eleventh Plan concedes that progress implementing the objectives of health 'have been slow'. The Report gave the particulars of the rates of infant mortality (per 1000 live births) for India as 60 against Sri Lanka (13), China (30) and Vietnam (19). The rate of maternal mortality (per 1,00,000 deliveries) of India is 407 against Sri Lanka (92), China (56) and Vietnam (130).

Growth of Slum Capitals

IN his 2007-08 Budget Speech, Finance Minister Chidambaram put forth a proposal to promote Mumbai as a world class financial centre and to make 'financial services' the next growth engine of India.

Of its 13 million population, Mumbai city has 54 per cent in slums. It is estimated that 100 to 300 new families come to Mumbai every day and most land up in a slum colony. Prof R. N. Sharma of the Tata Institute of Social Science says that Mumbai is disintegrating into slums. From being known as the slum capital of India and the biggest slum of Asia, Mumbai is all set to become the slum capital of the world.

The population of Delhi is about 14 million of which nearly 45 per cent population lives in slums, unauthorised colonies, JJ clusters and undeveloped rural parts. During dry weather these slum dwellers use open areas around their units for defecation and the entire human waste generated from the slums along with the additional wastewater from their households is discharged untreated into the river Yamuna.

The cumulative FDI inflows (until September 2006) to the New Delhi region was of Rs 27,369 crores and to Mumbai Rs 24,545 crores. The two spots of New Delhi and Mumbai received 46 per cent of the total FDI inflows into India. The FDI inflows have in no way assisted in improving the health and environment conditions of the people. On the other hand, the financial capital of India and the political capital of India are set to become the topmost slum cities of the world.

Victims of Globalization

IN his Making Globalization Work, Nobel Laureate Stiglitz wrote: "Trade liberalisation—opening up markets to the free flow of goods and services—was supposed to lead to growth. The evidence is at best mixed. Part of the reason that international trade agreements have been so unsuccessful in promoting growth in poor countries is that they were often unbalanced. The advanced industrial countries were allowed to levy tariffs on goods produced by developing countries that were, on average, four times higher that those on goods produced by other advanced industrial countries."

In his foreword to The Dynamics and Impact of Globalization by Dr. M. V. Louis Anthuvan, Justice V. R. Krishna Iyer pointed out pithily: "The New World

Order is the product of what is now familiarly described as globalization, liberalisation and privatisation. The weaker sectors like the Asian and African countries are victims, whose economic welfare is slavery, at the disposal of the White world. When World War II came to a close, commercial conquest and trade triumph became the major goal of the United States and the other giant trade powers. Indeed, these mighty countries and companies even made world hunger as Big Business. The poorer countries with natural resources have been made banana republics and cucumber vassals. The Human Development Report 2006 recorded: "Globalization has given rise to a protracted debate over the precise direction of trends in global income distribution. What is sometimes lost sight of is the sheer depth of inequality—and the associated potential for greater equity to accelerate poverty reduction. Measured in the 2000 purchasing power parity (PPP) terms, the gap between the incomes of the poorest 20 per cent of the world's population and the $ 1 a day poverty line amounts to about $ 300 billion. That figure appears large, but it is less than two per cent of the income of the world's wealthiest 10 per cent."

To Make Globalization Work

UNDER the phenomenal growth of information technology which has shrunk space and time and reduced the cost of moving information, goods and capital across the globe, the globalization has brought unprecedented opportunities for human development for all, in developing as well as developed countries. Under the commercial marketing forces, globalization has been used more to promote economic growth to yield profits to some countries and to some groups within a country. India should pay immediate attention to ensure rapid development in education, health, water and sanitation, labour and employment so that under time-bound programmes the targets are completed without delay. A strong foundation of human development of all people is essential for the social, political and economic development of the country.

Though at present India appears to be dominant in some fields of development as in IT-ITES, this prosperity may be challenged by other competing countries which are equipping themselves with better standards of higher education. As detailed earlier, our progress in education has been slow and superficial, without depth and quality, to compete the international standards.

The government should take immediate steps to increase agricultural production and create additional employment opportunities in the rural parts, to reduce the growing inequality between urban and rural areas and to decentralise powers and resources to the panchayati raj institutions for implementing all works of rural development. Steps should be taken for early linking of the rivers, especially in the south-bound ones, for supply of the much-needed water for irrigation. It should be remembered that without a sustainable and productive growth of the agricultural sector, the other types of development in any sphere will be unstable and illusory. Despite the concerted development in manufacturing and service sectors, despite the remarkable inflow and overflow of foreign reserves, agriculture is still the largest industry providing employment to about 60 per cent of the workforce in the country.

Mere growth of the GDP and others at the macro level in billions does not solve the chronic poverty and backward level of living norms of the people at the micro level. The growth should be sustainable with human development and decent employment potential. The welfare of a country does not percolate from the top, but should be built upon development from the bottom.

MODERN GLOBALIZATION

Globalization, since World War II, is largely the result of planning by politicians to break down borders hampering trade to increase prosperity and interdependence thereby decreasing the chance of future war. Their work led to the Bretton Woods conference, an agreement by the world's leading politicians to lay down the framework for international commerce and finance, and the founding of several international institutions intended to oversee the processes of globalization. These institutions include the International Bank for Reconstruction and Development (the World Bank), and the International Monetary Fund. Globalization has been facilitated by advances in technology which have reduced the costs of trade, and trade negotiation rounds, originally under the auspices of the General Agreement on Tariffs and Trade (GATT), which led to a series of agreements to remove restrictions on free trade.

Since World War II, barriers to international trade have been considerably lowered through international agreements — GATT. Particular initiatives carried out as a result of GATT and the World Trade Organization (WTO), for which GATT is the foundation, have included:

- Promotion of free trade:
    - o elimination of tariffs; creation of free trade zones with small or no tariffs
    - o Reduced transportation costs, especially resulting from development of containerization for ocean shipping.
    - o Reduction or elimination of capital controls
    - o Reduction, elimination, or harmonization of subsidies for local businesses

- o Creation of subsidies for global corporations
- o Harmonization of intellectual property laws across the majority of states, with more restrictions
- o Supranational recognition of intellectual property restrictions (e.g. patents granted by China would be recognized in the United States).

Cultural globalization, driven by communication technology and the worldwide marketing of Western cultural industries, was understood at first as a process of homogenization, as the global domination of American culture at the expense of traditional diversity. However, a contrasting trend soon became evident in the emergence of movements protesting against globalization and giving new momentum to the defence of local uniqueness, individuality, and identity, but largely without success. The Uruguay Round (1986 to 1994) led to a treaty to create the WTO to mediate trade disputes and set up a uniform platform of trading. Other bilateral and multilateral trade agreements, including sections of Europe's Maastricht Treaty and the North American Free Trade Agreement (NAFTA) have also been signed in pursuit of the goal of reducing tariffs and barriers to trade.

World exports rose from 8.5% in 1970, to 16.2% of total gross world product in 2001.

Measuring Globalization

Looking specifically at economic globalization demonstrates that it can be measured in different ways. These centre around the four main economic flows that characterize globalization:

- Goods and services, e.g., exports plus imports as a proportion of national income or per capita of population
- Labour/people, e.g., net migration rates; inward or outward migration flows, weighted by population
- Capital, e.g., inward or outward direct investment as a proportion of national income or per head of population
- Technology, e.g., international research & development flows; proportion of populations (and rates of change thereof) using particular inventions (especially 'factor-neutral' technological advances such as the telephone, motorcar, broadband)

As globalization is not only an economic phenomenon, a multivariate approach to measuring globalization is the recent index calculated by the Swiss think tank KOF. The index measures the three main dimensions of globalization: economic, social, and political. In addition to three indices measuring these dimensions, an overall index of globalization and sub-indices referring to actual economic flows, economic restrictions, data on personal contact, data on information flows, and data on cultural proximity is calculated. Data is available on a yearly basis for 122 countries, as detailed in Dreher, Gaston and Martens (2008). According to the index, the world's most globalized country is Belgium, followed by Austria, Sweden, the United Kingdom and the Netherlands. The least globalized countries according to the KOF-index are Haiti, Myanmar, the Central African Republic and Burundi.

A.T. Kearney and *Foreign Policy Magazine* jointly publish another Globalization Index. According to the 2006 index, Singapore, Ireland, Switzerland, the Netherlands, Canada and Denmark are the most globalized, while Indonesia, India and Iran are the least globalized among countries listed.

Effects of Globalization

Globalization has various aspects which affect the world in several different ways such as:

- *Industrial*-emergence of worldwide production markets and broader access to a range of foreign products for consumers and companies. Particularly movement of material and goods between and within national boundaries. International trade in manufactured goods increased more than 100 times (from $95 billion to $12 trillion) in the 50 years since 1955. China's trade with Africa rose sevenfold during 2000-07 alone.
- *Financial*-emergence of worldwide financial markets and better access to external financing for borrowers. By the early part of the 21st century more than $1.5 trillion in national currencies were traded daily to support the expanded levels of trade and investment. As these worldwide structures grew more quickly than any transnational regulatory regime, the instability of the global financial infrastructure dramatically increased, as evidenced by the Financial crisis of 2007–2010.

As of 2005–2007, the Port of Shanghai holds the title as the World's busiest port.

- *Economic*-realization of a global common market, based on the freedom of exchange of goods and capital. The interconnections of these markets, however, meant that an economic collapse in any one given country could not be contained.

  Almost all notable worldwide IT companies are now present in India. Four Indians were among the world's top 10 richest in 2008, worth a combined $160 billion. In 2007, China had 415,000 millionaires and India 123,000.

- *Health Policy*-On the global scale, health becomes a commodity. In developing nations under the demands of Structural Adjustment Programs, health systems are fragmented and privatized. Global health policy makers have shifted during the 1990s from United Nations players to financial institutions. The result of this power transition is an increase in privatization in the health sector. This privatization fragments health policy by crowding it with many players with many private interests. These fragmented policy players emphasize partnerships, specific interventions to combat specific problems (as opposed to comprehensive health strategies). Influenced by global trade and global economy, health policy is directed by technological advances and innovative medical trade. Global priorities, in this situation, are sometimes at odds with national priorities where increased health infrastructure and basic primary care are of more value to the public than privatized care for the wealthy.

Britain is a country of rich diversity. As of 2008, 40% of London's total population was from an ethnic minority group.

The latest official figures show that in 2008, 590,000 people arrived to live in the UK whilst 427,000 left, meaning that net inward migration was 163,000.

- *Political*-some use "globalization" to mean the creation of a world government which regulates the relationships among governments and guarantees the rights arising from social and economic globalization. Politically, the United States has enjoyed a position of power among the world powers, in part because of its strong and wealthy economy. With the influence of globalization and with the help of The United States' own economy, the People's Republic of China has experienced some tremendous growth within the past decade. If China continues to grow at the rate projected by the trends, then it is very likely that in the next twenty years, there will be a major reallocation of power among the world leaders. China will have enough wealth, industry, and technology to rival the United States for the position of leading world power.
- *Informational*-increase in information flows between geographically remote locations. Arguably this is a technological change with the advent of fibre optic communications, satellites, and increased availability of telephone and Internet.
- *Language*-the most popular language is Mandarin (845 million speakers) followed by Spanish (329 million speakers) and English (328 million speakers).
    - o About 35% of the world's mail, telexes, and cables are in English.

- o Approximately 40% of the world's radio programs are in English.
- o About 50% of all Internet traffic uses English.

- *Competition*-Survival in the new global business market calls for improved productivity and increased competition. Due to the market becoming worldwide, companies in various industries have to upgrade their products and use technology skillfully in order to face increased competition.
- *Ecological*-the advent of global environmental challenges that might be solved with international cooperation, such as climate change, cross-boundary water and air pollution, over-fishing of the ocean, and the spread of invasive species. Since many factories are built in developing countries with less environmental regulation, globalism and free trade may increase pollution. On the other hand, economic development historically required a "dirty" industrial stage, and it is argued that developing countries should not, via regulation, be prohibited from increasing their standard of living.

  The construction of continental hotels is a major consequence of globalization process in affiliation with tourism and travel industry, Dariush Grand Hotel, Kish, Iran
- *Cultural*-growth of cross-cultural contacts; advent of new categories of consciousness and identities which embodies cultural diffusion, the desire to increase one's standard of living and enjoy foreign products and ideas, adopt new technology and practices, and participate in a "world culture". Some bemoan the resulting consumerism and loss of languages.
  - o Spreading of multiculturalism, and better individual access to cultural diversity (e.g. through the export of Hollywood and, to a lesser extent, Bollywood movies). Some consider such "imported" culture a danger, since it may supplant the local culture, causing reduction in diversity or even assimilation. Others consider multiculturalism to promote peace and understanding between people. A third position gaining popularity is the notion that multiculturalism to a new form of monoculture in which no distinctions exist and everyone just shift between various lifestyles in terms of music, cloth and other aspects once more firmly attached to a single culture. Thus not mere cultural assimilation as mentioned above but the obliteration of culture as we know it today.
  - o Greater international travel and tourism. WHO estimates that up to 500,000 people are on planes at any one time. In 2008, there were over 922 million international tourist arrivals, with a growth of 1.9% as compared to 2007.

- o Greater immigration, including illegal immigration. The IOM estimates there are more than 200 million migrants around the world today. Newly available data show that remittance flows to developing countries reached $328 billion in 2008.
- o Spread of local consumer products (e.g., food) to other countries (often adapted to their culture).
- o Worldwide fads and pop culture such as Pokemon, Sudoku, Numa Numa, Origami, Idol series, YouTube, Orkut, Facebook, and MySpace. Accessible to those who have Internet or Television, leaving out a substantial segment of the Earth's population.
- o Worldwide sporting events such as FIFA World Cup and the Olympic Games.
- o Incorporation of multinational corporations in to new media. As the sponsors of the All-Blacks rugby team, Adidas had created a parallel website with a downloadable interactive rugby game for its fans to play and compete.

- *Social*-development of the system of non-governmental organisations as main agents of global public policy, including humanitarian aid and developmental efforts.
- *Technical*.
  - o Development of a Global Information System, global telecommunications infrastructure and greater transborder data flow, using such technologies as the Internet, communication satellites, submarine fiber optic cable, and wireless telephones
  - o Increase in the number of standards applied globally; e.g., copyright laws, patents and world trade agreements.
- *Legal/Ethical*
  - o The creation of the international criminal court and international justice movements.
  - o Crime importation and raising awareness of global crime-fighting efforts and cooperation.
  - o The emergence of Global administrative law.
- *Religious*
  - o The spread and increased interrelations of various religious groups, ideas, and practices and their ideas of the meanings and values of particular spaces.

Cultural Effects

Globalization has had an impact on different cultures around the world. Japanese McDonald's fast food as an evidence of corporate globalization and the integration of the same into different cultures. "Culture" is defined as patterns of human activity and the symbols that give these activities significance. Culture is what people eat, how they dress, beliefs they hold, and activities they practice. Globalization has joined different cultures and made it into something different. As Erla Zwingle, from the National Geographic article titled "Globalization" states, "When cultures receive outside influences, they ignore some and adopt others, and then almost immediately start to transform them."

One classic culture aspect is food. Someone in America can be eating Japanese noodles for lunch while someone in Sydney, Australia is eating classic Italian meatballs. India is known for its curry and exotic spices. France is known for its cheeses. America is known for its burgers and fries. McDonald's is an American company which is now a global enterprise with 31,000 locations worldwide. This company is just one example of food causing cultural influence on the global scale.

Another common practice brought about by globalization is the usage of Chinese kanji in tattoos. These tattoos are popular with today's youth despite the lack of social acceptance of tattoos in China. Also, there is a lack of comprehension in the meaning of Chinese characters that people get, making this an example of cultural appropriation.

The internet breaks down cultural boundaries across the world by enabling easy, near-instantaneous communication between people anywhere in a variety of digital forms and media. The Internet is associated with the process of cultural globalization because it allows interaction and communication between people with very different lifestyles and from very different cultures. Photo sharing websites allow interaction even where language would otherwise be a barrier.

Negative Effects

Globalization has been one of the most hotly debated topics in international economics over the past few years. Globalization has also generated significant international opposition over concerns that it has increased inequality and environmental degradation. In the Midwestern United States, globalization has eaten away at its competitive edge in industry and agriculture, lowering the quality of life in locations that have not adapted to the change.

Effect on Disease

Globalization, the flow of information, goods, capital and people across political and geographic boundaries, has also helped to spread some of the deadliest infectious diseases known to humans. Starting in Asia, the Black Death killed at least one-third of Europe's population in the 14th century. Modern modes of transportation allow more people and products to travel around the world at a faster pace, they also open the airways to the transcontinental movement of infectious disease vectors. One example of this occurring is AIDS/HIV. Approximately 1.1 million persons are living with HIV/AIDS in the United States, and AIDS remains the leading cause of death among African American women between ages 25 and 34. Due to immigration, approximately 500,000 people in the United States are believed to be infected with Chagas disease. In 2006, the tuberculosis (TB) rate among foreign-born persons in the United States was 9.5 times that of U.S.-born persons.

Brain Drain

Opportunities in richer countries drives talent away from poorer countries, leading to brain drains. Brain drain has cost the African continent over $4.1 billion in the employment of 150,000 expatriate professionals annually. Indian students going abroad for their higher studies costs India a foreign exchange outflow of $10 billion annually.

Economic Liberalization

The World today is so interconnected that the collapse of the subprime mortgage market in the U.S. has led to a global financial crisis and recession on a scale not seen since the Great Depression. Government deregulation and failed regulation of Wall Street's investment banks were important contributors to the subprime mortgage crisis.

A flood of consumer goods such as televisions, radios, bicycles, and textiles into the United States, Europe, and Japan has helped fuel the economic expansion of Asian tiger economies in recent decades. However, Chinese textile and clothing exports have recently encountered criticism from Europe, the United States and some African countries. In South Africa, some 300,000 textile workers have lost their jobs due to the influx of Chinese goods. A total of 3.2 million – one in six U.S. factory jobs – have disappeared since the start of 2000.

Effect on Income Disparity

A study by the World Institute for Development Economics Research at United Nations University reports that the richest 1% of adults alone owned 40% of global assets in the year 2000. The *three* richest people possess more financial assets than the poorest 10% of the world's population, combined. The combined wealth of the 10 million millionaires grew to nearly $41 trillion in 2008. In 2001, 46.4% of people in sub-Saharan Africa were living in extreme poverty. Nearly half of all Indian children are undernourished.

Effect on Environmental Degradation

Burning forest in Brazil. The removal of forest to make way for cattle ranching was the leading cause of deforestation in the Brazilian Amazon from the mid 1960s. Recently, soybeans have become one of the most important contributors to deforestation in the Brazilian Amazon.

The Worldwatch Institute said the booming economies of China and India are planetary powers that are shaping the global biosphere. In 2007, China overtook the United States as the world's biggest producer of CO_2. At present rates, tropical rainforests in Indonesia would be logged out in 10 years, Papua New Guinea in 13 to 16 years. A major source of deforestation is the logging industry, driven spectacularly by China and Japan. Thriving economies such as China and India are quickly becoming large oil consumers. China has seen oil consumption grow by 8% yearly since 2002, doubling from 1996–2006. Crude oil prices in the last several years have steadily risen from about $25 a barrel in August 2003 to over $140 a barrel in July 2008. *State of the World* 2006 report said the two countries' high economic growth hid a reality of severe pollution. The report states: The world's ecological capacity is simply insufficient to satisfy the ambitions of China, India, Japan, Europe and the United States as well as the aspirations of the rest of the world in a sustainable way.

Without more recycling, zinc could be used up by 2037, both indium and hafnium could run out by 2017, and terbium could be gone before 2012. It said that if China and India were to consume as much resources per capita as United States or Japan in 2030 together they would require a full planet Earth to meet their needs. In the longterm these effects can lead to increased conflict over dwindling resources and in the worst case a Malthusian catastrophe.

Food Security

The head of the International Food Policy Research Institute, stated in 2008 that the gradual change in diet among newly prosperous populations is the most important factor underpinning the rise in global food prices. From 1950 to 1984, as the Green Revolution transformed agriculture around the world, grain production increased by over 250%. The world population has grown by about 4 billion since the beginning of the Green Revolution and most believe that, without the Revolution, there would be greater famine and malnutrition than the UN presently documents (approximately 850 million people suffering from chronic malnutrition in 2005).

It is becoming increasingly difficult to maintain food security in a world beset by a confluence of "peak" phenomena, namely peak oil, peak water, peak phosphorus, peak grain and peak fish. Growing populations, falling energy sources and food shortages will create the "perfect storm" by 2030, according to the UK government chief scientist. He said food reserves are at a 50-year low but the world requires 50% more energy, food and water by 2030. The world will have to produce 70% more food by 2050 to feed a projected extra 2.3 billion people and as incomes rise, the United Nations' Food and Agriculture Organisation (FAO) warned. Social scientists have warned of the possibility that global civilization is due for a period of contraction and economic re-localization, due to the decline in fossil fuels and resulting crisis in transportation and food production. One paper even suggested that the future might even bring about a restoration of sustainable local economic activities based on hunting and gathering, shifting horticulture, and pastoralism.

The journal *Science* published a four-year study in November 2006, which predicted that, at prevailing trends, the world would run out of wild-caught seafood in 2048.

Drug and Illicit Goods Trade

The United Nations Office on Drugs and Crime (UNODC) issued a report that the global drug trade generates more than $320 billion a year in revenues. Worldwide, the UN estimates there are more than 50 million regular users of heroin, cocaine and synthetic drugs. The international trade of endangered species is second only to drug trafficking. Traditional Chinese medicine often incorporates ingredients from all parts of plants, the leaf, stem, flower, root, and also ingredients from animals and minerals. The use of parts of endangered species (such as seahorses, rhinoceros horns, saiga antelope horns, and tiger bones and claws) has created controversy and resulted in a black market of poachers who hunt restricted animals. In 2003, 29% of open sea fisheries were in a state of collapse.

Sweatshops

It can be said that globalization is the door that opens up an otherwise resource-poor country to the international market. Where a country has little material or physical product harvested or mined from its own soil, large corporations see an opportunity to take advantage of the "export poverty" of such a nation. Where the majority of the earliest occurrences of economic globalization are recorded as being the expansion of businesses and corporate growth, in many poorer nations globalization is actually the result of the foreign businesses investing in the country to take advantage of the lower wage rate: even though investing, by increasing the Capital Stock of the country, increases their wage rate. One example used by anti-globalization protestors is the use of sweatshops by manufacturers. According to Global Exchange these "Sweat

Shops" are widely used by sports shoe manufacturers and mentions one company in particular – Nike. There are factories set up in the poor countries where employees agree to work for low wages. Then if labour laws alter in those countries and stricter rules govern the manufacturing process the factories are closed down and relocated to other nations with more conservative, laissez-faire economic policies.

There are several agencies that have been set up worldwide specifically designed to focus on anti-sweatshop campaigns and education of such. In the USA, the National Labour Committee has proposed a number of bills as part of the The Decent Working Conditions and Fair Competition Act, which have thus far failed in Congress. The legislation would legally require companies to respect human and worker rights by prohibiting the import, sale, or export of sweatshop goods.

Specifically, these core standards include no child labour, no forced labour, freedom of association, right to organize and bargain collectively, as well as the right to decent working conditions.

Tiziana Terranova has stated that globalization has brought a culture of "free labour". In a digital sense, it is where the individuals (contributing capital) exploits and eventually "exhausts the means through which labour can sustain itself". For example, in the area of digital media (animations, hosting chat rooms, designing games), where it is often less glamorous than it may sound. In the gaming industry, a Chinese Gold Market has been established.

3

The Global Compact and Human Rights

REFRESHER ON THE GLOBAL COMPACT

The Global Compact was introduced in 1999 because many felt that globalization was not delivering all it had promised. In particular, its benefits were dramatically unevenly distributed. Although the primary responsibility for implementing international agreements on human rights, labour standards, the environment and anti-corruption lies with governments, business was seen as having an important role to play. In fact, one of the founding premises of the GC is that without active involvement of business, there is the danger that universal principles, including those embodied in international human rights instruments, will remain unimplemented.

The Global Compact emphasizes the business case for improved social and environmental performance and business' own operations and activities not the traditional CSR concept that is based on philanthropy. We believe that the largest impact that business can have is through conducting their business in a sustainable way that respects human rights and limits their environmental impact, treats their workers well and avoids corruption.

The Compact, itself, is both a set of universal principles and a network-based multi-stakeholder initiative with a change model for how to raise the level of business' social and environment performance. The Secretary-General derived the principles from international instruments that enjoy wide consensus like the UDHR, ILO Declaration, Rio Declaration, and UN Convention Against Corruption.

Businesses initiate their participation through a commitment by their CEO endorsed by their Board expressing their support for the principles and their intention to work towards their implementation within their own operations.

This is a key element of the Compact's leadership model. Effective positive change requires a leadership commitment and it is our intention that change agents inside companies will use their CEO's expression of commitment to help them to more easily make necessary changes inside the company to improve its social and environmental performance. The Global Compact is not a seal of approval for or endorsement of the companies or other organizations participating in it. Nor is it a regulatory or compliance based model. The Global Compact Office has neither the mandate nor the resources for that. As a result, we encourage improved performance and positive change through the means available to us as an initiative inside the UN Secretariat: learning, dialogue, networks, initiatives, projects and promoting greater transparency around company social and environmental efforts. We also work with the financial incentive system within which companies operate to encourage the mainstream financial community to take into account companies' social and environmental performance in making their valuations.

Global Compact Office was established in July 2000 with less than 50 companies. Today, there are 2268 participating companies in 87 countries, dozens of civil society and labour organizations and more than 40 local networks engaged.

ADDED VALUE PROVIDED BY THE HUMAN RIGHTS APPROACH TO POVERTY REDUCTION

Some poverty reduction strategies already have features that reflect international human rights norms. For example, the emphasis placed on civil society participation in the Poverty Reduction Strategy Paper approach advocated by the World Bank and the IMF reflects the right of individuals to take part in the conduct of public affairs, as well as the related rights of association, assembly and expression. The introduction of social safety nets resonates with the rights to a reasonable standard of living, food, housing, health protection, education and social security. Anti-poverty strategies that demand transparent budgetary and other governmental processes are consistent with the right to information, while the insistence that strategies are "country-owned" corresponds to the right of peoples to self-determination.

This congruence between features of existing poverty reduction strategies and the international human rights framework gives rise to two important points. First, the departure represented by the introduction of a rights-based approach to poverty reduction should not be overstated. Second, the application of human rights to poverty reduction reinforces some of the existing features of anti-poverty strategies. The value added by the human rights approach to poverty reduction consists both in the manner in which it departs from existing strategies and in the manner in which it reinforces them. The major elements of this process may be enumerated as follows.

By introducing the dimension of an international legal obligation, the human rights perspective adds legitimacy to the demand for making poverty reduction the primary goal of policy-making. The last decade has witnessed a move towards poverty reduction as the focus of international cooperation as well as of national policy-making. The human rights perspective adds strength to this movement by drawing attention to the fact that poverty signifies non-realization of human rights so that the adoption of a poverty reduction strategy is therefore not just desirable but obligatory on the part of States that have ratified international human rights instruments.

Recognition of the principles of equality and non-discrimination, which is a central premise of the human rights approach, helps to highlight the fact that a great deal of poverty originates from discriminatory practices – both overt and covert – at the international, national and local levels. This recognition calls for the reorientation of poverty reduction strategies from a tendency to focus on narrow economic issues towards a broader strategy that also addresses socio-cultural and political-legal institutions that sustain the structures of discrimination.

Recognition of complementarities between civil and political rights, on the one hand, and economic, social and cultural rights, on the other, adds impetus to the process of strengthening and broadening the scope of poverty reduction strategies. In particular, it helps dispel the misconception that civil and political rights and freedoms are luxuries and relevant only to relatively affluent societies. Accordingly, the human rights approach demands that measures be taken to ensure civil and political rights are integral components of poverty reduction strategies.

Unlike old-style approaches to poverty reduction, the human rights approach attaches as much importance to the processes whereby developmental goals are achieved as to the goals themselves. In particular, it emphasizes the importance of ensuring people's participation, especially participation by the poor and otherwise marginalized groups, in all aspects of decision-making. The importance of participation is being increasingly recognized. The human rights approach reinforces this recognition by drawing attention to the fact that participation is valuable not just as a means to other ends but also as a fundamental human right that should be realized for its own sake.

Making trade-offs among alternative goals in the light of social priorities and resource constraints is an integral part of any approach to policy-making.

The human rights approach is no exception, but it offers the poor better protection by ruling out certain kinds of trade-offs that are potentially harmful to them. In particular, it rules out any trade-off that leads to retrogression of a human right from its existing level of realization or to non-achievement of certain minimum levels of realization that have been identified as core obligations.

Perhaps the most important source of added value in the human rights approach is the emphasis it places on the accountability of policy-makers and other actors whose actions have an impact on the rights of people. Rights imply duties, and duties demand accountability. It is therefore an intrinsic feature of the human rights approach that institutions and legal/administrative arrangements for ensuring accountability are built into any poverty reduction strategy.

In sum, the human rights approach has the potential to advance the goal of poverty reduction in a variety of ways: (a) by urging speedy adoption of a poverty reduction strategy, underpinned by human rights, as a matter of legal obligation; (b) by broadening the scope of poverty reduction strategies so as to address the structures of discrimination that generate and sustain poverty; (c) by urging the expansion of civil and political rights, which can play a crucial instrumental role in advancing the cause of poverty reduction; (d) by confirming that economic, social and cultural rights are binding international human rights, not just programmatic aspirations; (e) by adding legitimacy to the demand for ensuring meaningful participation of the poor in decision-making processes; (f) by cautioning against retrogression and non-fulfilment of minimum core obligations in the name of making trade-offs; and (g) by creating and strengthening the institutions through which policy-makers can be held accountable for their actions.

The word "guideline" is understood differently by different people and institutions. The set of Guidelines presented here should be seen as elaborating and clarifying certain principles that should guide the process of formulating, implementing and monitoring a poverty reduction strategy if it is to be consistent with a human rights approach. The expectation is that once the principles are understood, the actors involved in poverty reduction will be able to implement them in practice, keeping in view the specificities of their own context. In other words, this is not a manual that purports to teach in a mechanical, comprehensive and directive way how to implement human rights in the context of poverty reduction.

While the principles of the rights-based approach to poverty reduction enunciated in these Guidelines are broadly applicable to both rich and poor countries, the primary focus is on poverty in poorer countries. In part, this is in recognition of the obvious fact that poverty is a much more serious problem in these countries. But it is also partly because poverty in rich countries has special features that need to be addressed separately. Perhaps these Guidelines could be expanded in the future to address those issues. The Guidelines presented here do not address all aspects of human rights with equal emphasis, because they are formulated for the specific context of poverty reduction, which is only a part of the broader human rights agenda. The rationale of the choice of rights, of the relative emphasis placed on different rights, and of the targets, indicators and strategies to be found in these Guidelines should be understood in this context.

The choice of human rights to be addressed in these Guidelines was based on a judgement as to which rights are most relevant to the context of poverty. This judgement was in turn guided by the understanding that human rights can be relevant to poverty in different ways. [5] Of special significance in the context of poverty reduction are rights that have either constitutive or instrumental relevance.

The idea of constitutive relevance of human rights derives from our understanding of what it means to be poor. According to a widely accepted view, a poor person is one who is deprived of basic capabilities – such as the capability to be free form hunger, to live in good health, to be literate, and so on. In the language of rights, one may say that a poor person is one for whom a number of human rights remain unfulfilled – such as the rights to food, health, education and so on. Such rights have constitutive relevance for poverty if a person's lack of command over economic resources plays a role in causing their non-realization. Some human rights are such that their fulfilment will help realize other human rights that have constitutive relevance for poverty. For example, if the right to work is realized, it will help realize the right to food. Such rights can be said to have instrumental relevance for poverty. The same human right may, of course, have both constitutive and instrumental relevance. These Guidelines address the rights that are considered to be most relevant to poverty – on either constitutive or instrumental grounds or on both.

The Guidelines are divided into three sections. Section I sets out the basic principles of a human rights approach that should inform the process of formulating a poverty reduction strategy. Section II sets out the human rights approach to determining the content of a poverty reduction strategy. It identifies, for each of the rights relevant to poverty reduction, the major elements of a strategy for realizing that right. Here the rights are classified under two broad headings – national and international – depending on the level at which action will have to be taken. Section III explains how the human rights approach can guide the monitoring and accountability aspects of poverty reduction strategies. Like the principles discussed in Section I, accountability is also one of the basic principles of a human rights approach to poverty reduction. But because of its special significance in the context of human rights and poverty reduction, it is singled out for discussion in a separate section.

In Section II of the Guidelines, the discussion of each right is structured around four parts. Part A outlines the relevance of the right in the context of poverty. Part B sketches the scope or content of the right as set out in international human rights instruments. For ease of reference, boxes reproduce some of the most relevant international human rights provisions; they also refer to recent world conferences, as well as the most relevant General Comments or Recommendations adopted by United Nations human rights Treaty-bodies. (General Comments and Recommendations offer guidance to State parties on the contours and content of human rights and the measures that might be taken to better secure their implementation.)

Part C identifies key targets in relation to each right and lists, for each target, some indicators that will help assess the extent to which these targets are being achieved over time. Part D sets out key features of a strategy for achieving the specified targets. Some brief comments are in order regarding the targets, indicators and strategies identified in these Guidelines.

For each right, the targets were derived from the scope of the right as set out in international human rights law (and discussed in Part B under each right).

The choice of targets was guided by the following question: given the scope of the right, what are the major targets whose fulfilment would ensure realization of that particular right for the poor? Achieving these targets, for all the rights that are relevant to poverty, should be the ultimate goal of the human rights approach to poverty reduction. Many of the targets draw upon, and are similar to, those set out in the Millennium Development Goals (MDGs) adopted by the United Nations General Assembly in September 2000.

These targets may not all be achievable immediately – they may be subject to progressive realization. Nevertheless, a human rights approach to poverty reduction requires States to move as expeditiously as possible towards fulfilment of the targets. In the light of progressive realization, States should identify appropriate indicators, in relation to which they set ambitious but realistic benchmarks (i.e. intermediate targets) corresponding to each ultimate target, so that the rate of progress can be monitored and, if progress is slow, corrective action taken. Thus, indicators measure progress towards both intermediate and ultimate targets.

Several points relating to indicators are worth noting. First, the construction of human rights indicators is an ongoing enterprise and this document does not claim to have entirely resolved the matter. Nonetheless, an attempt has been made to derive from the existing literature, including that on Millennium Development Goals, a set of indicators that seem most appropriate for the targets in question, keeping in view the context of poverty. It is important to bear this poverty context in mind when inquiring why certain targets and indicators have been chosen, and not others.

Second, even in the context of poverty, the proposed list of indicators is by no means exhaustive. At the same time, it is not expected that all the indicators proposed here are applicable to all countries at all times. The list is intended for reference only. Each country must decide for itself which indicators are most appropriate for its specific circumstances.

Third, while using the indicators, it should be borne in mind that the objective is to indicate the conditions of the poor, and of specific disadvantaged groups among the poor, and not the average condition of the population as a whole. Some indicators are such that even if they refer to the overall population, any improvement or deterioration indicated by them will basically reflect changes in the condition of the poor – for example, the proportion of all children with access to primary education, or the proportion of homeless people in the country. Other indicators do not have this property – for example, the rate of specific crimes against women. These will have to be disaggregated to reflect the condition of the poor and of specially disadvantaged groups among them, e.g. poor women, minorities, indigenous peoples and so on. Exactly what type of disaggregation is appropriate will depend on the nature of the target in question and the particular circumstances of the country.

Fourth, most of the indicators proposed in these Guidelines have a striking resemblance to the standard indicators of socio-economic progress. So this raises the question, in what sense can they be characterised as human rights indicators? In brief, a human rights indicator derives from, reflects and is designed to monitor realisation or otherwise of a specific human rights norm, usually with a view to holding a duty-bearer to account. Thus, because there is overlap between human rights targets and socio-economic progress, there is likely to be a resemblance between human rights indicators and the standard indicators of socio-economic progress - although it should be observed that some human rights indicators, especially those relating to civil and political rights, do not usually figure in measures of socio-economic progress. Essentially, what tends to distinguish a human rights indicator from a standard disaggregated indicator of socio-economic progress is less its substance than (i) its explicit derivation from a human rights norm and (ii) the purpose to which it is put viz human rights monitoring with a view to holding duty-bearers to account.

Some remarks should be made to clarify the strategies proposed in connection with each right. First, the intention is not to offer a complete strategy for implementing the right in question. A strategy is offered only to the extent that it is relevant to poverty reduction. Even in the context of poverty, the idea is not to formulate comprehensive and detailed prescriptions, but to identify some broad principles that follow from human rights concerns. The details are to be worked out by the people engaged in preparing poverty reduction strategies, and these details are bound to vary depending on the context.

Second, for each right the proposed strategy consists of two distinct types of recommendation. First, there are recommendations that follow directly and clearly from the explicit human rights laws and their elaboration by the UN human rights Treaty-bodies. Second, there are recommendations that may not be explicitly stated in any treaties or human rights jurisprudence, but are considered to be consistent with the spirit and intention of the law. In general, a prescriptive tone is adopted here for the first set of recommendations, while the second is presented rather as a set of suggestions. It should be understood, however, that when the prescriptive tone is used it is only because the recommendations are in the nature of legal obligations. Moreover, these obligations have not been imposed from outside; they have been voluntarily incurred by States with a view to upholding the dignity and freedom of their people. The prescriptive language is intended merely to remind States of what they have voluntarily undertaken to do.

Third, even taking the prescriptive and suggestive elements together, the proposed strategy for any particular right cannot be regarded as comprehensive in any sense. This is partly because of the interdependence of human rights discussed earlier. Thus, the strategy proposed for implementing the right to food will not succeed for everyone unless progress is made in realizing the right to work, because most people who are not directly involved in food production have to work to purchase food from the market. Furthermore, successful implementation of any right will depend on the institutions for participation, monitoring and accountability – issues that are common to all rights and have therefore been discussed in separate sections instead of being repeated for each right. Thus, the strategy proposed for each right has to be seen as part of a comprehensive approach rather than as being adequate in isolation.

Fourth, a comprehensive approach does not prevent a State from prioritizing among rights. It is not expected that any country will find it feasible to implement all the recommendations with respect to all the rights simultaneously and immediately. Each State is free to set its own priorities and take up some of the recommendations for immediate implementation, while deferring others, so long as it abides by the principles of progressive realization. In choosing priorities, however, each State should be alert to the interdependence of human rights so as to maximize the effectiveness of its policies.

These Guidelines address large, complex, multisectoral issues of far-reaching importance. Clearly, this document represents one stage in a long-term project. While the Guidelines draw on some practical experience, they should be subjected to a piloting process and revised accordingly. In this way, they can be refined and become increasingly operational.

United Nations specialized agencies, programmes and other bodies have a wealth of material and expertise bearing upon the issues addressed in this document. Thus, they are in an excellent position to help States formulate, implement, monitor and evaluate strategies, policies, programmes and projects that reflect these Guidelines. It is to be hoped that the various United Nations agencies and programmes will coordinate closely with a view to assisting States that may wish to use the Guidelines as a way of enhancing their poverty reduction strategies.

THE GLOBAL COMPACT'S APPROACH TO HUMAN RIGHTS

Two of the Global Compact's ten principles are devoted to human rights. However, the labour standards principles are also human rights related. The two human rights principles are positive and negative, that is, they emphasize doing good as well as not doing harm. Human rights is a major priority area of the UN Global Compact Office as it remains one of the newest and least familiar for many of the company participants. We've been doing a fair bit of work in this area and plan to continue doing so. We feel we are making an important contribution although much more clearly remains to be done.

Our main partner in all our human rights work has been and will remain the OHCHR. They are clearly the guardians of the two human rights principles. We also work with a number of other organizations in this area, including BLIHR and the Danish Institute for Human Rights.

Located within the UN Secretariat-the Secretary-General's office to be precise-the Global Compact Office must be as pragmatic and non political as possible. We focus on the practical "How" question, namely, how to implement human rights within a business's own operations and activities, especially on what businesses can do to eliminate their potentially negative human rights impact. Two recent publications that we have produced in this area are: Raising the Bar; and Embedding HR in Business Practice. One of our major activities in this area has been fostering tool development and recommending proven tools to help with the implementation process. Rather than reinvent the wheel, we help disseminate information about existing tools with a proven track record, such as the Business & Human Rights Resource Centre's website, the Danish Institute Human Rights Compliance Assessment quick check tool, and the BLIHR matrix.

We are also working on a human rights training package and, with partners, on a business guide to human rights impact assessment and, with BLIHR, on guidance for managers on how to implement human rights. One of our most significant contributions to the area continues to be our efforts to build consensus among companies, other societal actors and even governments that human rights are an important business issue. Our leadership model is key here. The process for initiating involvement (CEO commitment with endorsement from the Board) means that many boardroom and/or senior executive discussions about human rights have taken place because of the Global Compact. Moreover, 2268 companies are on record as having expressed support for and intention to implement human rights. Importantly, these are companies in 87 different countries, helping to demonstrate the universality of human rights. Governments have also collectively and individually recognized the contribution of the Global Compact in a number of contexts, most recently in the 2005 World Summit Outcome document.

We are pleased to report that much learning is going on at the local level. We know that some Global Compact local networks have used our human rights publication as the basis for running their own learning activities on human rights. Many Global Compact local networks have also invited local chapters of human rights NGOs to come and speak with them to help them learn about human rights in a business context. In some countries where governments are not very supportive of human rights, business has been taking a keen interest and are slowly helping their governments to see that human rights are important.

We have also contributed to the business and human rights debate through helping to develop and refine its lexicon. As already mentioned, we helped popularize the concepts of "sphere of influence" and "complicity" as key terms that have helped focus and advance the business and human rights debate. We also collect and disseminate case studies of the real dilemmas that companies are facing and provide opportunities for companies and others to come together to work on solutions. E.g. Supply chain, business in conflict zones (Enabling economies of peace), managing diversity and non-discrimination, and contributing to OHCHR's consultation process last year. As the UN, we can bring to the table audiences that others sometimes can't.

Is our approach having an impact? McKinsey & Company's impact assessment in 2004 found that the Compact has existential power and has had significant incremental impact in the sense of helping change to happen faster and more easily-which is our modest aim. Among the other findings were that half of all participating companies reported having changed their policies with respect to the principles. Many companies from OECD countries have signed on to Global Compact to learn about how to improve their human rights performance. For nearly two-thirds of the companies from developing countries, the Global Compact is the first corporate citizenship initiative in which they have engaged. Many do so to learn how to improve their social and environmental performance and thus enhance their ability to enter into supplier relationships with larger global firms.

There is no doubt that much more remains to be done. One of our most exciting upcoming challenges is that we're bringing our multi-stakeholder approach to China with a big Summit there later this year.

ROLE OF THE GLOBAL COMPACT

A word or two is also warranted on the role of the Global Compact in the context of calls for greater legal accountability for business. The first point to note is that the Global Compact is a voluntary initiative without a mandate or resources to monitor compliance. Nevertheless, protecting the integrity of the UN and of the initiative is a legitimate concern. We therefore introduced a stricter logo protection policy and new integrity measures covering misuse of the GC logo and a complaint procedure for systematic and egregious abuse of the GC's overall aim and principles. The policy goes as far as UN legal office will allow given our status as voluntary initiative of UN Secretariat.

We also introduced a procedural requirement that all company participants communicate to their stakeholders on a regular basis their progress in implementing all ten principles. Companies not doing so for two years in a row are designated "inactive" on our website until they start communicating.

This has already started to show results with media calling attention to "inactive" companies, prompting them to start communicating. Most importantly of all, we cannot emphasize enough that the Global Compact's voluntary initiative is not intended to be a total solution. It is positioned as complementary to and not a substitute for other approaches, including for international law. Human rights issues are complex and a multitude of approaches is clearly needed.

HISTORY OF HUMAN RIGHTS

The idea of human rights, that is the notion that anyone has a set of inviolable rights simply on grounds of being human regardless of legal status, origin or conviction for crimes, emerges as an idea of Humanism in the Early Modern period and becomes a position in the 18th century Age of Enlightenment. The human rights movement emerged in the 1970s, especially from former socialists in eastern and western Europe, with major contributions also from the United States and Latin America. The movement quickly jelled as social activism and political rhetoric in many nations put it high on the world agenda. By the 21st century, Moyn has argued, the human rights movement expanded beyond its original anti-totalitarianism to include numerous causes involving humanitarianism and social and economic development in the Third World.

Some notions of righteousness present in ancient law and religion is sometimes retrospectively included under the term "human rights". While Enlightenment philosophers suggest a secular social contract between the rulers and the ruled, ancient traditions derived similar conclusions from notions of divine law, and, in Hellenistic philosophy, natural law.

Ancient Near East

While it is known that the reforms of Urukagina of Lagash, the earliest known legal code (c. 2350 BC), must have addressed the concept of rights to some degree, the actual text of his decrees has not yet been found. The oldest legal codex extant today is the Neo-Sumerian *Code of Ur-Nammu* (ca. 2050 BC). Several other sets of laws were also issued in Mesopotamia, including the Code of Hammurabi (ca. 1780 BC), one of the most famous examples of this type of document. It shows rules, and punishments if those rules are broken, on a variety of matters, including women's rights, men's rights, children's rights and slave rights.

Antiquity

Some historians suggest that the Achaemenid Persian Empire of ancient Iran established unprecedented principles of human rights in the 6th century BC under Cyrus the Great. After his conquest of Babylon in 539 BC, the king issued the Cyrus cylinder, discovered in 1879 and seen as some today as the first human rights document. The cylinder has been linked by some commentators to the decrees of Cyrus recorded in the Books of Chronicles, Nehemiah, and Ezra, which state that Cyrus allowed (at least some of) the Jews to return to their homeland from their "Babylonian Captivity".

In opposition to the above viewpoint, the interpretation of the Cylinder as a "charter of human rights" has been dismissed by some historians and characterized by some others as political propaganda devised by the Pahlavi regime. The German historian Josef Wiesehöfer argues that the image of "Cyrus as a champion of the UN human rights policy... is just as much a phantom as the humane and enlightened Shah of Persia.", while historian Elton L. Daniel has described such an interpretation as "rather anachronistic" and tendentious. The cylinder now lies in the British Museum, and a replica is kept at the United Nations Headquarters.

A declaration for religious tolerance on an egalitarian basis can be found in the Edicts of Ashoka, which emphasize the importance of tolerance in public policy by the government. The slaughter or capture of prisoners of war was also condemned by Ashoka. Some sources claim that slavery was also non-existent in ancient India. Others state, however, that slavery existed in ancient India, where it is recorded in the Sanskrit Laws of Manu of the 1st century BC.

Early Islamic Caliphate

Many reforms in human rights took place under Islam between 610 and 661, including the period of Muhammad's mission and the rule of the four immediate successors who established the Rashidun Caliphate. Historians generally agree that Muhammad preached against what he saw as the social evils of his day, and that Islamic social reforms in areas such as social security, family structure, slavery, and the rights of women and ethnic minorities improved on what was present in existing Arab society at the time. For example, according to Bernard Lewis, Islam "from the first denounced aristocratic privilege, rejected hierarchy, and adopted a formula of the career open to the talents." John Esposito sees Muhammad as a reformer who condemned practices of the pagan Arabs such as female infanticide, exploitation of the poor, usury, murder, false contracts, and theft. Bernard Lewis believes that the egalitarian nature of Islam "represented a very considerable advance on the practice of both the Greco-Roman and the ancient Persian world." Muhammed also incorporated Arabic and Mosaic laws and customs of the time into his divine revelations.

The Constitution of Medina, also known as the *Charter of Medina*, was drafted by Muhammad in 622. It constituted a formal agreement between Muhammad and all of the significant tribes and families of Yathrib , including Muslims, Jews, and pagans.

The document was drawn up with the explicit concern of bringing to an end the bitter inter tribal fighting between the clans of the Aws (Aus) and Khazraj within Medina. To this effect it instituted a number of rights and responsibilities for the Muslim, Jewish and pagan communities of Medina bringing them within the fold of one community-the Ummah.

The Constitution established the security of the community, freedom of religion, the role of Medina as a haram or sacred place (barring all violence and weapons), the security of women, stable tribal relations within Medina, a tax system for supporting the community in time of conflict, parameters for exogenous political alliances, a system for granting protection of individuals, a judicial system for resolving disputes, and also regulated the paying of blood-wite (the payment between families or tribes for the slaying of an individual in lieu of lex talionis).

Muhammad made it the responsibility of the Islamic government to provide food and clothing, on a reasonable basis, to captives, regardless of their religion. If the prisoners were in the custody of a person, then the responsibility was on the individual. Lewis states that Islam brought two major changes to ancient slavery which were to have far-reaching consequences. "One of these was the presumption of freedom; the other, the ban on the enslavement of free persons except in strictly defined circumstances," Lewis continues. The position of the Arabian slave was "enormously improved": the Arabian slave "was now no longer merely a chattel but was also a human being with a certain religious and hence a social status and with certain quasi-legal rights."

Esposito states that reforms in women's rights affected marriage, divorce, and inheritance. Women were not accorded with such legal status in other cultures, including the West, until centuries later. *The Oxford Dictionary of Islam* states that the general improvement of the status of Arab women included prohibition of female infanticide and recognizing women's full personhood. "The dowry, previously regarded as a bride-price paid to the father, became a nuptial gift retained by the wife as part of her personal property."

Under Islamic law, marriage was no longer viewed as a "status" but rather as a "contract", in which the woman's consent was imperative. "Women were given inheritance rights in a patriarchal society that had previously restricted inheritance to male relatives." Annemarie Schimmel states that "compared to the pre-Islamic position of women, Islamic legislation meant an enormous progress; the woman has the right, at least according to the letter of the law, to administer the wealth she has brought into the family or has earned by her own work."

William Montgomery Watt states that Muhammad, in the historical context of his time, can be seen as a figure who testified on behalf of women's rights and improved things considerably. Watt explains: "At the time Islam began, the conditions of women were terrible-they had no right to own property, were supposed to be the property of the man, and if the man died everything went to his sons."

Muhammad, however, by "instituting rights of property ownership, inheritance, education and divorce, gave women certain basic safeguards." Haddad and Esposito state that "Muhammad granted women rights and privileges in the sphere of family life, marriage, education, and economic endeavours, rights that help improve women's status in society." However, other writers have argued that women before Islam were more liberated drawing most often on the first marriage of Muhammad and that of Muhammad's parents, but also on other points such as worship of female idols at Mecca.

Sociologist Robert Bellah (*Beyond belief*) argues that Islam in its 7th-century origins was, for its time and place, "remarkably modern...in the high degree of commitment, involvement, and participation expected from the rank-and-file members of the community." This is because, he argues, that Islam emphasized the equality of all Muslims, where leadership positions were open to all. Dale Eickelman writes that Bellah suggests "the early Islamic community placed a particular value on individuals, as opposed to collective or group responsibility."

Middle Ages

Magna Carta is an English charter originally issued in 1215. Magna Carta was the most significant early influence on the extensive historical process that led to the rule of constitutional law today. Magna Carta influenced the development of the common law and many constitutional documents, such as the United States Constitution and Bill of Rights.

Magna Carta was originally written because of disagreements amongst Pope Innocent III, King John and the English barons about the rights of the King.

Magna Carta required the King to renounce certain rights, respect certain legal procedures and accept that his will could be bound by the law.

It explicitly protected certain rights of the King's subjects, whether free or fettered — most notably the writ of habeas corpus, allowing appeal against unlawful imprisonment.

For modern times, the most enduring legacy of Magna Carta is considered the right of habeas corpus. This right arises from what are now known as clauses 36, 38, 39, and 40 of the 1215 Magna Carta. The Magna Carta also included the right to due process: "No Freeman shall be taken or imprisoned, or be disseised of his Freehold, or Liberties, or free Customs, or be outlawed, or exiled, or any other wise destroyed; nor will We not pass upon him, nor condemn him, but by lawful judgment of his Peers, or by the Law of the Land. We will sell to no man, we will not deny or defer to any man either Justice or Right." —*Clause XXIX of the Magna Carta*

ISSUES OF HUMAN RIGHTS

The Internally Displaced due to Conflicts

The large-scale internal migration caused by political violence has created classes of internal refugees. During the years of militancy in the Punjab, after the anti-Sikh riots in 1984, and the movement of Kashmiri Pandits out of the valley have provided visible evidence of such migration. While the violence that preceded the migration has been squarely addressed in human rights terms, the rehabilitation and return of the migrants after displacement appears to have been only on the margins of the human rights movement.

Refugees

India has not ratified the 1951 UN Convention on Refugees, nor has it signed the 1967 protocol. The Indian state has generally resisted visits from the UNHCR to camps where refugees are housed. Activists say that the Indian state has been relatively benign towards refugees. One non-governmental source, in 1999, India hosted more than 2,92,000 refugees; which includes more than 16,000 persons from Afghanistan, 65,000 Chakmas from Bangladesh, 30,000 Bhutanese of Nepali origin, 50,000 Chin indigenous people from Myanmar and about 39,000 pro-democracy student activists from Rangoon and the Mandalay region, 1,10,000 Sri Lankan Tamils of whom 70,000 are in camps and 40,000 outside, 1,10,000 Tibetans and around 7000 persons from other countries.

The assassination of Rajiv Gandhi in 1991 has reportedly altered the treatment meted out to the Sri Lankan refugees. A fact-finding report of a civil liberties organisation in Tamil Nadu, Sri Lankan refugees fall into three categories: those who are in the 133 refugee camps; refugees who maintain themselves outside the camps; and those who have been identified as belonging to militant groups who were kept in virtual rigorous confinement in the three special camps. In August 1995, 43 inmates of the Special Camp at Tippu Mahal, Vellore escaped and a one-man commission set up by the state describes the structure and administration of the camps.

The refugees were found to be prisoners in these camps and, as even the state appointed commission had remarked, 'admittedly these inmates or most of them are in rigorous confinement in the special camps for five or six years continuously.' The testimony of the two inmates to the fact-finding team also revealed that the camp in Vellore had among its inmates at least 12 disabled persons.

The Government of India does not appear to have any policy on how to deal with refugee-prisoners in their camps.

The protection of Chakma refugees in the state of Arunachal Pradesh, and their right to have their claim for citizenship considered, was canvassed by a civil liberties group before the NHRC. The Supreme Court, approached by the NHRC, directed that the threats held out to the Chakmas by the local citizens be dealt with by the state. It also asserted that their applications for being granted citizenship be considered under the Citizenship Act. The difficulties besetting refugees even after long years of residence in a state, with state acquiescence, were in evidence here.

Land Alienation

The loss to communities of right over land is widespread, and various movements to recover control over land and related resources have been active particularly in the past decade and a half, though some movements go back many decades. The issue of tribal land alienation was linked with that of displacement, and the judicial system was used to get an order declaring unconstitutional the transfer of land from a tribal to a non-tribal through the medium of the state (in its land acquisition capacity).Recent efforts to delete this constitutional protection given in Schedule V of the Constitution are being resisted as a denial of basic protection given to tribals, paving the way for their displacement and impoverishment.

The issue of land alienation was one of the primary issues in the struggle for separate statehood for Uttaranchal, and till today is identified as one of the main rights violations occurring in the state.

In Kerala, the issue is differently positioned. While the loss of land to the tribal is viewed as a violation of their rights and protection of those rights, the settlers are largely people who are themselves on the economic margins.

While groups from within the tribal communities have been demanding restoration of alienated land, and the High Court has supported their stand, other human rights advocates maintain an uneasy silence since the contest appears to be between two vulnerable communities.

Right Over Resources

The right of the forest dwellers to reside in forests, and for those dependent on forest produce to have access to forests, is contested terrain. Till recently, there were conservation groups which demanded that removing tribals from within forest areas was necessary in the interest of conservation. This stand has softened somewhat, and a more symbiotic relationship between the forest and the dweller recognised as possible. The problems are now spoken of in terms of overpopulation, and over-grazing, in the forest area.

State policy is, however, widely perceived as being inimical to the continuance of the forest dweller within the forest. 'Settling' of rights and interests is therefore met with deep suspicion, as is happening in Madhya Pradesh.

Activists have therefore been mobilising the grassroots - in MP, it was through a *padayatra* over a period of six months –to resist the conservation projects which may end up pauperising the dwellers, and, further, may denude the forest too. There have been attempts in the early '90s to prepare a new Forest Bill that will contain within it the interests of conservation, and of the people. Efforts such as this have stalled the legislation proposed by the state which groups and movements see as being opposed to rights - including the right to livelihood, to culture, to security, to shelter, among others - even while the alternative bills have hardly ever been adopted.

An activist identified the problem of land and resources being related to how possession and ownership of land are perceived.

There are three kinds of property he said:

1. Private property
2. Public property
3. Common property

What is held as 'public property' by the state, he said, has been treated as property owned by the state, and not held in trust by the state. It is the notion of common property that has to be resurrected and advanced.

The entry of mining interests into Orissa has, for instance, brought into the open the problem that is inherent in globalisation when it comes into conflict with local interest. The unequal, triangular contest between multinational mining interests, the state which binds itself to protecting the multinational interest on Indian territory, and the local dwellers–in the case of mining, it is often tribals - manifests itself as a human rights issue.

Aquaculture, which brings in corporations to exploit resources through prawn culture, for instance, has been resisted on grounds of loss of livelihood, long-term destruction of marine life and consequent degradation of the environment. Corporatised aquaculture and shrimp farms have been banned. Deep-sea trawlers have also been banned, and the livelihood and lives of fisher communities salvaged. So, too, with prawn culture. Human rights activists see setbacks to these efforts at preservation of community livelihoods and of the environment in the Aquaculture Bill that has been presented to the Parliament in 2000.

The Aruvari Sansad (Water Parliament) in Ajmer district in Rajasthan, which, with the help of the Tarun Bharat Sangh, an NGO, has wrested control over the river, the check dams it has built along it, the revived rivers and the fish that have sprung into being in the river is an uncommon assertion over water and water resources to the exclusion of agencies of the state.

The issue of land reforms and the redistribution of land was encountered in Andhra Pradesh. The Peoples War Group, for instance, avers that land reform is at the root of their attacks against the state. The problem of professional land grabbers, and the response of land invasion to take possession of land which should rightly belong to the invading community, was also seen in Andhra Pradesh. State response has been to treat the attacks, and invasion, as public order, or law and order, problems.

The loss of tribal land through land alienation - something that the law limits - has raised other issues in Kerala, for instance. The land had been bought from the tribals by settlers who are themselves economically and socially marginalised. A prolonged legal battle, where the court had directed the return of the land to the tribals, has not seen a solution to the contending interests of two communities, each in need of protection from expropriation.

Custodial Violence

Custody death, torture in custody and custodial rape have been subjects of much concern. Custodial violence has

been on the agenda of civil rights groups for over two decades, and reports documenting instances of violence and its systemic occurrence, have been instrumental in the campaigns against custodial violence. Although custody deaths have found an acknowledgment from the state, and the NHRC has issued directions to the states,

- To report of the NHRC any death in custody within 24 hours of the occurrence, and
- To videotape the post-mortem proceedings,

it is difficult to assess if this has resulted in any reduction in the incidence of custody deaths. NHRC reports show a marked increase in the reported cases of custody deaths each year. This is attributed, by the NHRC, to increased reporting and not to increased incidence of the crime; this, however, needs to be further investigated. The incidence of custody deaths demonstrates more undeniably the brutalisation of the processes of law enforcement by the police and armed forces. However, custodial torture (not resulting in death) is not at the focus of campaigns to reduce custodial violence. There are few places which have taken up the treatment of the victims of torture as victims of torture. The Indian state, in the meantime, has resisted attempts (including that of the NHRC) to have it ratify the Torture Convention In recent reported cases from the Gauhati High Court, it is 15 and 16-year olds who are found to have been victims of state violence, and the defence of the state has been that they were hardened militants.

Custodial rape has found an expanded definition - in terms of power rape - in the Penal Code, 1860.8 However, these provisions have hardly been invoked. In the meantime, most often, judicial perceptions of the victim of custodial rape have in significant measure, discredited the victim's version, and blamed the victim resulting in reduction of sentence for policemen convicted of rape to less than the minimum prescribed in law.

From Mathura to Rameeza Bi to Maya Tyagi to Suman Rani - these women have become symbols of patriarchal prejudices.

Campaigns in the matter of custodial rape have invoked their name, and they are now names that are etched into the history and legend of the women's movement.

In the meantime, the legal dictum that the identity of a victim of rape be not disclosed to protect her privacy has been set in place.

Project Displacement

Project displacement, for the construction of large dams or for power projects, for instance, have led to protest movements directly involving the affected people.

The NBA has utilised strategies and tactics of protest – including *jal samarpan*, human chains, working on the funders and the contractors to withdraw, participating in the proceedings before, and surrounding, the World Commission on Dams - which have refused to let the issue be drowned out.

This has also seen the manufacturing of conflicting forces, such as the pro-dam lobby which is believed to be largely state-sponsored.

Human rights issues that arise include:

- Displacement, *per se*
- The poverty of rehabilitation, and often, the impossibility of rehabilitation
- The impoverishment that results from displacement
- The non-reckoning of cultural and community identity and of rights.

What constitutes development has come into severe question in this arena. The Land Acquisition Act 1894 has been at the centre of protests. Among the strategies adopted to deal with the coercive nature of the law has been the drafting of alternative legislation. The obduracy of the state in not approving a policy for rehabilitation of the displaced has also been cause for protest.

Sexual Harassment at the Workplace

This issue acquired visibility with the decision of the Supreme Court in *Vishaka*. Earlier efforts at having the problem addressed, as, for instance, in the Delhi University, has drawn strength from the guidelines set out in the judgment. It was widely reported, however, that it was still proving difficult to get institutions to adopt the guidelines and act upon it. The Madras High Court, for instance, was reportedly averring that the guidelines did not apply to the court; and allegations of sexual harassment by a senior member of the Registry were given short shrift. The process of setting up a credible grievance redressal mechanism was reportedly being watered down in the recommendation of a committee to the Delhi University.

In Kerala, a Commission of Inquiry was set up after Nalini Netto, a senior official of the Indian Administrative Service, pursued her complaint of sexual harassment against a serving minister of the state cabinet - which is seen as a diversion from a representative investigative and redressal forum. P E Usha, in Kerala, faced hostility in her university when she followed up on her complaint of sexual harassment. There have been allegations of sexual harassment of women employees by senior persons within institutions working on human rights, and in progressive publications, which too have shown up the inadequacy of the redressal mechanisms.

- Translating the guidelines into norms in different institutions and workplaces;
- Finding support systems for women who are sexually harassed
- Breaking through thick walls of disbelief are reckoned to be the priorities. This has also been introduced into programmes on gender sensitisation for judicial officers.

Sexual harassment accompanied by violence has become a common feature with cases of acid throwing where there is unrequited love, and harassment which has culminated in the murder of a hounded girl.

Rape

In the '80s and into the early '90s:

- The definition of rape
- The meaning of consent in the context of rape

- Marital rape was widely discussed, and alternative drafts and definitions essayed. While following *Tukaram and Ganpat's* case, 'power' rape was partially introduced into the law. The definition of rape, consent and the status of marital rape in law has however not been altered. Again, while the campaign's gains are witnessed in the Supreme Court holding that, as a rule, the victim's version should not require corroboration and that it should be given credence
- The trauma of the trial continues,
- The law's sanction to delving into character evidence concerning the victim remains in the Evidence Act despite the flood of criticism and protest it has provoked.

In Uttaranchal, an issue not uncommon in investigations into, and trial of, rape surfaced. It was reported that women who were raped at Muzaffarnagar are being pressurised not to testify in the criminal cases not only by the police but also by their own community and political leaders, particularly since monetary compensation has been paid.

In 1994, the National Commission for Women (NCW) was asked by the Supreme Court to propose a scheme for establishing Rape Crisis Centres, and for a Criminal Injuries Compensation Board, which could care for victims of crime. This is yet to materialise.

In the meantime, the women's movement in Rajasthan has got the administration to provide monetary relief to victims of rape, unconnected with trial and conviction. Though this has, at least occasionally, resulted in the veracity of the accusation being challenged as having been made so as to obtain the sum in compensation, it is seen as a move to helping the woman recover.

Rape as reprisal was symbolised in Bhanwari Devi's experience. Bhanwari Devi, a *saathin* working in Rajasthan in and around her village, was part of a wider network of women who were involved in a state-sponsored programme of empowerment particularly of women and girls. Her intervention to thwart the practice of child marriage in the community around her is commonly acknowledged as having resulted in the gang rape that was inflicted on her - as punishment, by men of the dominant community who were outraged by her intervention.

The acquittal of the alleged rapists, more especially the reasoning of the court, based on caste and hierarchies of belief, accentuates the re-victimising of the woman.

The low rate of conviction for rape, and the protest from women's groups, were held out to justify a proposed amendment to criminal law to provide death penalty for the offence of rape. The conflict between provisions of the death penalty and human rights has surfaced, even if gradually, and the groups we met, as well as the National Commission for Women, have rejected the proposal for death penalty for the offence of rape.

Death Penalty

The civil liberties movement has been consistent in its opposition to the death penalty. For a brief while, there were some sections in the women's movement who supported - either vocally, or by their silence - the imposition of death penalty for rape. This too has been retracted, and death penalty for rape opposed. After the period in the early '80s, when the Supreme Court drew up the `rarest of rare' rule, there has been a downward slide, particularly discernible in the 1990s.

- Multiple death sentences,
- Death penalty to minors, and
- Death sentence while reversing acquittal are not uncommon.

The campaign against execution of two youths in Andhra Pradesh who had been convicted of burning a bus which killed 23 passengers saw concerted action, which resulted in their sentence being commuted by the President.

The confirmation of the sentence of death on women is a relatively recent phenomenon. Ramashri's sentence was reduced to life by the Supreme Court, even as the court rejected the right of the NCW to intervene. The sentence of death imposed upon Nalini, convicted in the Rajiv Gandhi assassination case, has been opposed by human rights groups, along with the sentence of death meted out to three others in the same matter. Death sentence confirmed despite dissent among judges of benches of the Supreme Court on the sentence that should be imposed is another, disturbing, occurrence. Even doubts about the age of the accused - whether he had been less than 16 years of age and therefore a juvenile - were not sufficient to dispense with death sentence where death was awarded by a majority of judges.

That the young accused was defended by legal aid lawyers and that 'It is reasonable to presume, in such circumstances, that the amicus curiae or advocate appointed on State brief, would not have been able even to see the petitioner, much less collect instructions from him, during the second and third tiers' was noticed only by the minority judge. Dearth of data, and difficulty of access to data is one obstacle to effectively countering the retentionists. In the meantime, the proliferation of death penalty in recent statutes, *viz..,*

- The Narcotic Drugs and Psychotropic Substances Act 1985 (and as amended in 1988),
- National Security Guards Act 1986,

- TADA 1987 (which lapsed in 1995, but trials under which continue),
- Arms Act 1950 (as amended in 1988),
- Indo-Tibetan Border Police Act 1992,
- The Scheduled Castes and Scheduled Tribes (Prevention of Atrocities) Act 1989,
- Commission of Sati (Prevention) Act 1987,
- Section 364 A IPC as introduced in 1993– 'kidnapping for ransom, etc.'

There has been a deafening silence from the NHRC on the issue of the death penalty.

Urban Shelter and Demolition

There has been a routinising of the emergency visible in the matter of cleaning up of the cities. In 2000-2001, Delhi has seen a spate of demolitions of 'slums'. The slum dwellers have been divided up into eligible and ineligibles, with the eligible being given very small plots of land on which they are required to construct houses within six months on a license basis. The size of the plot ensures that it is only a 'slum' that develops. The 'ineligibles' are not thereafter considered by state policy.

Housing rights activists too do not appear to have been able to identify what happens to the ineligibles when demolition occurs. In Bangalore, housing rights groups have been attempting to demonstrate the effort and money that 'encroachers' expend on the land on which they settle; and that they have worked for their entitlement to alternative plots.

In Bombay, and to a lesser extent elsewhere, there have been attempts to involve the slum dwellers in reconstructing the area in a manner which will let the slum disappear, while they are given places in high-rise tenements in the same area with the rest of the space to be used commercially. In Patna, an order of the High Court in a PIL, requiring the municipal corporation to demolish encroachments, resulted in a demolition spree that an embarrassed court had to step in to stop.

The illegal status of the urban dweller who cannot afford to purchase legality has been aggravated by B.N. Kirpal, J saying: 'Establishing or creating slums, it seems, appears to be good business and is well organised...Large areas of public land, in this way, are usurped for private use free of cost... The promise of free land, at the taxpayers' cost, in place of a jhuggi, is a proposal which attracts more land grabbers. *Rewarding an encroacher on public land with free alternate site is like giving a reward to a pickpocket.*'

Unlike South Africa, where the state's obligation to provide shelter before destroying even an illegal habitat was recognised, drawing upon international law, there is no such recognition in Indian law or judicial decisions. Activists and campaigners therefore face an unenviable, if unavoidable, task of combating the anti-poor stand of the state.

Pavement dwelling, and houselessness, was raised in the '80s and, though it may never really have disappeared, it has resurfaced more rigorously since the demolitions have begun in Delhi.

Migrant workers living on pavements have been particularly vulnerable to random attacks in areas of militant violence. Newspapers have reported such occurrences in the '90s. This issue affecting migrant labour particularly needs to be addressed. The 'clearing' of pavements by removing hawkers has been a phenomenon visible in most cities. Eviction of hawkers, and of dwellers, is a significant issue, and the demands include recognition not only of shelter, land and monetary compensation, but of livelihood too.

Livelihood

Apart from issues of rights over resources, and in the context of displacement and relocation, the death of cotton farmers has, for instance, raised questions about protection of livelihood. Liberalisation has resulted in loss of jobs to large numbers in the workforce, and we hear of deaths among the working classes. This is an area that seems to demand closer attention. The withdrawing of protective labour legislation, which is proposed, such as the 'abolition' part of the Contract Labour (Prohibition and Regulation) Act 1970, or the prohibition of night work for women except where specifically attempted, it is feared, is likely to shrink the rights of workers to a great degree.

Freedom of association is also being re-cast in a new Trade Unions Bill, which labour leaders and activists believe is meant to stifle the powers of labour to group together and be heard. The casualisation of labour which the changes portend are expected to drastically reduce the bargaining power of labour.

In 1989, a PIL filed by two social/political activists from Orissa, led to the express recognition of starvation as a violation of fundamental rights. In 1994, the NHRC acknowledged that starvation is a violation of human rights and ordered the state to pay compensation to the families of victims of starvation in Kalahandi in Orissa.In March/April 2001, academics/researchers from the Delhi School of Economics and the Madras Institute of Development Studies have asked for distribution of buffer stocks that the government has stored in its godowns, to stem the tide of hunger among those with low purchasing power.

The juggling with the public distribution system, and the defining and re-defining of the poverty line and consequently of 'below poverty line' is causing particular concern. The death of 17 protesters chased by the police into the Tamaraparani river, and over 200 injured in the incident has been compared to the killing of innocent persons by the British at Jallianwallabagh 80 years ago. On July 23, 1999, a solidarity procession organised by several political parties proceeded to the Collectorate in Tirunelveli Town in South Tamil Nadu, demanding an early solution of the wage dispute that had been the cause of discontent and agitation among tea workers in the Manjolai Tea Estate.

The also demanded the immediate and unconditional release of 652 tea estate workers who had been kept in the Tiruchi jail for six weeks following a demonstration before the same Collectorate on June 7 and 8, 1999.

Talks on the labour dispute having failed, the political parties decided to present a charter of demands to the Collector. As the processionists neared the Collectorate, the police attempted to prevent the jeep which had the leaders of the agitation in it from proceeding further. As the crowd milled around, the events that ensued included a lathi charge by the police, the lobbing of tear gas and the police also opened fire. A video footage shows an injured person, bleeding, being carried away by four policemen. This injured person remains unaccounted for. The police then chased the people down the banks of the river Tamaraparani forcing the people to jump into the water to save themselves from the police force. Photographs graphically reveal the pursuit of the people by the police into the river, even pushing the people back into the water. People drowned. There were injuries on the person of the drowned victims, testifying to ante-mortem police brutality.

This episode constitutes a new threshold to police violence and brutality in labour related agitation and protest. The 'clearing' of pavements by removing hawkers has been a phenomenon visible in most cities. Eviction of hawkers, and of dwellers, is a significant issue, and the demands include recognition not only of shelter, land and monetary compensation, but of livelihood too.

Fake Encounters (Extra-judicial killings)

In India, extra-judicial killings by the police or the security forces are called 'encounter killings', meaning that the killing occurred during an armed encounter between the police or security forces and the victim. The killing by the state forces is most often declared to be defensive, cases of attempted murder and other related offences are registered against the victims, and the cases closed without further investigation since criminal cases come to an end upon the death of the accused.

Despite being 'unnatural deaths', and the victim having being killed, no investigation ensues to determine whether the death was in fact in an actual encounter, nor whether the use, and the extent of use, of force was justified. This is an acknowledged strategy of the state for eliminating certain kinds of opposition to the state and the established order. In Andhra Pradesh, for instance, the naxalites have been the targets; in Punjab, it was the militant; in Mumbai, it is those who are alleged to be part of the underworld.

Civil liberties groups, journalists and lawyers have consistently challenged this practice over the past two decades.

The demand as it has been articulated after recent episodes has been:

- For doing away with state violence in the form of killings in fake encounters, and
- That all cases of encounter killings ought to be registered as first information reports (FIRs) and investigated before the case is closed. The practice of registering cases against the deceased and terminating the proceedings even before it begins is being vigorously challenged. The NHRC too has issued directions endorsing this recommended practice, but to little effect. These court, and out-of-court, battles have carried on throughout the '80s and the '90s to the present.

The Committee of Concerned Citizens (CCC), a group of individuals in Andhra Pradesh, has approached encounter killings differently. Addressing both naxalite groups and the state, the CCC has been working at de-escalation of violence. While the naxalite response has taken the CCC to the issue of land reforms as being fundamental in understanding violence of the opposition, the state, it is widely believed, is pursuing the path of unbridled unleashing of the use of encounters. The numbers killed in encounters have increased in the two years when the process of reconciliation was being negotiated by the CCC, making some of them ask if intervention by the human rights actors was actually prompting the state to escalate the violence.

The human rights community has had to contend with the issue of impunity which is immediately seen as arising from thee non-registration and the non-investigation of cases.

Involuntary Disappearances

The Punjab disappearances were brought into the open by two human rights defenders, Khalra and Kumar. Khalra was himself thereafter 'disappeared'. Investigations into these disappearances - which were uncovered when mortuary records in three districts of the Punjab were scrutinised and 'unidentified' and partially identified persons were found to have been cremated without informing the families of the deceased - was handed over by the Supreme Court to the NHRC.

The manner in which the matter was reduced to a point where the State of Punjab agreed to pay compensation of ₹. 1 lakh (*without admitting liability*) to the families of 18 persons who had been disappeared and the NHRC's tolerance of this stand of the state, is striking in the *general denial of the phenomenon of disappearances*.

This was after the CBI had found that bodies of several persons had been cremated surreptitiously in the late '80s and early '90s–585 persons who had been subsequently identified had been cremated after being labelled as unidentified. Around 330 of them had been partially identified and over 1200 remained to be identified. The deficiency of compensation as a measure of reconciliation is also evident.

Disappearances appear to be a pattern where there is militant resistance to the state. Case law speaks of this phenomenon in the Northeast. In fact, the first major case of compensation for disappearance after being picked up by the armed forces was from the Northeast.33 On February 27, 2001, newspapers reported that it was alleged in the Lok Sabha, without being effectively countered, that the number of persons missing from the custody of the security forces and the police has risen to 2174 in Jammu and Kashmir; 76 cases had been registered and only one person had been challaned so far.

- Acknowledgment of involuntary disappearances
- Investigation, and seeking to establish what happened to the disappeared so that families and the community can finally know
- Prosecution and punishment, for reasons of deterrence too, and
- Compensation as a measure of atonement are being sought to be worked into the system. It was also reiterated that reconciliation would be impossible to achieve without such acknowledgment, identification of the disappeared and reparation.

That Khalra disappeared even while the matter was being taken to the Supreme Court is a statement on impunity. The theme of impunity was laid out when K.P.S. Gill, the policeman in-charge in Punjab through the waning years of militancy, lashed out in protest when a policeman, Sandhu, committed suicide while facing multiple charges of excesses committed during the years of militancy. The schizophrenic attitude of the process which rewarded him when he killed 'terrorists', and later sought to prosecute him for abuse of power even amounting to murder, stood exposed. Gill;

- Blamed the judiciary for having been inactive, or of playing safe, when captured terrorists were brought before it, and
- Held out the threat that if pursued by prosecution, the police would be unavailable to deal with militancy another time.

Preventive Detention

When the Constitution came into being in 1950, preventive detention laws were avowedly intended to be a transient measure. During the emergency, the Maintenance of Internal Security Act 1971 (MISA) was among the more infamous laws which allowed for preventive detention of persons in the avowed interest of maintenance of internal security. There are now a number of legislations which permit preventive detention, in the states and at the centre.

The National Security Act 1980 (NSA) is an instance of the latter. The A.P Prevention of Dangerous Activities of Bootleggers, Dacoits, Drug Offenders, Goondas, Immoral Traffic Offenders and Land Grabbers Act 1986 is an example of the former.

Public protest against the continuance of these laws is almost inaudible despite:

- The long periods, sometimes up to two years, that a person may be kept in preventive detention
- The tardiness of the procedure prescribed - *e.g.*, the executive may be given up to three months to get the opinion of the Advisory Board which may effectively have a person in custody under executive order up to ninety days
- The range of activities that are allowed to be covered by preventive detention laws that are unconnected with public order or law and order.

Unlike the challenge to the TADA, preventive detention laws have not engaged the human rights community in any sustained manner.

Detention

A range of detentions including those that were plainly illegal came to light during the course of our work:

- The incarceration of persons deemed to be 'non-criminal lunatics' (NCLs) or the wandering mentally ill in jails was investigated in a PIL before the Supreme Court. These are persons picked up under the Police Acts of the states, or under police powers in other laws such as the Indian Lunacy Act 1912, or its successor law, the Mental Health Act 1987.

  They are treated as `nuisances', or bracketed as being dangerous, this providing the rationale for putting them away. The term NCL is in contradistinction to `criminal lunatics', that is, those accused of crime but found to be mentally ill or suffering from mental disorder. For years NCLs were received in jails as places of 'safe custody' under the Indian Lunacy Act 1912 and later under the Mental Health Act 1987.

  In the states of West Bengal and Assam, where the Supreme Court sent

Commissioners to investigate, it was found that many of those in jails as NCLs were in fact not mentally ill at all, but had been placed there deviously, to serve some completely unrelated purpose. For instance, a 70-year woman was found to have been put away as an NCL apparently because her landlord was using it as a means of evicting her. We heard resonances of this reasoning from a lawyer-activist in Chennai.

- The Supreme Court declared, in August 1993, that using jails as places of safe custody to house non-criminal mentally ill persons (NCMI) is unconsti-tutional. Apart from the state of Assam, which admitted in an affidavit in the Supreme Court to continuing the practice, the NHRC has intermittently reiterated that NCMI should be housed in places other than jails. It is plain that the practice continues.
- This is an area that has not been widely addressed within the human rights community. NHRC's recognition of the issue too has been desultory.
- There is evidence in law reports, and activists have admitted to have knowledge of, the practice of hostage taking by the police where the person to be apprehended is not within reach of the police. Relatives of the person sought are then picked up and kept in custody till he surrenders. This appears to have happened with some regularity in Punjab, but we also heard of it in Delhi and Andhra Pradesh, for instance. This breach of the law needs further investigation and response.
- There have been reports of people spending long years in jail, which could have been averted if prisons were not as inaccessible as they are. *Rudul Sah,*37 the man who spent fourteen years in jail because he had been considered unfit to stand trial, and continued to remain untried despite having been declared fit, is one wellknown instance. Recent instances from Bihar38 and West Bengal reveal that the neglect that occasions such illegal incarceration continues. The incapacity of a person to follow up on his trial and sentence, and to procure orders in time has been known to keep him in prison long after he was due to have been released.

The inability to furnish bail or sureties was reportedly one such reason for the large undertrial population.

- It is evident that systemic changes are imperative if these questions of personal liberty are to be addressed.
- In custodial institutions other than prisons - in 'protective homes' for women, for instance, the problem of custody versus shelter has been raised. Protective homes are established under the Immoral Traffic (Prevention) Act 1956 (ITPA). Since they are the only statutory

institutions that can house women for 'protection' as also for 'correction',41 they act as places of custody, operating within the executive-magistracy system. We met women in 'protective custody' in the Agra Protective Home, who were witnesses in a case to be tried in Jhansi; they desired to leave and they had been in the institution for nearly two years. But the law would not let them. 'Rescued' women were placed in these institutions, but the purpose of 'rehabilitation' was found to be too inadequate to make the difference.

- Prison jurisprudence since the late '60s recognises that prisoners do not lose all their rights because of imprisonment. Yet, there is a loss of rights within custodial institutions which continue to occur. For instance, it was found that the HIV status of all the women in the Agra Protective Home was public knowledge, and there was no confidentiality attaching to this information. There was segregation within the institutions of those found to be HIV positive, and, for a while, the Supreme Court too endorsed this. The rules governing women in these institutions uncannily resemble prison rules - such as those concerning visitors, letters, and even punishment for conduct within the institutions.
- Persons working in this area said that this was an area which called for an injection of human rights experience and perspectives.
- The non-release of persons cured of mental illness from institutions was also reported to be a problem. We repeatedly met the need for halfway homes and support services which could help a person be restored to liberty.
- In Delhi, we heard of persons who had been picked up as being persons of Bangladeshi origin, who were kept in custody in a night shelter till they could be repatriated if they were, in fact, found to belong to Bangladesh and the Foreigners Act 1946 could be invoked to effect this move. There was concern that even the basis of identifying them as possible foreigners was not clear and that dispelling suspicion of nationality could well be more difficult for the poor and the dispossessed.

It is also found that it is common practice to pick up people for questioning, and not record their presence in the police station till the police is ready to present them before a magistrate - a way of thwarting the constitutional requirement that every person taken into custody be produced before a magistrate within 24 hours.

Apart from the illegality of such detention, it also makes difficult proving torture in custody during the period of illegal, unrecorded, detention. Human rights activists suggest that telegrams be dispatched to the Chief Minister, the

Director General of Police, the Superintendent of Police, and the Governor for instance, when information about such illegal detention is obtained, to establish the time of detention. The conditions of persons with mental illness in institutions have been cause for human rights concern. In Gwalior Mental hospital, for instance, it was found that persons with mental illness were left in nakedness; the explanation was that they tore their clothes if they were given them. The press raised the issue. Chaining of mentally ill patients was also a practice, and this was outlawed by an order of the court.

One difficulty in ensuring that such violations do not occur, and in getting the law implemented, is access. The human rights community has not engaged with the problems faced within the walls of custodial institutions. Imaginative answers which will make open institutions of what are now bureaucratic, and closed, institutions is an imperative. The hysterectomy controversy in the early 1990s in Pune represents another aspect of the control and decisionmaking within custodial institutions. The hysterectomy of girls below 18 years of age, who were mentally retarded, raised controversy about the decision made by the professionals.

The professionals involved in making the decision neither denied that the hysterectomy was being done, nor did they did see it as a violation. It was justified as being in the best interests of the hygiene of the mentally retarded girl, as making practicable the care of the mentally retarded. The response did not rule out the possibility of sexual abuse when within the institutions, but said it would protect the girls from pregnancy in the event of such an encounter.

The persons responsible for the decision responded angrily to the charges of human rights violations. The Medical Council of India, however, distanced itself from this position, and declared the practice as being against their norms. The intervention of the media and the human rights community precluded further hysterectomies from being done.

THE INTERNET AND HUMAN RIGHTS: AN OVERVIEW

The Internet is a unique communications medium. Like no other medium before, it allows individuals to express their ideas and opinions directly to a world audience and easily to each other, while allowing access to many more ideas, opinions and information than previous media have allowed. Consequently, there is a vital connection between the Internet and human rights.

Through the Internet, citizens from the most repressive regimes are able to find information about matters concerning their own governments and their human rights records that no newspaper may dare print, while denouncing the conditions under which they live, for the world to hear. The Internet allows an intimate look at other countries, other people and other cultures that few before were ever able to attain. This power to give and receive information, so central to any conception of democracy, can be truly achieved on the Internet, as nowhere before.

Further, through the use of encryption technology, citizens can have instantaneous communications with individuals all over the world that are much more resistant to government and private surveillance.

On the Internet, citizens are not mere consumers of content but also creators of content. This fundamental shift in power has created a possibility for every individual to be a publisher. Consequently, the content on the Internet is as diverse as human thought. Individuals and communities have been using the new-found freedom online to link, interact and work collectively in this global work space.

The effect of access to and use of this global interactive medium has been to promote and defend civil and political rights worldwide. This unprecedented power, however, can be very threatening to repressive regimes. The experiences of communities in different countries indicates that few things could be more threatening to authoritarian regimes than access and use of a medium that knows no boundaries and is very hard to control. While traditional methods of censorship-embargoing newspapers and closing down presses-do not work on the Internet, the online censoring techniques that these regimes attempt can be just as destructive.

While the Internet is technologically resistant to government control, it is not immune from such control. Indeed, some countries have been quite sophisticated in exploiting the control and surveillance potential to great effect, at least in the short run. Just because the younger generation may know how to "hack" through proxy servers to avoid censorship does not mean that the youth are safe. These actions should be understood in the technological context--that such hacking is probably obvious to government system administrators, and may make people vulnerable to being identified and prosecuted. Meanwhile, nations around the world are seeking to exploit the surveillance potential of this new medium, including by asserting control over the design and development of communications networks to maximize their surveillance capabilities.

For these reasons, governments and regional and international bodies should enact enforceable free expression guarantees, promote widespread access to and use of strong cryptographic tools that will enable real security, and provide legal protections of privacy, including controls on government surveillance.

The Internet and Human Rights Work

The Internet is one of the best means for communicating on human rights, because it is inexpensive and global. E-mail makes point-to-point communication between human rights workers and among NGOs (non-governmental organizations) cheap and easy, and allows for better coordination of actions. Furthermore, the Internet has the potential of reaching global audiences, including those most in need of such information. The Internet is important to those working for human rights, as it can provide a secure means of communicating between and coordinating the work of human rights groups. Consequently, human rights activists were among the first to make use of the Internet to--

- Coordinate actions and make contacts. Perhaps the most important application of the Internet in human rights is as a great tool for NGOs and activists to be in touch with each other, to share information privately, and to coordinate actions.
- Expose human rights violations and let people know about them. Many human rights organizations throughout the world have instituted e-mail lists to propagate their press releases, alerts and denunciations vis a vis human rights violations. Many of these groups also use Usenet to post their information, or it is posted there by others, and many groups have instituted web pages to make information available.
- Solicit action. Many organizations now use e-mail to distribute action alerts calling for letters to be written on behalf of specific issues.
- Gather information. The amount of human rights information online is extraordinary-beginning with the University of Minnesota web site, and now with the UNHCHR (United Nations High Commissioner on Human Rights) site online, it's much easier to do human rights research.

By enabling early access to information, immediate dissemination of calls for campaigns, and the organization of wide international pressure, the Internet greatly increases the lobbying capacities of human rights groups.

It is vitally important, therefore, to promote freedom of expression and privacy as central elements of the development of the information society.

Internet Freedom in the US

Unfortunately, the US government's domestic policy has not been fully supportive of human rights on the Internet. The US Congress has twice enacted censorship legislation attempting to control content on the Internet. Under our strong constitutional protection of free speech, these laws have been ruled unconstitutional by the courts. Yet Members of Congress continue to press other restrictive measures, and proposals are pending to make Internet Service Providers (ISPs) liable for removing allegedly illegal or improper content. On the privacy side, the Communications Assistance for Law Enforcement Act of 1994 (CALEA) requires that telecommunications systems be designed to accommodate government surveillance, and that law has been perverted by the Department of Justice and the Federal Communications Commission to not merely preserve but to enhance government wiretap capabilities.

Only recently has the US government begun to turn away from its efforts to control the spread of encryption, which is crucial to security and privacy on the Internet.

Still, officials in the Justice Department are trying to preserve their access to decryption keys, and the surveillance debate in the US is not over. Meanwhile, the US government refuses to publicly discuss its international eavesdropping activities, amid growing domestic and international concern over the nature of surveillance in a digital world and, in particular, the US government's "Echelon" surveillance system.

Internet Access Is Important to the Promotion of Human Rights

The most often disregarded impediment to the achievement of the Internet's democratic potential is the problem of access. Accessing the Internet requires either the possession of a computer and payment to an Internet Service Provider or access to a facility where one can connect. This means that, generally, only the affluent will have access. Governments can control freedom of expression of sections of the population by hindering their access to the Internet. This may be done directly by imposing high taxes on computer products and supporting telephone monopolies that keep phone rates high and thus discourage the use of the Internet, or indirectly by failing to support community centres where people may have low-cost access to the Internet.

However, augmented Net access without civil liberties guarantees ? in technology and in law ? may not benefit individuals and may be coupled with government control and extended surveillance capability.

Freedom of Expression

The Universal Declaration, the European Convention and other international human rights agreements enshrine the rights to freedom of expression and access to information. These core documents explicitly protect freedom of expression "regardless of frontiers," a phrase especially pertinent to the global Internet:

> *"Everyone has the right to freedom of opinion and expression; this right includes freedom to hold opinions without interference and to seek, receive and impart*

information and ideas through any media, and regardless of frontiers." Article 19, Universal Declaration of Human Rights.

"Everyone shall have the right to freedom of expression; this right shall include freedom to seek, receive, and impart information and ideas of all kinds, regardless of frontiers, either orally, in writing or in print, in the form of art, or through any other media of his choice." Article 19, International Covenant on Civil and Political Rights.

"Everyone has the right to freedom of expression. This right shall include freedom to hold opinions and to receive and impart information and ideas without interference by public authority and regardless of borders." Article 10, European Convention for the Protection of Human Rights and Fundamental Freedoms.

No matter what the means, government restrictions on speech or access to speech of others violate basic freedom of expression protections. In addition to direct government censorship of Internet communications, or privatized censorship, freedom of speech in the Internet is threatened by diverse factors.

Blocking, filtering, and labelling techniques can restrict freedom of expression and limit access to information. Government-mandated use of blocking, filtering, and label systems violates basic international human rights protections. Global rating or labelling systems squelch the free flow of information. Efforts to force all Internet speech to be labelled or rated according to a single classification system distort the fundamental cultural diversity of the Internet and will lead to domination of one set of political or moral viewpoints. Diversity and user choice are essential: To the extent that individuals choose to employ filtering tools, it is vital that they have access to a wide variety of such tools. "Self-regulatory" controls over Internet content, which have been promoted by some as an alternative to government regulation, ought not to place private ISPs in the role of police officers for the Internet. With regards to content, what is being suggested in the name of "self-regulation" is not that ISPs should as a group regulate their own behaviour, but rather that they should regulate the speech of their customers. This is not true "self-regulation." The role of an Internet Service Provider is crucial for access to the Internet and because of the crucial role that they play, ISPs have been targeted by law enforcement agencies in many countries to act as content censors. While ISPs ought to provide law enforcement reasonable assistance in investigating criminal activity, confusing the role of private companies and police authorities risks substantial violation of individual civil liberties.

Privacy

The Universal Declaration, the European Convention and international human rights instruments enshrine the right to privacy. These core documents explicitly protect the privacy of correspondence and communication:

"No one shall be subjected to arbitrary interference with his privacy, family, home or correspondence, nor to attacks upon his honour and reputation. Everyone has the right to the protection of the law against such interference or attacks." Article 12, Universal Declaration of Human Rights

"No one shall be subjected to arbitrary or unlawful interference with his privacy, family, home or correspondence, nor to unlawful attacks on his honour and reputation." Article 17, International Covenant on Civil and Political Rights

"Everyone has the right to respect for his private and family life, his home and his correspondence." Article 8, European Convention for the Protection of Human Rights and Fundamental Freedoms

Privacy is becoming increasingly important for citizens in the information society. Electronic communications can be very easily intercepted by anyone who wants to. Sending an e-mail message is thus the equivalent of sending a postcard. In the human rights arena especially, many matters discussed among NGOs are extremely confidential. Names of witnesses to human rights violations, for example, need to be kept from those who would harm them. Repressive governments commonly use their intelligence services to tap the phone communications of human rights groups and intercept their mail. It is very likely that they are also intercepting electronic mail.

How Privacy can be Protected on the Internet: Unlike phone calls and paper mail, however, electronic mail can be easily encrypted so that only those to whom it is directed can read it. This means that anyone, such as NGOs, wanting to communicate delicate information freely can do so, without having to fear the consequences of others, such as governments, accessing it.

Therefore, we believe that policies concerning cryptography should be based on the fundamental right to engage in private communication.

Unfortunately, national governments have already taken steps to detain and harass users and developers of cryptography. Nonetheless, strong cryptography is already in use by human rights advocates and its further widespread use should be affirmatively promoted. We oppose efforts that would lead to the development of communications infrastructures designed for surveillance.

Anonymity: Central to free expression and the protection of privacy is the right to express political beliefs without fear of retribution and to control the disclosure of personal identity. Protecting the right of anonymity is therefore an essential goal for the protection of personal freedoms in the online world. The right of anonymity is recognized in law and accepted by custom. It has been an integral part of the growth and development of the Internet. Some governments are working to extend techniques for anonymity. But other efforts are underway to establish mandatory identification requirements and to limit the use of techniques that protect anonymity. For example, the G-8 recently considered a proposal to require caller identification for Internet users. Some local governments have also tried to adopt legislation that would prohibit access to the Internet without the disclosure of personal identity.

Governments should not require the identification of Internet users or restrict the ability to express political beliefs on the Internet anonymously. Efforts to develop new techniques to protect anonymity and identity should be encouraged. ISPs should not establish unnecessary identification requirements for customers and should, wherever practicable, preserve the right of users to access the Internet anonymously.

THE EFFECTS OF HUMAN RIGHTS VIOLATIONS ON THE ENVIRONMENT

Conditions in occupied Tibet demonstrate a prominent feature of environmental human rights. Environmental human rights encompass not only substantive protections such as the right to life, health, traditional livelihood, and culture, but they also include procedural rights. The procedural protections of environmental human rights include the right to information about the environment; the right to express opinions about environmental issues; the right to environmental and human rights education; the right to associate peacefully with others for the purpose of protecting the environment; the right to participate in decisions affecting the environment; and the right to administrative or judicial redress for violations of protected rights. These fundamental freedoms anchor the full realization of all human rights in an open and just society.

When Tibetans are systematically excluded from decisions affecting the Tibetan plateau's environment, and when Tibetans are not given information about actions that affect the environment nor permitted to exchange freely the information they have, there is no check on the environmental harm that results. The procedural protections of environmental human rights are as important as its substantive guarantees.

Uranium mining is taking place at nine known uranium mines on the Tibetan plateau to fuel China's nuclear weapons program and development of nuclear power. Due to the conditions of China's occupation, Tibetans are excluded from the decisions regarding where and how such mining is taking place, and have no access to information about the significant health risks associated with exposure to waste from the mining operations. As a result, rural Tibetan villages in the vicinity of uranium mines, which have experienced illness and "mysterious" deaths among villagers and domestic animals, still have no verifiable knowledge of what risks they are living with, and no recourse for the harms their communities have suffered. The dual nature of environmental human rights not only calls attention to the environmental harm that has occurred, but also asks the question, "how did this happen?" By focusing on what decisions were made, who had access to information about them, and who took part in the decision, the social conditions under which environmental harm occurs can be better understood. Only when the people who are directly affected by environmental harm have a voice in what—and in what manner—environmentally significant actions are taken, is lasting environmental protection possible. This touches on one of the most innovative aspects of human rights and the environment. Linked in a rights-based approach, environmental human rights create a mechanism to hold polluters accountable for environmental harm. Giving the people personally affected by environmental harm a voice in an international forum creates accountability. It also melds one of the greatest strengths of human rights law to one of the weakest areas of environmental law: universal standards.

The large differences in levels of environmental protection between countries is one factor that is accelerating the exploitation of labour and natural resources around the world. As trans-national corporations and governments alike search for the cheapest means of production, the lack of environmental safeguards also means lower production costs. Low-priced goods sold on the international market often come at the expense of polluted air, fouled rivers, and deforested slopes. China has capitalized on Tibet's resource base to build part of its industrial infrastructure and place products on the world market. Similarly, one of China's most powerful foreign policy tools is its inexpensive labour pool and the role of its enormous population as a potential market for low-priced goods.

While the lack of universal standards is one of the biggest hurdles to environmental protection, this is one of the greatest strengths of human rights law. Fundamental notions of basic human rights have been articulated by the global community since 1948, when the Universal Declaration of Human Rights entered into force. Environmental human rights use global human rights norms to state a universal standard of minimum environmental protection that applies equally to every country. In this way environmental harm is cast in terms of its toll in human suffering, which leverages human rights standards to universalize our understanding of unacceptable environmental harm.

ENVIRONMENTAL HUMAN RIGHTS AS INTERNATIONAL LAW

These connections between human rights and the environment are evolving as international legal norms. In the twenty years between the United

Nations (U.N.) Stockholm Declaration on the Human Environment in 1972 and the 1992 U.N. Conference on Environment and Development in Rio de Janeiro (the "Earth Summit"), increasing attention has been paid to the impact of environmental problems on human rights. Even in 1972, the Stockholm Declaration stated the human right to "adequate conditions of life, in an environment of a quality that permits a life of dignity and well-being." By 1992 with the Earth Summit's adoption of the Rio Declaration on Environment and Development, concepts of sustainable development and the rights of future generations to a healthy environment had been added: "environmental protection shall constitute an integral part of the development process and cannot be considered in isolation from it."

One of the most encouraging steps in this direction has been the work in the U.N. Sub-Commission on Prevention of Discrimination and Protection of Minorities over the last seven years. Since first taking up the issue in 1989, under the able leadership of the Sub-Commission's Special Rapporteur, the Sub-Commission has established that there exists meaningful precedent in international law for environmental human rights. The Sub-Commission explored the environmental dimension of human rights, and articulated the links between sustainable development, environmental protection and respect for human rights.

One of the most significant events of the Sub-Commission's study on human rights and the environment was a meeting of an international group of experts in May 1994 at the U.N. in Geneva, Switzerland. This meeting was called for by the Sub-Commission's Special Rapporteur and organized by the Sierra Club Legal Defence Fund, an American environmental non-governmental organization (NGO) that has played a role in the inception and progress of the Sub-Commission's work. This meeting had the ambitious goal of stating a set of principles that embodied the environmental dimension of human rights and grounded environmental rights firmly in human rights law.

The Geneva meeting achieved this goal, and produced the Draft Declaration of Principles on Human Rights and the Environment. The Draft Declaration is incorporated into the Sub-Commission's Final Report, and stands as the current reference point for environmental human rights.

4

Social Development and Human Rights

HUMAN RIGHTS

The natural law, in its original conception, was intended to include both rights and duties. The exclusive emphasis on the rights of man belongs to the eighteenth century. In our own time, a considerable change of feeling has occurred. Modern man seems to be willing to admit that rights are conditional on duties. This change of feeling is obvious with respect to property rights. A natural right of doing with one's property whatever one pleases can no longer be claimed. Social legislation interfering in the ways a man runs his factory is supported by public feeling everywhere. The rights of property imply duties.

Hence it seems that any modern formulation of a bill of natural rights should be supplemented by a bill of duties. Any formulation, however, of these obligations of man encounters difficulties far greater than the formulation of a bill of rights. If we assume that the principle of natural law should be respected by, or find an expression in, positive law, any formulation of such obligations will provide the actual power–holder not only with the mural excuses and the intellectual tools but also with the legal instruments to disregard the rights of man.. It is he who decides whether the obligations have been respected. There is only one such obligation, the legal recognition of which may do not harm (though perhaps not much good either). It is everybody's duty to recognize the human rights of his fellow citizen. This would mean, in practice, that whoever advocates the disregarding or abolishing of these rights loses the moral claim to, and the legal protection of his own human rights.

If, however, these duties of man should be duties towards the 'public welfare' the 'Society' and the State, and rights are made conditional on the fulfilment of these duties, the duties will uproot the rights. The rights will wither away. Whoever is in a position to interpret the *salus publica* or to act in the name of Society or State can use the allegedly unfulfilled duties to shove aside the rights.

A bill of duties of the citizens towards the State would require as its counterpart a formulation of the duties of the 'sovereign' State towards the citizen. However, though the State can compel the citizen, the citizen cannot compel the State to respect these duties.

Hence the possibility that a government transgresses the rights or fails in its duties would logically require not only a right, but a duty, of rebellion or revolution on the side of the citizen–a thing completely empty under modern technological conditions. As this right and duty of revolution can be misused, the State will again have a right and the duty to suppress such revolutions. That means the theoretical justification of civil war by natural law.

THE HUMAN RIGHTS SYSTEM

In order to explore the potential of the human rights framework to achieve social development, it is necessary to briefly describe the human rights system. The essential components of the system are ideology, substantive rights, functions, beneficiaries, actors, institutions, procedures and the levels at which it operates. The human rights system is rich in texts, rhetoric and institutions, but it is lacking in material resources to make rights effective. States place interests such as national security or economy, and the cultivation of international relations. Popular consciousness of rights is often dulled by ethnic conflicts or the burden of traditional values and authority.

Ideology

Surprisingly, there is no great consensus on the ideology of rights. There is substantial agreement that the purpose of human rights is to protect human dignity, but there are different views on the source of that dignity. The principal difference lies between those who seek a religious basis for that dignity, and those who seek a secular basis. There is a widespread perception that the origins of the concept of human rights lie in Western, individualist or liberal philosophy and for that reason some in the East argue that it is alien to their own cultures.

Even in the West there is criticism of the individualistic bias of human rights. There are also historical and pragmatic explanations for rights the former consisting of an analysis of the growth of classes and their relationship to the state, and the latter justifying rights in terms of fairness, stability and peace. These differences bear on the acceptance and realization of rights, but perhaps their importance has diminished with the elaboration of rights under the auspices of the United Nations. It has been possible to reach broad agreement on the scope and substance of rights, and the key international instruments have been ratified by a large number of countries adhering to differing religions and cultural traditions.

The ideology of human rights is one of the most powerful forces today largely at the level of rhetoric, but also as justification for action, particularly the collective interventions by the international community in oppressive states. The ideology of rights and the acceptance that the international community has the overriding responsibility for their protection has been invoked to justify limits on state sovereignty, a cornerstone of the international system.

Levels: International, Regional and National

The national, regional and international levels constitute the global system of rights. Historically, the concept and practice of human rights developed in national systems. Before the establishment of the United Nations, a number of states provided for the protection of rights in their constitutions. The League of Nations and the International Labour Organization facilitated the internationalization of specific rights of workers and minorities, but it is only since the existence of the United Nations that there has been an exponential growth in international human rights law. The United Nations Charter committed its members to the promotion and protection of human rights. The United Nations marked its entry into this area in 1948 by adopting the Universal Declaration of Human Rights since then many conventions have been negotiated and ratified by member states.

The growth of conventions and institutions at the international level was paralleled by the establishment of the European Convention of Human Rights, providing the first instance of the protection of rights at the regional level. The Convention is enforced by the European Court of Human Rights. Since then, regional systems of human rights have been established for Africa and the Americas, though there are differences in the scope of rights and the method of enforcement.

Another regional system has developed in recent years under the auspices of the OSCE, in which Canada and the United States also participate so far the progress has been in developing norms and in the method of persuasion. There are many advantages in having regional systems: for instance, they take the load off the international system, and bring the pressure of friendly, neighbouring states to bear on offending states. Equally important, they represent the consensus of the states as to the standards of government behaviour acceptable in the region. Perhaps the absence of regional systems in

Asia and Pacific-Australasia is due to the lack of this regional consensus. Consequently, regional systems are uneven, wiTheurope's being the best integrated and certainly the most effective.

The third level is the national. It is the most important level for giving legal effect to human rights norms, which is done by guarantees in the constitutions and laws, and by giving effect to international or regional treaties. It is also the most important level for the enforcement of rights; most violations of rights are dealt with, at least in the first instance, in national courts or other human rights institutions. It is at this level that the key struggle for human rights is conducted and the resistance to it waged.

The different levels are being integrated through a regime of treaties that are effective at the national level but supervised at the regional or international level, and through the respect paid by national governments and judiciaries to elaborations of rights by regional or international tribunals. Nevertheless, there is a division of labour between these levels as regards the different functions of the human rights system, to which I now turn.

Functions

One of the most important functions is developing a consensus on rights and interests to be protected. This is often done by interest groups women, minorities, migrants, corporations and so on. In recent years NGOs have played an important role in lobbying for the recognition of particular interests many norms on indigenous peoples, minorities and protection against torture owe their origin to the efforts of NGOs. Sometimes regional or international conferences have also performed this role.

Once there is a substantial consensus, the task of norm setting can be undertaken. This involves the elaboration of treaties or legislation and has historically been the role of national governments and legislatures. However, in recent years the international system has played a crucial role. The United Nations has provided the forum for negotiating treaties on human rights. By its nature, norm setting is the responsibility of official bodies, but NGOs have also played a significant role in developing treaties or legislation.

The promotion of respect for rights consists of various activities including information on and education about human rights, and support for the institutions that uphold them. This function is the responsibility of official and non-official bodies. In many countries official human rights commissions have a special responsibility for the propagation of rights. In more authoritarian states, the primary responsibility is discharged by NGOs and social groups, including trade unions.

Closely connected to the respect for rights is mobilization of groups on the basis of rights. Claims of rights have constituted forms of protest and challenges to authority. In so far as one function of rights is the empowerment of vulnerable groups, mobilization is crucial and, since the aim of mobilization is to organize social groups and challenge authorities, human rights defenders are often harassed or even oppressed. Human rights also provide the basis for networking, nationally and internationally. Indigenous peoples and women have been particularly successful in networking, which is almost always the preoccupation of non-official bodies.

Protecting rights is the primary responsibility of the state which together with other official bodies is generally bound to respect human rights and most legal actions are directed at the state's violations of rights. Protecting rights takes various forms, ensuring that:

- There is law and order in which people can enjoy their rights;
- The police and army are trained in human rights norms, and respect and uphold people's rights;
- Institutions in the front line of securing rights, like the judiciary and human rights commissions, are independent and adequately resourced; and
- There are effective sanctions against those who violate the rights of others.

The United Nations has played a limited role in protecting rights. The principal UN agency for this purpose formerly the United Nations Centre for Human Rights, now incorporated into the Office of the United Nations High Commissioner for Human Rights has had very limited resources, and had a low profile until the appointment of the current Human Rights Commissioner, Mary Robinson. Unlike other UN agencies, it had no field offices until recently it now has over 20, supervising the protection of rights and offering technical assistance. The task that receives most attention is enforcing rights, most typically through the judicial process. In recent years other institutions, such as ombudsmen, and human rights or equality commissions, have been established for the protection of human rights. These institutions tend to follow less adversarial procedures than courts, and offer mediation and reconciliation. Access to these bodies is also easier, cheaper and more informal than it is to courts, and they tend to be multifunctional, with information and education being a primary responsibility. However, courts remain the final arbiters of violations, and the ultimate authorities for the interpretations of human rights provisions. Therefore the interpretation of judges and legal practitioners, who have a key role in access to the courts, and a well functioning legal system are indispensable for an effective system of enforcement of rights.

The primary institutions for the enforcement of rights are national, but in countries that are part of a regional system of human rights, regional commissions or courts can play an important, supplementary role. The role of the European Court of Human Rights is crucial in that it makes the final interpretations of the European Convention, which are binding on national governments and courts. The international system plays little role in the enforcement of rights. The first steps in international enforcement have been taken with the establishment of tribunals for war crimes in Rwanda and the former Yugoslavia, and with the imminent establishment of the permanent international tribunal as agreed in Rome three years ago.

The international system has an important, or, more accurately, a potentially important, role in the supervision of the protection and enforcement of rights. This supervision takes two forms: one is primarily political and is the responsibility of the OHCHR and the mechanisms associated with it, such as special rapporteurs for countries including Afghanistan and Cambodia, or on themes such as extrajudicial killings, disappearances and violence against women. The other form of supervision is more judicial., the task being performed by specialist, independent bodies set up under human rights treaties.

Most major treaties provide for periodic reports to these bodies; this is the principal means of supervising a state's performance of its treaty obligations. But some treaties also provide for a complaints mechanism, either at the insistence of another state or of a person who alleges that his or her rights have been violated. Even when there is a complaints procedure, the decision of the body is not strictly enforceable, although it provides a valuable opportunity for the body to elaborate the provisions of the treaty and explain the scope of rights protected by it and the permissible derogations.

This has been a particularly valuable aspect of the work of the United Nations Human Rights Committee, set up under the International Covenant on Civil and Political Rights. However, the potential of the supervisory role of the international system has yet to be realised. Until now meagre resources have been provided to the United Nations and the treaty bodies, many of whom can only meet once or twice a year for a fortnight or so and have inadequate secretariat support and virtually no follow-up machinery. This state of affairs is ample evidence of the low priority accorded to human rights by the international community, as is the fact that the international supervisory system is highly fragmented, incoherent and largely ineffective.

Supervision is also exercised at the regional level for states that are members of regional systems, and also at the national level. Some national human rights commissions may be required to produce an annual report but more often this task is performed by national and international NGOs. Of the latter, Amnesty International and Human Rights Watch are well known. It is also worth mentioning that the United States Department of State produces an annual report on the state of human rights in other countries which is an important aspect of its foreign policy.

Actors and Institutions

The preceding subsections have given some account of the actors and institutions that form part of the human rights system. Here it is sufficient to recapitulate that actors exist at various levels and include official and unofficial bodies. There has been considerable emphasis on strengthening national institutions for the protection of rights since the World Conference on Human Rights, held in Vienna in 1993. The OHCHR has played an important role in the promotion of human rights commissions. As discussed in the upcoming subsection on Democratization: The record, considerable foreign assistance has been given for the strengthening of judicial and legal institutions.

A significant set of actors are civil society institutions, which operate nationally and internationally. The framework of human rights has provided a powerful basis for their growth and networking, and they have played an important role in popular mobilization and aggregating demand. In authoritarian states, they have kept alive the demand for democratization, and brought violations of rights to world attention. They are an important lobby for the protection of human rights, and play a significant supervisory role. They were once seen as troublemakers by governments and international agencies, but now enjoy considerable legitimacy in official circles, and are accepted as an indispensable partner in the pursuit of human rights.

Beneficiaries of Rights

The beneficiaries of rights are human beings. However, most legal systems extend human rights to corporations and other entities at least to the extent that they are capable of exercising them. It used to be that rights were traditionally restricted to citizens, and many constitutions still so restrict their scope. International instruments are ambiguous; they speak as if rights belong to everyone., with only the political rights being restricted to citizens, but they do not seem capable of enforcing the wider view of entitlement to rights. However, an increasing number of states extend non-political rights to all residents, although some still discriminate against immigrants in civil, economic and social rights. In a globalizing world, the restriction of rights to citizens, especially when citizenship is conceived of in narrow racial or ethnic terms, is a serious limitation on people's exercise of rights.

So long as rights were attached to citizenship, there was a notion of a uniform set of rights. After the international covenants on civil and political, and on economic, social and cultural rights were adopted, available to everyone., the international community turned its attention to specific groups of people. Conventions for the protection of vulnerable groups racial minorities, women, children, indigenous peoples and migrant workers were adopted. For the most part, they reiterate the rights that these groups allegedly already enjoy under the two Covenants, but provide a basis for affirmative action, special policies and protective institutions, and networking. These developments were in some cases presaged in national systems for example, India, which adopted special constitutional protection of historically disadvantaged minorities.

The concern with vulnerable groups, particularly minorities, has promoted the concept of group rights. In the classical traditions of human rights, only individuals had rights; those who adhere to this approach are uncomfortable with rights of groups and newfangled ideas such as the right to development. But the notion of group rights has assumed a particular importance in multi-ethnic societies, where it has in some cases become the organizing matrix of society.

Internationalization of Human Rights and State Sovereignty

From the perspective of the Declaration and the prospects of international action, the degree of internationalization of human rights is a significant factor. The expression internationalization of human rights refers to the process whereby human rights are encapsulated in international instruments, most of which have become binding on signatory states. The process encompasses the elaboration of human rights, binding states to respect and enforce these rights, and setting up an international system of supervision and enforcement of the obligations of states in respect of human rights. Internationalization of rights also refers to the norms by which states conduct their relations with other states and which international organizations must follow in their work, and it is deemed to have established a new international morality. Because international human rights have been established in what passes for a consensual process, it is often assumed that they are universally valid, as opposed to, for example, democracy, where it is conceded that there is no uniform, universal form. The result is that states may be more willing to intervene to promote or protect rights than to support democracy or criticize political systems that look authoritarian.

The process has resulted in the translation into international instruments of human rights originally developed in national systems and adopted in several state constitutions. The inscription of these rights in international instruments has expanded the scope of the operation of human rights, bringing an important change in the character and purpose of international law and making individuals and their rights its central concern.

The manner in which a state treated its citizens used to be regarded as an internal affair; it was no business of other states or international organizations. The concept of state sovereignty provided a shield for states against external intervention and even external comment. State sovereignty and non-intervention in the domestic affairs of a state are still the cornerstone of the international order under the United Nations Charter. But the notion of what is domestic has changed under the Charter's imperative to promote and protect human rights. International instruments have placed special responsibilities on the state with regard to minorities and indigenous peoples, and other vulnerable communities or groups. This change in international law has been reinforced by international and regional instruments, which have placed obligations on states to respect human rights and to account to the international community for the performance of this responsibility. A number of institutions and procedures have been established since the United Nations was founded to address the question of the violation of human rights by a state. The right of states, regional organizations and the international community to criticize states that violate the human rights of their nationals is increasingly recognized. The eruption of civil wars, often centring on ethnic conflicts, has increased the involvement of the international community in the affairs of states; this involvement is most dramatically manifested in humanitarian intervention, but also takes the form of mediation and conciliation, strengthening national capacity for the promotion of and respect for human rights, monitoring the observance of treaty obligations, and imposing sanctions. The lack of immunity for heads of state for torture and similar crimes, and the establishment of an international criminal court, reinforces this trend.

However, it is important to note that this qualification on state sovereignty is not universally accepted. A number of states, among them those that have been victims of imperialism, argue that state sovereignty and a strong state is essential for the protection of the rights of citizens. Foremost among the proponents of this view is China. Sometimes this pragmatic argument is combined with a doctrinal view of state sovereignty, drawing its inspiration from pre-UN days. Russia has, for example, tried to fend off criticism of its conduct in unleashing a brutal war on the Chechens on the grounds that what it does to its own citizens is its own business, squarely within its sovereignty.

The Association of South-East Asian Nations refused to condemn Indonesia for the atrocities that its troops perpetrated in East Timor. The resistance of states to the notion that human rights anywhere is a matter of international concern, justifying international action, is a serious impediment to the enforcement of human rights. It prevents speedy remedial action by or through the United Nations Security Council. Sanctions or interventions follow only upon brutal repression of groups, resulting in great loss of life. An international consensus on the grounds and modalities for intervention is necessary to prevent extreme violations of human rights. Hesitation about a forthright commitment to the role of the international community in the enjoyment of rights, particularly humanitarian intervention, is no doubt induced by anxieties about the hegemonic power of some states, and the fear that interventions will be selective to serve the interests of powerful countries like the United States.

The Human Rights Industry

Despite the complex structure of the human rights system, those involved in the propagation and promotion of human rights form a small group. At the unofficial level, there are a handful of international NGOs that dominate the scene, enjoy a favoured status with the United Nations and receive most of the media publicity.

National NGOs are frequently dependent on them as interlocutors for fundraising and for guidance on tactics and organization. There are also a small number of Western foundations that sustain this movement and thus exercise a disproportionate influence on the orientation and even the possibility of the human rights movement and a small number of official international, regional and national organizations with human rights mandates.

There is a considerable circulation of personnel between these NGOs, foundations and organizations, and a strong bonding. The term human rights industry is often used, pejoratively, to refer to the self-interest of the aforementioned groups and the way they organize the production, dissemination and implementation of rights. It suggests that their primary commitment is to their own organizations and their dominance of the system, not the protection of rights.

There is no need to buy into all of this cynicism, but there is little doubt that the human rights movement has become highly bureaucratized, hierarchical, even narrow. The industry having become highly legalistic due to the proliferation of rights, and the mushrooming of the jurisprudence of courts, tribunals and committees, the leadership has passed to lawyers, who for the most part are less concerned with mobilizing mass social movements around rights than with advocacy and lobbying.

The framework of human rights will serve the agenda of the Social Summit only if it is carried to the people, if they believe that their own oppression is clearly linked to the violation of rights, and if they are organized to claim their rights and to base their agenda and organization on them. It is ironic that the people in whose name the legitimacy of rights is claimed are for the most part isolated from participation in human rights movements.

SOCIAL AND PEOPLE RIGHTS

The general picture of a colony, is of a territory where economic subordination entails political disability; where political disability may bring with it severe restrictions upon civil liberty and an exceptional widening of the legal meaning at the word 'sedition' (such restrictions being at their most severe when the metropolitan authorities regard the native culture as backward or inferior: and where official anxiety about sedition and allied offences leads to judicial and police practices which in the metropolitan country would be regarded us unusually harsh.

The consequence is that the subject peoples as a whole, and particularly their more cultivated and better educated representatives, exhibit to a marked degree the frustrations, and the corruptions of importance. For it should not be forgotten that, true as it may be that absolute power corrupts absolutely, the psychological effects of absolute powerlessness are no less damaging.

Formulations of human rights naturally tend to reflect the major frustrations of those who make them, If a right declared and claimed, is to be more than an empty aspiration if it is to serve as 'a working conception and effective instrument,' it will express the natural demands of dissatisfied groups and of the have-nots of the social order Liberty is the cry of the bond, equality the cry of the victim of discrimination, fraternity the cry of the outcast, progress and humanity are the cry of those whom their fellows use as means instead of respecting as ends, full employment is the cry of the worker whose daily job or lack of job stunts his soul and mocks his capabilities, social planning is the cry of those who are trampled underfoot when privilege and power strive to make the world safe for themselves. That is why declarations of the rights of man are strong allies of social progress, at least when, they are first promulgated. For social progress is reorganisation in the interests of the unprivileged.

Hence it might be predicted that when colonial peoples about drafting a bill of rights their claims will tally generally with those of depressed and disabled groups everywhere, but will also show a special distribution of emphasis corresponding to the special character of colonial disabilities. And in fact, wherever colonial discontent achieves articulate form, it shows a keen awareness both of the fundamental significance of an equity-less economy, with its necessary corollary of political subordination, and of the organic connection between these and the denials of civil liberty common m colonial territories. It is, further, ready enough to subscribe to the traditional democratic slogans of liberty, equality and fraternity, partly because colonial peoples have wide experience of being used as means to other people's ends, and partly because such slogans are handy for embarrassing the metropolitan authorities.

But all these diverse sentiments and attitudes arc given a particular colouring, they wear a particular, livery, distinctive of colonial experience. This colour, this livery, is the claim to equal rights with citizens of she metropolis, the protest against a discrimination that appears, to those on whom it falls, to be as arbitrary as it is comprehensive. For this reason progressive movements among colonial peoples tend to assume a nationalist and liberationist form. They are liberationist because their awakening political consciousness sees the established constitutional ties with the metropolis as emblems of foreign domination.

They are nationalist because separate nationhood is the repository of state power, and without state power at their disposal the liberationists can neither sever their political and economic dependence on the metropolis nor take over the administrative functions of the metropolis after the severance has been made.

We should, therefore, see the colonial peoples both as aggregations of individuals repressed and thwarted by specific forms of disprivilege, and as emergent nations struggling to attain equal status with the so-called independent countries in point of sovereignty and international recognition. The claim–we emphasise this — is to formal equality of status. It is not to material equality of function.

Nor is it necessarily to full national sovereignty inthe classical signification of the term. Colonial peoples object to limitations of sovereignty when they are fastened on them from without, and appear as badges of inferiority. They might well accept limitations, provided they could do so of their own choice in the interests of effective international organisation, and provided they were assured that the majority of other free countries were genuinely making the same acceptance.

Such is the position of the dependent peoples, and such are their needs or rights. The needs cannot be satisfied by legislative enactment, nor can the rights be guaranteed by constitutional charter. Attempts to give the force of unalterable law to the claims of particular groups or communities have often been made. But since no legislators can bind their successors for ever, the attempts prove in the end either fruitless or superfluous.

For the hope of seeing their claims acknowledged in practice the colonial peoples must rely on the establishment and maintenance of certain broad politico-economic conditions inside and outside their own countries. Of such conditions perhaps the most indispensable are:

(a) an international system of co-operative peace and defence, without which the security and integrity of small countries tend to be merely nominal;

(b) social planning of the lend-lease type, under which the colonies could draw on the richer countries for capital needed for colonial development, without surrendering the equity in that development, and without creating such vested interests in the colonies themselves as may impede the growth of popular responsibility in either the economic or the political field;

(c) a working system of political and economic organi-sation both in the metropolitan countries and in the colonies, such that social power and responsibility may be given the widest possible distribution; education in the colonies widens the compass of popular responsibility, so political advances extend the opportunities for its exercise;

(d) full employment both in the metropolitan countries and in the colonies; and this not merely in the sense of a productive job of some kind for every every man and woman able and willing to take it, but also in the ampler sense of work offering scope for the highest skill that each individual, in the given social conditions, is capable of developing.

CLASSICAL DOCTRINE OF THE RIGHTS

Even in the twentieth century political thought and activity are determined largely by the classical doctrine of the rights of man. According to this doctrine each individual by virtue of belonging to the gens humana, has inalienable rights. Indeed, if one does not let oneself be misled by day-to-day events, it becomes apparent that the great political controversy between Liberal Democracy and Communism is pursued under the rubric of human rights. It is pursued moreover in such a way that both sides to the quarrel consider themselves the appointed guardians of these rights, and mutually reproach each other with their violation. If, for some, the system of economic exploitation hiding according to them, behind the facade of Liberal Democracy is in total contradiction to human rights, for others the so-called liberation of the proletariat and the development towards true humanity in the Communist sense are really a pretext leading to slavery and to the establishment of the totalitarian power of party and State, to which the rights of the individual are exposed without protection. Finally one also cannot deny that the third great political movement which is being realized in our time, the emancipation of the colonial peoples, is being carried out under the banner of the doctrine of human rights, that national self-determination and human rights are seen as linked together.

In these circumstances the question of the content of the classical doctrine on the one hand, and of the present-day doctrine on the other, is particularly pressing. Perhaps the expression, 'the rights of man', should mean for us something quite different from what it meant in the eighteenth century. Or rather, would it not be worth interpreting present tendencies in the light of their historical origin, unless we want to risk getting lost in the primeval forest of political phrases and slogans? The classical doctrine of the rights of man, which was developed in the Anglo-Saxon countries, in France, and in Germany, cannot be interpreted either exclusively as an unconditional negation of the State, or exclusively as an unconditional affirmation of the State. The 'cases' of unconditional negation and affirmation of the State must, however, be considered as extreme positions in relation to the classical doctrine. (1) According to the anarchist point of view, the State constitutes the danger which threatens the spread of liberty and equality. (2) According to the Jacobin point of view, the State appears as the creator of liberty and equality, because it has the monopoly of education and of force.

It follows from this that one also cannot identify the classical doctrine of the rights of man with a completely liberal doctrine, according to which the only things that matter are the emancipation of the middle classes and a reduction in the power of the State. Both in the American Constitution and in the French Declaration of 1789, there appears quite clearly a desire to compromise between the freedom to live without interference from the State and the freedom to participate in its affairs, and also between freedom and security. As for the German doctrine, one can cite Kant's theory of the constitutional State, which, starting from the axiom of liberty and equality, demands that the State should possess the right of constraint, regulated by laws, and that there should be a separation of powers.

It would be just as false to interpret the classical doctrine of the rights of man as an unlimited individualism. Indeed, one must not forget that the classical doctrine of the rights of man is determined by the conviction that, independently of his social or national affiliations, independently of his belonging to the 'class' of rich or poor, the individual enjoys autonomy because he is or ought to be a member of the gens humana and a rational being. But, in addition, it must be noted that even Rousseau has accepted Montesquieu's theory of 'the general in the particular'.

So it is not surprising that, in the classical doctrine of the rights of man, the freedom of the individual is in an case identical with freedom from all obligation. Hobbes's theory about the 'natural' unlimited liberty of the individual, according to which liberty and 'the freedom to devour and be devoured' are one and the same thing, entails the absolutist theory of the State, which is clearly opposed to the classical doctrine of the rights of man. The classical theory of natural law, which is connected with the classical doctrine of the rights of man, presents natural law as a system of individual rights and obligations (cf. Raphael's essay). In the realm of German culture, one can again refer to Kant's theory, according to which natural law, like positive law, ought to bring about the co-ordination of those who possess liberty at the same time. According to this theory, too, everyone has the duty to respect the liberty of others, as well as the right to demand respect for his own liberty in conformity with the universal law and to obtain in by compulsion.

Moreover, the classical theory of natural law does not exclude the duty of mutual aid. According to Kant, the individual ought not only to respect the aspiration of others to 'happiness', but even to encourage it. In addition to the duty of mutual aid which, in the framework of the family and the domestic community, for example, appears not only as a moral but also as a legal obligation, mention must be made here of the legal duty of the State to help the poor—a duty which is linked with the classical doctrine of the rights of man. In this connexion it must be remembered that, particularly according to the Jacobin conception, it is the duty of the State to create an economic equality. Finally it is relevant to point out that compulsory public education – this obligatory 'culture' – cannot be dissociated from the classical doctrine of the rights of man.

There is no doubt that the classical doctrine of the rights of man is concerned in the first instance with the relationship between individuals and the State. Nevertheless, two points must not be overlooked: first, that, as we have shown, classical natural law stems from legal relationship between individuals, which are guaranteed by the State. Secondly, that the family is generally envisaged as a natural community, and that, on the other hand, according to the principle of self-determination—taken along with that of the separation of powers – importance is given to social institutions which are not State-controlled.

All these considerations allow one to conclude that although the classical doctrine of the rights of man can be connected ideologically with extreme positions, it nevertheless found expression both in the American Constitution and in the French Declaration of 1789. In these, freedom from governmental interference and freedom to participate in government (die Freiheit vom Staat und die Freiheit zum Staat) complemented each other. We can also conclude that in their theoretical context there was no hint of domination by a radical individualism, blind to social obligations and social structures not organized by the State. And there was just as little domination by a theory of liberty which confused liberty with doing as one pleased. Starting off from this finding, we can determine more exactly the connexion between the classical and the modern doctrines of human rights.

This connexion is not to be interpreted in the sense of an antimony, but in the sense of a gradual differentiation. Even if one can notice a clear movement away from economic liberalism and towards a Welfare State providing social services—the evolution of the judgements of the American Supreme Court in matters of social and labour legislation provides an impressive demonstration of this – one ought not to ignore the fact that already a Georg Jellinek, in his general theory of the State, did not look on the intensifying of the drive towards social security as in any way a weakening, but rather as a strengthening, of individual freedoms. There was accordingly a continuous and gradual evolution towards the idea of social solidarity, the idea that man is to be understood not as an isolated individual but as a 'person living in a community', that humanity means sympathy with one's fellow-men, that consideration must be given to Fraternity as well as to Liberty and Equality. Moreover the practical significance of such ideas became greater and greater, and this evolution would certainly not be intelligible but for violent changes and advances in radical movements.

From the idea of social solidarity there follows a much greater open mindedness, both in theory and in practice, in dealing with those situations in which even an adult individual is referred to the help of the community; it is better understood that it is not enough to proclaim general freedoms, that for many reasons it is essential first to create the prerequisites for the exercise of freedom. So there grew up a far-reaching network of social institutions, social insurances, such as old-age and dependents' pensions, initial help of all kinds, compensation funds, and provident schemes. All these are financed partly by the State and partly by private organizations. Legislative measures directed towards the equalization of material burdens belong to the same category. Finally all these measures and institutions are to be understood from the standpoint of a modern conception of human rights. For this conception, it is not enough to postulate, for instance, free expression of opinion as such; it is important not to interfere with the process of the formation of public opinion and to keep it free from monopolization.

On the other hand, there arises from this basic point of view an enhanced awareness of the significance of non-State social institutions, of the hazards and risks to individuals which they entail. For instance, the family is understood and encouraged not only as a necessary, natural community, but as that social structure in which the individual as a community-orientated person receives the basis of his education and the protection which no large organization is in a position to give him. The idea of self-government is given a considerable significance also under varying conditions, on the one hand in the form of local administrative autonomy, on the other in the form of economic and social administrative autonomy, which so far as the shaping of conditions of work is concerned, is taken care of by trade unions and employers' associations. The fact that more attention is paid to political parties and that they are increasingly an object of scientific analysis and legislative efforts is also comprehensible from this basic point of view.

Thus there is connected with the doctrine of human rights a doctrine of social pluralism, and the dangers of this must be recognized. First, one must point out the danger that theory and practice draw the individual more and more into a plurality of social structures which are not connected with the State but which, by their power and bureaucratic ways, often resemble State institutions; consequently the individual can only acquire recognition in the category of outsiders, of the maladjusted. On the other hand there is the danger that individual selfishness will be replaced by a group selfishness which has nothing at all to do with the idea of fraternity, of the brotherhood of man. This danger – it can be indicated as the opposite danger to totalitarianism – corresponds to the danger of anarchy, which has in the threatened the classical doctrine of the rights of man.

In harmony with this attitude, the point of view of social security and justice is stressed in the important declarations of human rights in our day, side by side with the so-called liberal rights. Already in the Atlantic Charter of 14 August 1941 the aim was clearly declared of guaranteeing improved working conditions, economic equality, and social security for all, by means of the closest economic co-operation between nations.

In the Preamble to the United Nations Charter, there is mentioned the belief in fundamental human rights, in the dignity and value of the human person, as well as in social progress and a higher standard of living with greater freedom. In the Universal Declaration of Human Rights of 10 December 1948 along with liberal and political rights and the claim to legal protection, there is mentioned, amongst other things, the right to social security, to the economic, social, and cultural means indispensable for free development, the right to work, to appropriate payment and measures of social protection, to recreation and leisure, to security in case of illness, disablement, old age, and the right to education, beginning with free elementary education. In the Convention of 4 November 1950, on the Protection of Human Rights and Fundamental Freedoms; reference is made to the so-called Universal Declaration and to the rights contained therein, including social rights. In the catalogue of rights guaranteed by the Convention, however, there are no guarantees corresponding to the social rights of the Universal Declaration. In the Declaration of New Delhi, which was formulated in New Delhi by the International Commission of Jurists, the first section says: 'It is the duty of the Legislature in a free society under the role of law to create and maintain condition which safeguard the dignity of man as an individual. That dignity requires not only the recognition of his political and civil rights, but also the creation of social, economic, educational, and cultural conditions which are essential for the full development of the personality.' Unlike the Universal Declaration of Human Rights, and in agreement with the European Convention, the New Delhi Declaration makes no attempt to draw up a list of the social rights of individuals and the corresponding social duties of States.

Let us discuss the difficulties and the problems inherent in the realisation of the postulate of 'fraternity' and social rights by the example of the Bonn Basic Law. The Basic Law is directed towards the central value of human dignity. According to Article 1, § 1, the dignity of man is regarded as inviolable, and it is a duty of all State power to respect and to defend human dignity. The basis and the limit of the power of the State are thus determined by human dignity.

First of all, human dignity is significant as the foundation of human rights. Because they constitute the basis and limit of State power, the German people recognizes inviolable and inalienable human rights 'as the foundation of every human community, of peace and justice in the world'.

From the theoretical point of view, it is worth noting that the authors of the Basic Law try to make it clear that the basic structure, not only of order within the State, but also of order between States, of international order, derives from the idea of human dignity and human rights. Moreover the same attempt can be seen in the European Convention on Human Rights, in which reference is made to the basic freedoms 'which constitute the foundations of justice and peace in the world'. One may think little of the practical value of such formulae: nevertheless they give expression to the effort to break down the rigid barriers between national and international law, and to conceive of legal order as a whole, as an indivisible system of values.

On the other hand, there is eminent practical value in Article 1, § 3, of the Basic Law: 'The following basic rights are obligatory for legislation, administration, and judicial decision, as directly valid law.' This formula opposes the opinion that basic rights only represent a programme, which it is the task of the legislator to put into effect. On the other hand, it is not opposed to the opinion that the list of basic rights is to be thought of as an open list, that not only are the rights mentioned in it guaranteed by the Basic Law, but rather that all individual rights which can be derived from the principle of human dignity and which are capable of realization one day, are so guaranteed.

If one scrutinizes the whole list of basic rights, it is clear that it enumerates essentially the so-called classical rights of liberty, the to free development of the personality, the principle of equality, freedom of faith and creed, freedom of speech, the right to private property, etc. There is hardly any mention, however, of basic social rights in the sense of claims to State provision. On the other hand there are in this list prescriptions for the protection of the family (that is to say, of a non-State social structure), prescriptions which can hardly be put into the framework of individual rights. Moreover, amongst these prescriptions is one covering the mother's claim to the protection and care of the community, a social right from two points of view: social in so far as it points to social action, and social in so far as it cannot be described as a right which belongs to the individual as an individual, but as one which is derived from a social relationship and function. But more of that in another context.

In the catalogue of basic rights listed in the Basic Law there is, for example, no mention of right to a minimum economic subsistence. Consequently the question arises whether such a right can be directly derived from the principle of human dignity. The question is controversial. Nevertheless it is indisputable that Artide 1, § 1, together with the principle of the social State, which is firmly established in Article 20 of the Basic Law, implies that this right is to be described as fundamental. It is further indisputable that where the legislator has imposed on the State obligations for social action, the individual has at his disposal rights for which he can obtain satisfaction in a court of law.

It follows that, according to the view of the authors of the Basic Law, it is, in the first place, the business of the legislator to put into effect the principle of the social State, to impose on the State obligations for social action and to grant corresponding individual rights. This attitude of the authors of the Basic Law corresponds to the fact that where declarations of human rights are directed towards practical implementation, as the European Convention or the New Delhi Declaration are directed towards the task of satisfying social claims, this task is either marginally indicated or considered as a duty of the legislator. It is also significant that the almost, euphoric joy of the authors of the Universal Declaration of Human Rights in specifying social rights has noticeably abated in the light of the efforts to draw up a universal convention on human rights. The reason for this is that it is easier to forbid State measures, in the form of subjective, terse rights, with intelligible consequences, than to decree them. Two examples: freedom of speech on the one hand, the right to work on the other. It is relatively easy to procure observance for a prohibition addressed to the State against interference with freedom of speech. On the other hand it would be enormously complicated to give effect to a right to work. Apart from the fact that such a right would only too easily come into conflict with the freedom to choose one's own profession, it cannot be given effect without the erection of a whole apparatus of authorities provided with far–reaching powers. On the other hand, of course, such structural objections must not be given too much weight.

One must not overlook the fact that a group of publicly-recognized, subjective rights, which, as it happens, the European Convention and the Declaration of New Delhi have specially stressed, are linked, of logical necessity, with measures to be taken by the State. It is a question of the so-called claims for the safe-regarding of right. The right to the judge prescribed by statute implies, for example, a differentiated judicial organization. On the other hand one must not overlook the fact that giving effect to freedom of speech, for instance in the domain of television and radio, requires legislation in order to eliminate risks to the formation of opinion coming from public as well as from private quarters.

Nevertheless the whole body of opposing structures justifies the formula: prohibitions against interference by the State can be better expressed in the form of subjective rights than as commands to intervene.

An exception is formed by claims for the safeguarding of rights, which are guaranteed in the tradition of the constitutional State, claims such as the right to a minimum subsistence, which necessarily stems from the principle of human dignity and that of the social State. A further exception can be recognized in the right to education, which corresponds to compulsory schooling. At times it is presented as the right to share in the school arrangements which provide for elementary education. But then again it is presented as the right to share in them without being subjected to undue material burdens. Here it can be a question of the claim to the means of elementary education without charge, to grants in order to obtain teaching materials; finally it can be a question also of the right to the provision of educational establishments for children in remote districts, or at least to the provision of the necessary transport so that they can travel to existing schools. It goes without saying, that in this context, too, the realization of the right (or rights) depends on numerous legislative measures and administrative arrangements, and that a wide differentiation of claims is impossible. Yet it must be accepted that the principles set forth in the area of application of the Basic Law are presented in the form of subjective rights guaranteed by the constitution.

But besides – let us repeat – it appears to be simply the task of the legislator, resulting from the tenets of the social State and the principle of human dignity, to make arrangements to create social equality between different sections of the population, and social security, and to supplement formal equality by material equality.

The Basic Law assumes man to be a social person and not an isolated individual. This follows from the dignity of man and the principle of the social State. From this point of view one can understand the prescriptions which recognize the rights of non-State social structures or demand their protection. First of all, attention must again be drawn to the regulations for the protection of marriage and the family.

These regulations are not, indeed, in opposition to those which guarantee the freedoms of the individual. The principle of monogamy is intimately linked with the principle of equal rights of husband and wife. The right of parents to educate their children clashes with totalitarian ideas which consider young people as belonging to the State, and is based on the hypothesis that the education of social persons is most easily assured in the family group, as being the group in which as a rule the personality comes completely to fruition. Finally, the prescriptions for the protection of the family are also inspired by the thought that relative security in the family group will reduce the risk that individuals will be exposed to totalitarian tendencies. The 'federalism domestique', which was attacked by Robespierre, is accordingly at the service of the right to individual autonomy. In so far as one can derive subjective rights from the regulations of Article 6 of the Basic Law, it is not a question of rights which were originally individual, but of those which come from belonging to a group, of social rights in the sense of group rights.

Similar considerations apply in the realm of the right to self-government. The corporate bodies set up by Public Law, which are provided with rights of self-government and consequently with a certain independence from the State, are on the one hand useful for the fulfilment of necessary communal tasks and on the other hand serve the principle of vertical division of powers. If the principle of community self-government serves political freedom primarily, that of university self-government serves the freedom of teaching and research. Political freedom is again served by the granting of privileges to political parties as compared with other associations, according to Article 21 of the Basic Law. To be sure, legal practice and theory show that it is not altogether simple to understand adequately the position of political parties. The view that they are to be ranked with State-controlled bodies is untenable. It is more a question of non-State social structures to which has been delegated the public duty of facilitating the action of the politically active citizen, and which, as far as this duty is concerned, are entitled to specific, constitutionally guaranteed, social rights (in the sense of group rights). Their existence and effectiveness are nevertheless always: dependent on the initiative and agreement of individual citizens.

Through group rights the Basic Law also gives an assured position to workers' and employers' organizations. It protects the so-called right of association by declaring null and void agreements which limit this right (Article 9, § 3). Further, it also gives a legal basis for the view that these organizations perform a public duty in protecting and improving conditions of work and industry. From this, it is also intelligible that the legislator delegates to the so-called social partners a certain legal power in matters of wage-regulation.

Finally one must ask what is the connexion between the different categories of rights which have been discussed by means of these few examples.

Both the classical rights of the individual which protect him from interventions and encroachments by the power of the State, and also the political rights which assure to the individual a share in that power, derive from the principle of human dignity. They guarantee to the individual the possibility of self-determination economically, culturally, and politically. The same is true also of those social rights which oblige the State to do things for individuals, such as the right to a minimum subsistence, by means of which an existence fit for human beings is assured to every individual, and such as the right that corresponds to compulsory education, which is one of the foundations of self-determination. No hierarchy of values, as between these rights, is laid down. They are of equal rank. One would also not be justified in acknowledging a lesser rank for the specific group rights. Surely they too are finally directed towards an image of man as a social being.

Amongst these rights the relationship or interdependence, of reciprocal conditioning, is very important. They serve to develop the principle of human dignity. Political rights demand the so-called defence rights, and vice versa. Without elementary guarantees in economic matters, the other rights lose their meaning. Without an entitlement to elementary education, there can be no question of self-determination. Without freedom of association, the economic freedom of the worker is a mere formality. The right of parents to have their children educated assures the development of self-reliant and socially minded persons.

Nevertheless the structural differences between the different categories of rights must not be ignored. It is no accident that social rights, in the form of entitlements to benefit and of group rights, are often described as creating the conditions under which the individual can achieve self-determination. Where these conditions are fulfilled, they cease to be urgently significant. This is particularly so in respect of claims to assistance from the State. The supposition that these conditions are not fulfilled is by no means, valid everywhere. Rather the opposite is true, that the adult man who is adapted to his milieu and surroundings is capable of action on the basis of those rights which assure him freedom from State interference, as well as in the realm of political rights.

This explains the rule, which is firmly established in administrative and constitutional procedure, that the individual must prove he have claim to State provision, for example, while conversely, in the case of the limitation of economic freedoms, for example, it is the State which must provide the proof that there is a case for intervention, that without intervention there would be a serious danger for an important communal good.

From this point of view, one can talk of a primacy of the so-called defence rights and political rights, as opposed to entitlement rights, which take on a subsidiary significance. If one were to reverse this relationship, which concerns not the value-rating of the rights in question but the mode of their realization, man would, unawares, be changed from a responsible subject into an object of State care and provision.

The situation is similar for the relationship between classical rights of liberty and political rights on the one hand, and group rights on the other. From the view that the individual cannot be conceived of without multiple group connexions, it does not follow that these groups are of primary importance. Even although the economic freedom of the individual worker cannot develop significantly without freedom of association, and without associations, the trade union does not replace the individual as the subject of economic freedom. In the same way, the individual is not replaced by the political party as the bearer of political rights because, without political parties, the active rights of citizens cannot be developed. Even if, from the recognition of the fact that man is a social being, one can derive a special category of group rights, these cannot be substituted for the primary individual rights, but take their place beside them. For this reason too it would be impossible, without suppressing the freedom of decision of individuals, to enforce compulsory membership of a party or a trade union.

The rights which allow to the individual freedom from governmental interference and freedom to participate in government (Freiheit vom Staat und Freiheit zum Staat) have primary importance in this sense, as against social rights in their double significance, although they are based on the same conception of values.

Even if the rights which guarantee freedom from governmental interference are usually attributed to man as a member of the gens humane, and those which assure freedom of participation are attributed to man as a member of the State, there is nevertheless no difference in category between the rights of man and the rights of the citizen.

A doctrine of human rights which originates in the conception of the fundamental value of human dignity must comprehend as a unity the rights of man, the rights of the citizen, and social rights, in all their interdependence and in all their differences. The answer to totalitarian conceptions, which also appeal to the doctrine of human rights, can only be effective on the basis of a differentiating theory of man and code of law, which recognize unity in diversity, and look on man as a social being.

HUMAN RIGHTS IMPACT ASSESSMENTS

Rights & Democracy (International Centre for Human Rights and Democratic Development) is an independent Canadian institution created by an Act of Parliament. It has an international mandate to promote, advocate for and defend the democratic and human rights set out in the International Bill of Human Rights. In cooperation with civil society and governments in Canada and abroad, Rights & Democracy initiates and supports programmes to strengthen laws and democratic institutions, principally in developing countries.

Emphasis on Accompaniment

Communities and local research teams require reliable moral and professional support throughout the course of the human rights impact assessment process and its follow-up. This is important for capacity building, but also for the personal security of the community members and researchers themselves.

Realistic Budget and Time Allocation

Methodologies for human rights impact assessments should include a time and budget guide as part of the initial assessment process. Such a guide would flag potential costs that might not otherwise be considered and would provide the accompanying organization and research team members with a better estimate of the amount of time they require for each stage of the assessment process.

Revise the Methodology and Research Guide

The ten-step methodology should be broken down into smaller, better-defined tasks that provide explicit guidance on implementation. Some elements of the methodology were not sufficiently developed, such as how to structure the final reports. There is a tension between producing a user-friendly research guide and a comprehensive research guide. There should be a simpler way of selecting questions appropriate to each case study, perhaps by developing a digital tool.

The Case Study Reports

In three cases (Argentina, Peru, Philippines) the research teams were able to link human rights impacts directly to the investment project. In the two others (Democratic Republic of Congo and Tibet) enough information was produced to merit additional study and action.

Philippines

In 2005, the Canadian company TVI Pacific Inc. officially opened the Canatuan mine on the island of Mindanao in the Philippines. The mining operations displaced many families; divided the local indigenous people, known as the Subanon; deprived thousands of small-scale miners of their livelihood; and negatively affected rice farmers and fishers living downstream because of increased levels of sediment and metals in local rivers and creeks. One of the most controversial aspects of the mine is that it is located on the peak of Mount Canatuan, which the Subanon living in the area consider as sacred.

The research team focused heavily on the rights of Indigenous People as described in the UN Declaration on Indigenous Peoples. The central finding of this report is that the investment has had a negative impact on the ability of the Subanon to enjoy the human right to self-determination, to human security, to an adequate standard of living, to adequate housing, to work and to education.

Tibet

In March 2005, the Canadian company Nortel announced it had entered into an agreement with China's Ministry of Railways to provide a digital wireless communications network for a new railway being built in Tibet. The technology, called the Global System for Mobile Communications for Railways, is a key component in the railway's communication system. Railway communications systems are themselves part of China's Golden Shield Project, an all-encompassing surveillance network that monitors and controls the flow of information and people. The case study is ex-ante; it looks at the potential future impacts of the communications technology on the Tibetan people's rights to privacy, to security of the person, to freedom of expression and to self-determination.

The case study raises the issue of corporate complicity within public-private partnerships, particularly in non-democratic states where human rights violations are systemic. It also looks at the human rights obligations of the company's home state with regard to the export of dual-use technology.

Democratic Republic of Congo (DRC)

In 2001, SOMIKA, a processor of heterogenite (copper and cobalt), set up operations in the Katanga region of the DRC. The company processes ore from various neighboring sites where extraction is contracted out to artisanal miners. SOMIKA's installations are located on a major water table that supplies drinking water to 70% of the population of Lubumbashi. There is a risk that the water could potentially be contaminated by SOMIKA's operations. In addition, there are persistent concerns about discriminatory hiring procedures and working conditions including health and safety risks that have not been adequately addressed. This case study remains incomplete. A number of difficulties were experienced during the research process and therefore it is not possible to present definitive conclusions of the impact assessment here. Nevertheless, preliminary results indicate that there is reason for concern that violations of labour rights and the rights to water and health may have occurred as a result of the investment.

Argentina

In 1993, the government of Argentina created what was then the largest privatized water concession in the world when it awarded a contract to Aguas Argentinas S.A., a consortium of European and Argentine companies, to operate the water and sewage systems in Buenos Aires and surrounding municipalities. The research team studied the performance of both Aguas Argentinas and the Republic of Argentina over the life of the contract, which was terminated by the Argentine government in early 2006. This case study is the only one in the project that focuses on one specific human right - the human right to water. The conceptual framework of the report draws heavily upon General Comment 15, an interpretive statement issued by the United Nations about the human right to water. The central finding of this research is that the public-private partnership had a negative impact on the ability of the people of Buenos Aires to enjoy access to sufficient, safe, acceptable, accessible and affordable water.

Peru

In 1997, Doe Run Peru S.R.L. purchased a state-owned smelter complex in La Oroya, a Peruvian town in the Andes Mountains. The complex, in operation since 1922, produces copper, lead, zinc, silver, gold, and other products, and emits a toxic cocktail of pollutants. In 2006, La Oroya was named one of the 10 most polluted areas in the world. The case study looks in particular at the impact of the smelter complex on the human rights of women, including the human right to health, housing and water, as well as the human right to work, to information, and to freedom of expression.

The key finding of this case study is that the operations of Doe Run Peru, and the failure of the state to take appropriate steps, have had a negative impact on the ability of the people of La Oroya, especially women, to enjoy their human rights. When we launched a three-year project in 2004 to develop and test a human rights impact assessment methodology for investment, we knew that the task ahead would not be simple. We had been examining the links between human rights and economic globalization for many years and concerns related to foreign investment were impossible to avoid. We were receiving an ever-increasing number of appeals from communities around the world who often held dramatically different opinions about the benefits of foreign investment than did their governments or the corporations involved.

While we acknowledge that investment itself is neither inherently good nor bad for human rights, these stories illustrated that if foreign direct investment projects are to contribute towards sustainable and equitable development, their human rights impacts will have to be both acknowledged and addressed. This requires a process through which the impacts of specific investment projects can be understood in human rights terms. At its first meeting in November 2004, the project's international advisory committee grappled with the challenges presented by such an ambitious idea. They understood that governments, businesses and the affected communities each have distinct roles and responsibilities with regard to the protection of human rights, albeit with very different levels of influence.

They agreed also that basic human rights principles emphasize attention to the most vulnerable and that a process aimed at community empowerment would therefore be the most appropriate.

As a result of these deliberations, Rights & Democracy and the project's international advisory committee, decided to develop a draft methodology and research guide aimed at empowering communities to conduct human rights impact assessments of foreign investment projects. The model they developed was subsequently tested in five case studies, the results of which are presented here in two parts: our reflection on the experience (part one); the case study reports (part two).

The case study reports are the result of a year-long process that involved members of the affected communities, local researchers and our international advisory committee. It is unfortunate that the richness of that experience cannot be fully represented in these few pages. However, the information provided is faithful to the experience and to the data generated by using the draft methodology, although some editing of the final reports has been done by Rights & Democracy for the purposes of consistency.

You will find additional background information about this initiative on the Rights & Democracy website at www.dd-rd.ca, including the original versions of the draft methodology and the research guide. A revised methodology and research guide, based on lessons learned from this process, will be provided in a forthcoming publication.

HUMAN RIGHTS NGOS

Having set out the nature of the topic of human rights enforcement, it remains to define what a human rights NGO, an INGO, and a DNGO. The meaning of the term "NGO" tends to vary just as to who is using the term, and in what context. The two main usages of the term are within international law and by the international human rights movement, although the term also has some currency in social science studies of human rights. In international law, the definition of an NGO in the "Encyclopaedia of International Law" is very useful.

An NGO is a private organization, not established by a government or international agreement, which is capable of playing a role in international affairs by virtue of its activities, and whose members enjoy independent voting rights. Similarly, the European Convention on the Recognition of the Legal Personality of International Non- Government Organizations, defines NGOs as associations, foundations and other private institutions, which have a non-profit making aim of international utility; have been established by law; carry on activities in at least two states, and have their official offices in the territory of one of the parties to the Convention. The criteria of ECOSOC at the United Nations are very similar. Overwhelmingly the term "NGO" is thus used to include non-government entities at both international and national levels.

There is a view, however, based on the tradition of the Union of International Associations and the Institut de Droit International that the term NGO applies only to genuinely international associations. In this definition, an entity is a human rights NGO as long as its 'private' character is unquestionable, and its work is guided by the same idea of human rights as set out in international human rights law. In more social science based human rights research, such as that of van den Berg, the term "NGO" is favoured for being more neutral than terms such as "action group" or "protest group".

It is defined as consisting of groups of like-minded citizens that are independent of government; which act in counterpoint to governments and international institutions; do not seek government office themselves; and are non-profit making entities. An important question that is relevant to the data set out below is the extent to which the political nature of an unquestionably private organization defending human rights disqualifies it from being described as an NGO. In a famous article in 1989, Neier argued that a human rights NGO must be apolitical to be an NGO. Van den Berg, on the other hand, notes that in Holland DNGOs involved in human rights issues within foreign policy are often political, and yet their status as NGOs is not generally questioned. In the opinion of the author, Neier's approach leads to an unduly narrow definition of the term NGO.

Most organizations at the domestic level that have the defence of human rights as their main concern have a political agenda in one way or another. Furthermore, the self-identification of an organization, while important, should not preclude grouping for the purpose of scholarly analysis. It seems that whether an organization is explicit about its political position or not is more a matter of the norms of the domestic political culture and tactical considerations, rather than any indicator of its true nature. Further, because DNGOs are usually enmeshed more than INGOs in domestic political debates, an exclusion of groups with political agendas would have the undesirable effect of excluding from consideration a large number of groups that mobilize law in defence of human rights. To the author, as for Livezy, the political stance of an NGO goes more to its idea of what human rights are, rather than to its identity as an NGO.

For this reason, whatever the political stance of the group, for the purposes of this study an organization is not disqualified from being an NGO for having a political agenda. In order to properly understand human rights NGOs, it is also necessary to engage in a rudimentary taxonomy of them. The most rudimentary distinction between NGOs in the field of human rights is between domestic human rights NGOs and international human rights NGOs. Authors who use this common distinction generally do so on the basis that reliance on domestic law as opposed to international law, or working within the boundaries of one state rather than many, leads to functional and qualitative differences between NGOs. Unfortunately, most discussions do not distinguish whether an NGO is domestic or international with regard to the human rights problems it addresses, the nationality of its members, the location of its offices, where its human rights activities are conducted, or where its finance and support comes from. For the purposes of this study, an NGO is domestic, if the problems it addresses, its office, and its members all derive from a single country.

This is regardless of whether it undertakes enforcement or promotion work internationally, or in other countries, and regardless of whether it receives funding from outside the country. Similarly an NGO is international if the problems it addresses, its offices, and/or the nationality of its members all derive from more than one country. This is regardless of whether it undertakes promotion or enforcement within nations and regardless of whether it receives it's funding from a single country. The author has employed the commonly used distinction between DNGOs and INGOs in this study because it closely fits most of the data that was collected. The case studies situated in the United States and Germany concentrated on litigation in the US Supreme Court and the German Constitutional Court respectively to a degree that is extremely unusual in an INGO such as Amnesty International or Human Rights Watch.

Similarly, the case studies situated in Britain showed a concentration on policy work in the British Parliament to a degree that is also unusual among INGOs. In addition, it also seemed that these features were linked to similarities between the political and legal cultures of the United States, Britain and Germany and the organizational culture of the case studies situated in those countries.

In short, the category of a DNGO is employed not only because it is common in human rights literature, but also because the data confirmed that INGOs and DNGOs tend to operate in significantly different ways. It is also important, however, at the outset to concede that a clear cut distinction cannot always be drawn between DNGOs and INGOs. There is an inevitable degree of overlap between these categories when one considers real life human rights NGOs. Indeed, a minority of human rights NGOs show such a degree of overlap that they can almost be considered as DNGO/INGO hybrids. Nevertheless, individual human rights NGOs in practice a majority of the time show clusters of tactics and cultural features that are either predominantly domestic or international.

The author thus felt that in the vast majority of circumstances a demarcation between DNGOs and INGOs was true to the data he had obtained and analytically useful in the conclusions that it allowed to be drawn from data in the field. Some discussions of human rights NGOs also distinguish between local or regional NGOs within nation states, and DNGOs that cover the whole of a nation state. To the author, however, this is not as useful a distinction as that between DNGOs and INGOs, because each of the former operate in distinct legal and political environments which lead to distinct tactical environments. Local NGOs, on the other hand, might have distinct local concerns, but still operate in similar tactical environments to the other DNGOs in that national jurisdiction.

For this reason, local NGOs within nation states are designated DNGOs for the purpose of this research. Another distinction worth noting is between INGOs and regional human rights NGOs. The latter designation concerns NGOs that deal with situations in geographical regions encompassing more than one country, regardless of whether their funding and personnel are from one nation. This designation arose because of the existence of regional organizations in international law, such as the Council of Europe and the Organization of American States. These international institutions presented opportunities for NGOs to work within their ambit.

True INGOs are distinguished from regional NGOs in international affairs by their truly global concerns and struggles, and usually by a true internationalism among their staff and in their organizational design. Van den Berg distinguishes between public interest groups, which have altruistic or non-material objectives, and interest groups which strive for objectives that are predominantly derived from the economic and social position of the group. Within public interest groups, van den Berg distinguishes between general public interest groups with some interest in human rights, such as churches, and single issue groups that focus only on human rights or specific human rights.

This study focuses on what van den Berg calls single-issue public interest groups, but does not deny the influence of interest groups and general public interest groups on human rights standards. A further distinction among human rights NGOs is between membership organizations and non-membership NGOs. Membership NGOs have their policies decided by the vote of registered members. These policies are then usually carried out by a board, or by the staff. The majority of money for such organizations often also comes from members. Non-membership NGOs do not have their policies decided by the votes of members, but rather usually by an executive board, or even de facto by the executive director and staff.

While the author could have focused on membership and non-membership NGOs as a category in this research in preference to the DNGO/INGO distinction, he felt, on the basis of the data, that this distinction was not as decisive in influencing an NGO's entire functioning as whether its character was predominately domestic or international. While membership might be one factor in determining NGO functioning, the author felt that it was not as important as the DNGO/INGO distinction.

The data that the author collected seemed largely to confirm that this is the case. Nevertheless, where it is relevant below the author has taken into account the effects on a case study of it being a membership or non-membership organization.

The last debate on the taxonomy of human rights NGOs relevant to this study is the debate as to whether a human rights NGO must draw its human rights standards explicitly from international human rights law, or whether it can draw exclusively on domestic human rights standards. As Steiner points out, human rights NGOs themselves argue that whether an NGO draws on domestic or international standards should not affect its designation as a human rights NGO. They see the question of which standards are referred to as a tactical choice for the NGO concerned. To the author this seems a common sense stance and it will be adopted in this work.

The differences between indigenous rights traditions and the tradition of human rights in the international human rights movement is an important theoretical issue that will be dealt with in the following stage. However, for the purposes of this study it suffices to note that the U.S. Bill of Rights, the UK Human Rights Act, and the German Basic Rights in the Basic Law, all substantially reflect the aims of human rights protection embodied in the International Covenant on Civil and Political Rights. Thus, in this study, NGOs that rely exclusively on domestic human rights standards will be designated as human rights NGOs, and the reasons for their choice of international or domestic law standards will be treated as a tactical choice.

NON-GOVERNMENTAL ORGANIZATIONS AND HR

A non-governmental organization (NGO) is a legally constituted organization created by natural Variously, in jurisprudence, a natural person is a human being, as opposed to an artificial, legal or juristic person, *i.e.*, an organization that the law treats for some purposes as if it were a person distinct from its members or owner. Sometimes the legal situation limits the term by limits on age, psychiatric, medical, national, sex, sexual orientation, criminal record, official paperwork, and computer records (which may or may not be accurate).

For example, such legal provisions as Amendment XIX to the United States Constitution, which states a person can not be denied the right to vote based on gender, or Section 15 of the Canadian Charter of Rights and Freedoms, which guarantees equality rights, apply to natural persons only. In many cases fundamental human rights are implicitly granted only to natural persons; for example a corporation cannot hold public office, but it can file a lawsuit.) or legal persons(Legal personality (also artificial personality, juridical personalty, and juristic personality) is the characteristic of a non-human entity regarded by law to have the status of a person. A legal person (Latin: persona ficta), (also artificial person, juridical person, juristic person, and body corporate, also commonly called a vehicle) has a legal name and has rights, protections, privileges, responsibilities, and liabilities under law, just as natural persons (humans) do. The concept of a legal person is a fundamental legal fiction. It is pertinent to the philosophy of law, as is essential to laws affecting a corporation (corporations law) (the law of business associations).

Legal personality allows one or more natural persons to act as a single entity (a composite person) for legal purposes. In many jurisdictions, legal personality allows such composite to be considered under law separately from its individual members or shareholders. They may sue and be sued, enter into contracts, incur debt, and have ownership over property. Entities with legal personality may also be subject to certain legal obligations, such as the payment of tax. An entity with legal personality may shield its shareholders from personal liability.

The concept of legal personality is not absolute. "Piercing the corporate veil" refers to looking at individual human agents involved in a corporate action or decision; this may result in a legal decision in which the rights or duties of a corporation are treated as the rights or liabilities of that corporation's shareholders or directors. Generally, legal persons do not have all the same rights as natural persons—for example, human rights or civil rights (including the right to freedom of speech, although the United States has become an exception in this regard).

The concept of a legal person is now central to Western law in both common law and civil law countries, but it is also found in virtually every legal system) that operates independently from any government. The term is usually used by governments to refer to entities that have no government status. In the cases in which NGOs are funded totally or partially by governments, the NGO maintains its non-governmental status by excluding government representatives from membership in the organization.

The term is usually applied only to organizations that pursue some wider social A society or a human society is

- A group of people related to each other through persistent relations such as social status, roles and social networks.
- A large social grouping that shares the same geographical territory, subject to the same political authority and dominant cultural expectations.

The term society came from the Latin word societas, which in turn was derived from the noun socius ("comrade, friend, ally"; adjectival form socialis) thus used to describe a bond or interaction among parties that are friendly, or at least civil. Human societies are characterized by patterns of relationships (social relations) between individuals sharing a distinctive culture and institutions; a given society may be described as the sum total of such relationships among its constituent members. Without an article, the term refers either to the entirety of humanity or a contextually specific subset of people. In social sciences, a society invariably entails social stratification and/or dominance hierarchy. Used in the sense of an association, a society is a body of individuals outlined by the bounds of functional interdependence, possibly comprising characteristics such as national or cultural identity, social solidarity, language or hierarchical organization.

Like other groupings, a society allows its members to achieve needs or wishes they could not fulfill alone; the social fact can be identified, understood or specified within a circumstance that certain resources, objectives, requirements or results, are needed and utilized in an individual manner and for individual ends, although they can't be achieved, gotten or fulfilled in an individual manner as well, but, on the contrary, they can be gotten only in a collective, collaborative manner; namely, team work becomes the valid functional means, to individual ends which an individual would need to have but isn't able to get.

More broadly, a society is an economic, social or industrial infrastructure, made up of a varied collection of individuals. Members of a society may be from different ethnic groups. A society may be a particular ethnic group, such as the Saxons; a nation state, such as Bhutan; a broader cultural group, such as a Western society.

The word society may also refer to an organized voluntary association of people for religious, benevolent, cultural, scientific, political, patriotic, or other purposes. A "society" may even, though more by means of metaphor, refer to a social organism such as an ant colony or any cooperative aggregate such as for example in some formulations of artificial intelligence.) aim that has political (Politics is a process by which groups of people make collective decisions. The term is generally applied to the art or science of running governmental or state affairs. It also refers to behaviour within civil governments. However, politics have been observed in other group interactions, including corporate, academic, and religious institutions. It consists of "social relations involving authority or power" and refers to the regulation of public affairs within a political unit, and to the methods and tactics used to formulate and apply policy) aspects, but that are not overtly political organizations such as political parties.

Unlike the term "intergovernmental organization"An intergovernmental organization, sometimes rendered as an international governmental organization and both abbreviated as IGO, is an organization composed primarily of sovereign states (referred to as member states), or of other intergovernmental organizations.

Intergovernmental organizations are often called international organizations, although that term may also include international nongovernmental organization such as international non-profit organizations (NGOs) or multinational corporations.

Intergovernmental organizations are an important aspect of public international law. IGOs are established by treaty that acts as a charter creating the group. Treaties are formed when lawful representatives (governments) of several states go through a ratification process, providing the IGO with an international legal personality. Intergovernmental organizations in a legal sense should be distinguished from simple groupings or coalitions of states, such as the G8 or the Quartet. Such groups or associations have not been founded by a constituent document and exist only as task groups. Intergovernmental organizations must also be distinguished from treaties.

Many treaties (such as the North American Free Trade Agreement, or the General Agreement on Tariffs and Trade before the establishment of the World Trade Organization) do not establish an organization and instead rely purely on the parties for their administration becoming legally recognized as an ad hoc commission. Other treaties have established an administrative apparatus which was not deemed to have be granted international legal personality.), the term "non-governmental organization" has no generally agreed legal definition. In many jurisdictions, these types of organization are called "civil society organizations" or referred to by other names.

The number of internationally operating NGOs(The World Bank defines a non-governmental organization (NGO) as "private organizations that pursue activities to relieve suffering, promote the interests of the poor, protect the environment, provide basic social services, or undertake community development" An international non-governmental organization (INGO) has the same mission as a non-governmental organization (NGO), but it is international in scope and has outposts around the world to deal with specific issues in many countries.

Both terms, NGO and INGO, should be differentiated from intergovernmental organizations (IGOs), which describes groups such as the United Nations or the International Labour Organization. An INGO may be founded by private philanthropy, such as the Carnegie, Rockefeller, Gates and Ford Foundations, or as an adjunct to existing international organizations, such as the Catholic or Lutheran churches. A surge in the founding of development INGOs occurred during World War II, some of which would later become the large development INGOs like Oxfam, Catholic Relief Services, CARE International, and Lutheran World Relief.

International Non-governmental Organizations can further be defined by their primary purpose. Some INGOs are operational, meaning that their primary purpose is to foster the community based organizations within each country via different projects and operations. Some INGOs are advocacy-based, meaning that their primary purpose is to influence the policy-making of different countries' governments regarding certain issues or promote the awareness of a certain issue.

Many of the large INGOs have components of both operational projects and advocacy initiatives working together within individual countries is estimated at 40,000. National numbers are even higher: Russia has 277,000 NGOs; India is estimated to have around 3.3 million NGOs in year 2009 that is one NGO for less than 400 Indians, and many times the number of primary schools and primary health centres in India.

Terminology

NGOs are defined by the World Bank The World Bank is an international financial institution that provides loans to developing countries for capital programmes. The World Bank proclaims a goal of reducing poverty. By law all of its decisions must be guided by a commitment to promote foreign investment, international trade and facilitate capital investment.

The World Bank differs from the World Bank Group, in that the World Bank comprises only two institutions: the International Bank for Reconstruction and Development (IBRD) and the International Development Association (IDA), whereas the latter incorporates these two in addition to three more:International Finance Corporation (IFC), Multilateral Investment Guarantee Agency (MIGA), and International Centre for Settlement of Investment Disputes (ICSID).) as "private organizations that pursue activities to relieve suffering, promote the interests of the poor, protect the environment, provide basic social services, or undertake community development".

SOCIAL MOVEMENTS AND BROADENING THE FOCUS

The final trend brings us beyond the area of development cooperation narrowly spoken, but still concerns the deep linkages between development and human rights: it is the gradual emergence of a global, human rights-based focus on the way international economic and political relations affect development dynamics worldwide.

From a legal perspective, two processes are at play here. One is a coming together of economic law, human rights law and the law of development. The other is the extension of the parties concerned by legal obligations to include private corporations, individuals, and third states (if not the famously vague "international community" as well). The overall aim is to rethink and reorient the dynamics of international economic governance towards its impact on development – to add "development" as part of a "quality assurance" mechanism for the global governance system (Slinn 1999: 317).

This trend redirects the human rights spotlight back onto the rich countries and the global international political economy where rich country corporations and citizens occupy such a privileged position. Note that this implies a major extension of the human rights agenda as typically understood, for both human rights NGOs and development agencies. Human rights NGOs do have a long experience monitoring and publishing of civil and political rights violations in rich countries. At this level, however, they begin putting ESC rights on the agenda and consequently rethinking relations of trade, finance, investment, consumption, and aid between rich and poor countries and their citizens. Development agencies, on the other hand, have more willingness to address the domains covered by ESC rights. For them, the major change –apart from the already discussed re-conceptualization of their understanding and practice in such a ways as to incorporate human rights— is to place the behavior of rich country economic actors at center stage as much as that of Third World governments (Bunn 2000: 1453 ff.; Eide 1994:186-7). Anyone who reads the major ideological statements of the development enterprise – whether the Bank's World Development Report, or the much more "progressive" UNDP Human Development Report – will find that, with a few token exceptions, the exclusive focus of attention is on the Third World by itself. UNDP may have a few choice words to say about the need for debt relief, or the way structural adjustment programs designed by the Bretton Woods institutions are hurting the poor; the World Bank may briefly point out that rich country protectionist policies in agriculture and textile ought to be dismantled for they impose a cost on poor countries — but essentially, the nature of the game, the focus of attention, is on the Third World in isolation of the rest of the world, in isolation of history. In 1999, UNDP published its first Human Development Report that turned the focus away from the South, looking at patterns of global consumption and their impact on development. As a senior UNDP colleague told me, this was the most unsuccessful UNDP report ever, and it received much negative feedback.

Here, then, we see the emergence of a new conceptualization of development: it looks at development as a facet of a global process, and redefines the locus of change, at least partly, as being "at home" for the developed countries. It creates an imperative for donor agencies, citizens, NGOs, and corporations, to accept their responsibilities in this system. It extends the focus of development from dynamics in "the field" – that well-worn development term referring to poor places located in the Third World full of people with different skin colors and receiving assistance from us, the development enterprise – to a much broader conception of where the dynamics and constraints that affect development worldwide reside.

How should concerned parties act upon this conceptualization? Step one may be to connect "the field" directly with "the summit" in terms of the institutions of global governance that purport to promote development, especially the most contested of them: the World Bank, the International Monetary Fund, and the World Trade Organization. This means creating mechanisms of voice for those who are currently rarely if ever heard. Step two, closely related, is to put the development enterprise within the broader foreign policy context of which it is typically part. Some have termed this the search for coherence, whereby the aims of the development community are not undone by the behavior of the foreign policy or trade communities. In other words still, this implies a "moralization" of foreign policy and economic relations. Step three directly follows, and calls for examining the wide range of this moral focus, this seal of quality, to trade, finance, investment, production, intellectual property rights, and the like that affect development. Step four is to move away from the state as an entity, and focus directly on non-state actors – corporations, universities, NGOs, churches, and so on. The final step is to focus on ourselves as actors in global processes, not as members of the professional class of developers, but as citizens, consumers, and investors.

Michael Windfuhr, founder of FIAN, states it this way: a human rights approach to development "has to ensure that donors" own policies and programs do not limit states in implementing the right to food (2000: 29; 34). Development cooperation can create options as well as limit the choices of governments through conditionality. In that sense development cooperation influences the policies available to governments and is under these circumstances also responsible for possible problems in the implementation of rights. Governments are also responsible for their positions and decisions at international organizations such as the World Bank to the extent that they do influence Third World country policies. As a human rights scholar wrote:

The document makes the point repeatedly that it is States that bear the obligations with relation to the realization of rights but it might be appropriate to point out more forcefully that donors are also obliged to respect, protect and fulfill rights and that is what their programs are designed to do. They must therefore not only make every effort to prevent violations by others but also have a responsibility not to be the cause of violations. This has implications for donor governments with relation to the Bank and IMF of which they are executive board members. (Frankovits e-mail to the author, dated June 18, 2001. Also Frankovits & Earle 2000: 21)

One example among many the link between state policies and development relates to Uganda's debt. In a study of Uganda, Katarina Tomasevski, in her function as Special Rapporteur on the Right to Education, argued that Uganda's capacity to invest more in primary education was severely constrained by the country's debt burden, much of it dating from previous, dictatorial regimes. She recommended that "human rights impact assessments be institutionalized to identify international factors inhibiting or facilitating access to school and thus clarify the impact of international debt relief and structural adjustment polices." But the focus is not only on development policies: trade, financial, investment policies ought to be subject to the same requirements. By now, there exists a considerable body of international law that codifies the way human rights concerns shall shape international trade, production, investment, and financial relations. On August 26, 1999, the UN Commission on Human Rights adopted a resolution (PDHRE 2000: i: resolution 1999/30 on "trade liberalization and its impact on human rights") requesting that "all governments and economic policy forums take international human rights obligations and principles fully into account in international economic policy formulation."

Clearly, a problem with much of this is that the economics of debt relief, adjustment, and macro-economic policy is hotly contested; human rights standards supply relatively little specific information on the concrete policy choices required in this respect. Thus, many UN Commission on Human Rights reports dealing with ESC rights take on positions that are highly critical of the World Bank as well as rich counties for their lack of development assistance, the little progress made on debt relief, and the lingering protectionism against poor country exports. Often, these texts sound as if they could come straight from the anti-globalization protest movements the world has come to know in Seattle, Prague, and many other places. On the other hand, many other texts consist mainly of reaffirmations of the neo-liberal mantra that free trade and liberal economies are the best path to everything, including greater respect for human rights, environmental protection, and the like. Take article 12 in the Rio declaration, for example: "states should cooperate to promote a supportive and open international economic system that would lead to economic growth and sustainable development in all countries." As it currently stands, then, much of the human rights discussion, as it has been under the Cold War, is still a deeply ideological dialogue of the deaf.

Non-state actors

There are few clear instances of human rights language governing international economic relations, and none of these laws are directly aimed at restricting the behavior of corporations. The most detailed body of law laying out government commitments to ensure corporate accountability exists in the environmental field, and is codified in article 30 of Agenda 21. While not technically formal international law, Agenda 21 is, rather, soft or declaratory law, with significant moral force. States, having signed onto Agenda 21, have agreed to try to achieve its goals and to judged by them. Note that it, too, begins with a strong overall endorsement of liberal principles, and then proceeds to outline quite detailed commitments for sustainability that corporations ought to undertake.

Clearly, human rights law, and international law more generally, is rather limited in regard to citizens' movements. Non-state actors – including corporations – are generally not seen as subjects of international law: they have neither direct rights nor duties under international law. The rules and norms that do regulate their behavior extend from the power of states, though it is a well-founded principle of international law that states are liable for failing to protect the rights of individual citizens who might be affected by non-state actors within the jurisdiction of the concerned state. Sadly, there are precious few mechanisms to actually enforce the international human rights legal protections that exist, and no international legal mechanism control corporations directly. The limitations of the international legal order vis a vis corporations, meanwhile, exists along side what has come to be their historically unparalleled political and economic power. These firms now have the power not only to threaten relocation, but they can also make significant direct political contributions in many countries. In the U.S., for example, the top-500 corporations outspent both labor and environmental organizations by a ratio of seven to one. This power gives them the ability to deeply influence, if not constrain, state policy, and as a result, few states are ready to even consider extending international law or human rights law to corporations on their soil.

Indeed, some authors justify the extension of the focus to non-state actors through an argument of real-politik: in our current globalized and liberalized world, non-state actors, whether they be international organizations or multinational corporations, often wield more power than states. This power can be defined any way one wants: as the capacity to make other actors behave in the way desired by the powerful one; or as access to and control over scarce resources of capital, knowledge, organization. It therefore makes less and less sense to focus solely on states as the duty-holders for human rights claims. As Sano (2000: 752) states:

The means to achieve a realistic integration between human rights and development activities relate to creation of both entitlements and processes of empowerment. The International Covenant on Economic, Social and Cultural Rights establishes entitlements to basic living standards, primary health care, and basic education along with a number of other rights. But these entitlements are now directed towards nation-states that are often hampered by lack of resources, mismanagement, and restrictions imposed by international interventions. The scope of entitlements must be broadened in order to direct rights towards loci of real power exertion. This includes the nation-state, but also international organizations and firms that sometimes influence human rights realization to a considerably stronger degree than nation-states alone.

For this kind of approach to make headway, it needs to move beyond the professional human rights community and into the political, social, and economic mainstream – it needs to become an affair of citizens and not of experts. People can engage in these struggles as citizens (by voting and lobbying for the domestic and international government policies), as consumers (through the amount and type of products they consume), or as investors (through their use of shareholder power in corporations). They can do so through legal means – court proceedings, affecting public policies – or through non-legal means – support to social movements, choices of consumption, public education campaigns. They can do out of a sense of moral duty, global citizenship, or enlightened self-interest But in all of this, they can frame their engagements in human rights languages within an explicitly global context.

Schematically, there seem to be two ways in which citizens can promote and mainstream human rights within the international political economy of development. The most common approach is indirect, by influencing the behavior of the state. This makes most sense as states are in charge of setting the policy and regulatory frameworks of international trade and finance; they are the ones negotiating, ratifying, implementing, and verifying international commitments and translating these into national legislation; they are the ones voting on the policies of the IMF, the WB, or the WTO; they are the ones holding citizens and corporations accountable. Indeed, from an international legal perspective, states are basically the sole actors, and to the extent that specific behaviors of individuals or corporations are sought (as is the case in human rights law), such behavior ought to be protected and promoted by the state. From a political perspective, this also makes much sense: the capacity to influence state behavior translates into the capacity to enact and implement nation-wide policies.

Citizens, however, can and increasingly do affect the international political economy of development *directly* as well by bypassing the state. They can do this by wielding consumer power, engaging in shareholder activism, putting direct pressure on corporations, conducting general education and information campaigns, applying direct pressure on or collaborating with international organizations, or cooperating with people in communities. The options are many.

Here, again, a violations approach could provide a useful minimum standard, primarily because the approach widens the scope of monitoring from one focusing exclusively on nation-states to include other actors, (..) such as multinational corporations, NGOs and other international organizations. Much more is possible, however, and as we move further on these paths, we leave the traditional human rights community and move into the kind of activities development agencies such as Oxfam have always considered within their mandate, even though they have typically spent few resources on these activities. We are now moving into public education, advocacy and lobbying, alternative trade circuits, pressure on corporations and financial institutions, and the like. At these higher levels, there is a huge need for new social movements and specialized agencies.

HUMAN RIGHTS ON SOCIAL DEVELOPMENT AND PROGRAMME OF ACTION

The Copenhagen Declaration on Social Development recognizes the urgent need to address profound social problems, especially poverty, unemployment and social exclusion, that affect every country and sets as the task of the governments to address both their underlying and structural causes and their distressing consequences in order to reduce uncertainty and insecurity in the life of people.. It adopts a broad view of social development, as meeting the material and spiritual needs of individuals, their families and the communities in which they live.

This can only be achieved through social and people-centred sustainable development.. As an aspect of sustainable development, there is a commitment to the protection of the environment. Social development is inextricably connected wiTheconomic development, for some of its primary goals the eradication of poverty, unemployment and social exclusion depend on it.

The Declaration identifies a number of factors that have prevented the goals of social development from being achieved: chronic hunger, malnutrition, illicit drug trade, organized crime, corruption, foreign occupation, armed conflicts, illicit arms trafficking, terrorism, intolerance, xenophobia and incitement to racial, ethnic, religious and other hatreds. Many of these factors are connected with the violation of human rights. It is therefore not surprising that the Declaration places considerable emphasis on human rights and democracy in order to achieve these goals.

Indeed more than any other international declaration, with the exception of the Declaration on the Right to Development the Declaration places human rights at the centre of development. It states, for example, that democracy and transparent and accountable governance and administration in all sectors of society are indispensable foundations for the realization of social and people-centred sustainable development..

At another point it refers to the acknowledgment that social and economic development cannot be secured in a sustainable way without the full participation of women and that equality and equity between women and men is a priority for the international community and as such must be at the centre of economic and social development. The Declaration places particular emphasis on the eradication of poverty, and this is perhaps its closest connection with human rights. Poverty is the greatest cause of the denial of human rights. It is obvious that poor people enjoy a disproportionately small measure of economic rights such as education, health and shelter. However, they are equally unable to exercise civil and political rights, which would require not only an understanding of the dynamics of society and access to public institutions, but also confidence in themselves.

They are for the most part unable to use the legal process to vindicate their human and legal rights. Nothing destroys confidence so much as poverty. Poverty also compels people into the violation of the rights of others, particularly of their own children and women. Child labour is essential to the survival of millions of families throughout the Third World and, increasingly, so is prostitution. Bonded labour is a direct result of poverty, and its exploitation by the well off. Poverty produces massive inequalities, and the subordination of some groups to others in circumstances that deny them their basic dignity. The first of the principles and goals enunciated in the Declaration, and a central theme of the Programme of Action, is a commitment to a political, economic, ethical and spiritual vision for social development that is based on human dignity, human rights, equality, respect, peace, democracy, mutual responsibility and cooperation, and full respect for the various religious and cultural backgrounds of people. More specifically, governments have agreed to promote democracy, human dignity, social justice and solidarity at the national, regional and international levels; ensure tolerance, non-violence, pluralism and non-discrimination, with full respect for diversity within and among nations.

They have undertaken to promote universal respect for, and observance and protection of, all human rights and fundamental freedoms for all, including the right to development, and to ensure that disadvantaged and vulnerable persons and groups are included in social development.. Particular mention is made of the right of self-determination of all peoples, in particular of peoples under colonial or other forms of alien domination or foreign occupation and support for indigenous people in their pursuit of economic and social development, with full respect for their identity, traditions, forms of social organization and cultural values.

Without trying to exhaust the references to human rights in the Declaration, the last paragraph of the first Commitment is worth quoting: As suggested, reaffirm and promote all human rights, which are universal, indivisible, interdependent and interrelated, including the right to development as a universal and inalienable right and an integral part of fundamental human development, and strive to ensure that they are respected, protected and observed..

Several points about these formulations are worth noting. First, the importance of the language of rights. Repeated references to them might indicate a broad international consensus on human rights and freedoms and attest to the moral and political force of the idea of human rights or at least of its rhetoric. In recent decades the idea of respect for human rights seems to have become a driving force in international and regional policies and conduct, as in the intervention of the United Nations in the restoration of rights and democracy in Bosnia and Herzegovina, Cambodia, East Timor, Haiti and Nicaragua; or in the more specific regional mediations and interventions by the]Organization for Security and Cooperation in Europe.

Extensive references to democracy and human rights in the Declaration are evidence of the desire, if perhaps not necessarily the feasibility, of using human rights as a framework for sustainable development and solving other ailments of humankind. All of this enthusiasm and commitment to human rights must be taken with some caution, for the international human rights movement has been distinguished more by rhetoric than practice. Human rights are understood differently in different places, and the apparent consensus on rights conceals profound differences on, and even conflicts over, values and goals.

Second, the frequent invocation of rights in the different contexts in the Declaration attests to the enlarged scope of the concept and content of human rights. Rights have travelled a long distance from their origins in the emerging liberal economic orders of Europe and the United States since the seventeenth century, when the focus was on civil and political rights as the means to restrict the power of the government and enhance that of economic entrepreneurs.

Their philosophical foundations have broadened, fed by various political and intellectual traditions.

A large and diverse number of groups and interests have advanced their claims in the language of rights. The first additions to the classical liberal category of rights were economic, social and cultural rights. Since then specialized instruments have dealt with the claims and rights of vulnerable groups, such as women, children, refugees, migrants, indigenous peoples and people with disabilities. More broadly, but also ambiguously, there is the right to develop-ment, and notions of the preservation of the environment are being woven into the regime of rights. There is now a rich menu of rights, perhaps too rich as some complain, and the rights do not appear to be seamless. The regime of rights guarantees democracy and participation, and the accommodation of diversity. A fundamental assumption of contemporary human rights is social justice, and thus the alleviation of poverty, which is a primary concern of the Declaration.

Social justice has also promoted the idea of equity as between men and women, between groups, and between generations. There is a considerable widening of the range of entitlements of citizens and others, transforming people from supplicants into citizens. The broadening of human rights has focused attention on the state not merely as facilitator but also as provider. The logic of social, economic and cultural rights is positive obligations of the state, necessitating an active role, to ensure basic needs of people, and thus their dignity.

It is not surprising that these developments in the concept and scope of human rights have produced controversy. Behind the seeming consensus on the formulations in the Declaration on rights and democracy lurk several disagreements. How far the apparent disagreements reflect genuine differences of values is hard to say, for there is considerable hypocrisy and posturing in the position of governments. Human rights have become one of the frameworks for international relations, and the debates about them have become highly politicized. Having said that, it is possible to identify differences in approaches to human rights, and to their contents. These differences have been a major obstacle to a genuine consensus and the feasibility of consistent and effective international action to promote and protect human rights. The challenge to human rights of the Declaration is to achieve coherence of rights, founded on common values and understandings as to their purpose.

There are considerable advantages in using the human rights framework for social develop-ment. Despite the controversies that have prevented unified action on human rights, they seem to attract broad international support and few governments publicly condemn their values. The language of rights has the capacity to evoke a response and to provide moral and legal justification for certain forms of action. The ideology of, and claims based on, human rights have become increasingly effective ways to pressure governments and the international community. The regime of rights provides a basis for international or regional action and justifies the imposition of sanctions and, in extreme cases, humanitarian intervention. Human rights standards can also compensate for the weakness of international political institutions and machinery. In contradistinction to the growth of the idea and substance of rights in national systems where they followed the establishment of the apparatus of the state in the international system rights have developed with remarkable speed and are well ahead of the development of political institutions. However, that does not mean there is not sufficient authority or mechanism for their international enforcement.

The framework of rights is feasible because rights are now being defined in detailed terms and there are numerous decisions of courts and other tribunals that have elaborated the parameters of rights and their implications. They are no longer abstract formulations. Moreover, the regime of rights is now complex and multilayered, dealing with different kinds of claims and interests. It speaks to a variety of concerns, and provides doctrines as well as mechanisms for striking a balance between different claims.

Rights are a way to mobilize and empower the disadvantaged, and in many parts of the world this is their principal function. The language of rights makes people conscious of both their oppression and the possibility of change. Rights have been extraordinarily effective as a basis of networking in and across states and have demonstrated the possibility of international solidarity, particularly for women and indigenous peoples. Many non-governmental organizations justify their existence by the need to promote rights and it is the regime of rights that has enabled them to perform their promotional and investigative role, which has generally proved more effective than internal state mechanisms for accountability. It would be fair to say that the human rights regime has sustained civil society in its confrontation with the state.

Even more fundamentally, the regime of rights is crucial because it speaks in the language of entitlements. Poverty is not just a matter of a deprived economic situation; it is defined and sustained, on the part of the poor, by a sense of helplessness and dependence, and by a lack of opportunities, self-confidence and self-respect. It is increasingly being recognized that poverty can only be eradicated if the poor are given a greater share in decisions about programmes of poverty alleviation and their implementation. The language of rights makes it clear that the poor are not the subject of charity or benevolence, but are entitled to a decent standard of living and that civil and political rights are the vehicles for their participation and empowerment.

The effectiveness of the rights regime is, however, diminished by the fact that not all of them have been integrated into the international economic or financial systems, which are market oriented and primarily protect the interests of capitalists. Many types of rights are not favoured by the capitalist system. Historically only those rights have been upheld that support the interests of the dominant classes thus civil and political rights were propounded by a bourgeoisie coming into power. Today's economic and social rights speak to the claims of the oppressed and the powerless, and the chances of their fulfilment are slim. Developments in human rights have been at the level of rhetoric and to some extent the establishment of institutions, but they have not led to the redistribution of resources or to building the economic base that favours economic justice. Although norms of the human rights regime represent a serious challenge to the international market system, and an alternative vision, the material forces of the international market system are more powerful than the moral claims and rhetoric of human rights.

One further point needs to be made to establish the context for a rights-oriented strategy: it concerns globalization.. The Declaration correctly identifies the contradictory nature of globalization, on one hand opening up possibilities of increased economic growth, and on the other foreclosing options central to the Copenhagen aspirations, such as those of income redistribution, alleviation of poverty, employment opportunities and equity. It states that the global transformations of the world economy are profoundly changing the parameters of social develop-ment in all countries. The challenge is how to manage these processes and threats so as to enhance their benefits and mitigate their negative effects upon people.

There are grave doubts as to whether this challenge can be met successfully. The inherent tendency of economic globalization is to diminish democracy and to privilege market-oriented rights, reducing the importance and feasibility of social and solidarity rights. It is impossible to discuss the salience of the human rights strategy for the Copenhagen social development envisioned in Copenhagen without taking on board the impact of globalization and the redistributions of power that it has produced.

5

Social Justice and Human Rights

Each of three fields — health and human rights, social medicine, and social epidemiology — has valuable insights, and professionals working in these fields hold important roles in advancing the health of people in society. In particular, despite the comparatively recent establishment of the health and human rights field, it has made an enormous contribution to the advancement of global health equity. It has done so by providing an analytical framework to identify and protect the most vulnerable anywhere in the world from poorly conceived public health policies as well as from the egregious abuses that make them vulnerable to ill health and mortality. While health and human rights advocates have from the start taken a global perspective, social medicine and social epidemiology have been slower to catch up. Advancing global health and health equity against a wide variety of threats — including abusive actors, unjustifiable reasoning, and plain complacency of those who have the power to make a difference — will require coherent reasoning and coordination across the fields of social epidemiology, social medicine, and health and human rights. So it is welcome and commendable that this journal, the original publication of the health and human rights field, is taking the lead toward building such coherence and cooperation with a special issue on social determinants of health.

In this chapter, we examine the convergences and contrasts between social epidemiology, social medicine, and human rights approaches toward advancing global health and health equity. For the purposes of this article, we understand social medicine to be the practice of clinical medicine in a manner that demonstrates social awareness, while social epidemiology is the study of the social distribution of disease and causes of that distribution across groups and individuals. The first section of the article describes the goals and work of the WHO Commission on Social Determinants of Health. The second section discusses the role of human rights in the Commission's work. The third section evaluates, from the perspective of social epidemiology, two rights-based approaches to advancing health and health equity in comparison to a view that focuses more broadly on social justice. The article concludes by identifying four areas where social epidemiologists, practitioners of social medicine, and health and human rights advocates can and must work together in order to make progress on health and health equity.

SOCIAL JUSTICE

Arguments about social justice were shunned when the then Secretary of State for Education and Science, Kenneth Baker, proposed a radical restructuring of the school system. Introducing the Education Reform Bill at the 1987 Conservative Party Conference he declared 'the pursuit of egalitarianism is over'. The national goal was quality. The National Curriculum would deliver it 'for all our children, over all our country'. Effective opposition was contained by the language of access and entitlement but the idea of a common 'entitlement' curriculum was not new. HMI had been arguing for it since at least 1977. Feminist educators also supported the notion of a common curriculum experience, albeit one that encompassed the hidden curriculum of schooling and not one posited on a male educational paradigm. However this position is very different from the liberal reformist perspective that is limited by a failure to recognise that educational gender differentiation does not occur in a social and political vacuum. Knowledge is not a neutral commodity, but the emphasis on equal opportunities' serves to reinforce the illusion of neutrality. The National Curriculum gave equal entitlement to all pupils but gender hierarchies were reinforced by the privileging of maths, science and technology.

The status accorded male-centred forms of knowledge did little to challenge the values and practices of patriarchy/androcentricity:

- In short, while girls must be educated in the skills and attitudes to achieve an academic equality with boys—and to challenge inequalities within the labour market—the education of boys in the skills and attitudes to address their equal responsibilities within the family are of equal if not greater importance. And this is where the formal equality accorded by the National Curriculum is most lacking, in the 'masculinisation' of the schooling of girls with no corresponding 'feminisation' of the schooling of boys.

What this position represents is a concern to restructure boys' education in such a way as to break the circulation of stereotypical sex-role expectations. The views expressed emphasise that the majority of schooling operates for a particular form of hegemonic masculinity.

Arnot's review of gender research in British sociology of education highlights two theoretical traditions—the cultural and the political economy perspective. Whereas cultural analyses concentrate on different socialisation processes, political-economy theories use the method of historical materialism. In this latter tradition, reproduction theory is particularly influential, suggesting that schools reproduce the values and ideologies of the dominant social groupings, as well as the status rankings of the existing class structure. Building on this work, Arnot adjusts the theory to enable her to combine a class and gender analysis.

Here she develops the concept of gender codes, which is now fairly well established, to refer to 'the principles which govern the production, reproduction and transmission of gender relations and gender hierarchies'. Hegemony is put to the fore to show the possibility of accommodation and resistance, to allow us to explore the strategies and methods by which a particular way of seeing gender/power relations becomes projected as the 'natural' order. Sociological analysis can provide insight into how powerful groups within society maintain control, while showing how teachers, students and other human agents, can and do, play a crucial role in moderating or changing existing social norms. It is accepted that individuals within the school may generate counter-hegemonic forces and thereby offer routes to change in the name of, for example, women's rights.

Research undertaken for the Equal Opportunities Commission has revealed how English and Welsh education reforms of the late 1980s impacted on gender equality by institutionalising a National Curriculum which gave equal entitlement to all pupils to develop the same learning skills and experience the same subjects. Studying the figures on assessment performance for 1985–94, Arnot used a statistical construct of a 'gender gap' to consider comparative achievement figures. The time period covered the introduction of a new common examination, the General Certificate of Secondary Education, plus coursework assessment, seen to have improved the performance of girls noticeably, as they have the performance of boys, though less dramatically. In the compulsory sector, the pattern of male advantage was sustained in the increasing dominance of boys in chemistry, computer studies and economics.

On the other hand, a more balanced entry pattern was found in English, mathematics and history. Overall more girls than boys were entered for GCSE examinations and girls were more successful in terms of the proportion of A–C grades gained, though the elite minority of girls in private single-sex schools seemed to be at a substantial advantage. In the post-compulsory sector, the data showed sex segregation in subject choice was still marked. Far more young men completed A-levels in mathematics, physics and technology, and at 18 the gender balance in the pattern of examination performances had shifted. Similarly in vocational examinations and the various training schemes, the less prestigious types like business and commerce, hairdressing and beauty and service courses were mostly taken by women. Gender patterns in post school education show how being male or female impacts on career ambition.

They also suggest that:

- A girl's experience of gender cannot be abstracted so neatly from any other aspects of her life. Girls from different social backgrounds will not experience patriarchal culture in identical ways, and the adult lives they anticipate will promise different kinds of opportunity, responsibility and experience. Their priorities as girls will reflect these disparities.

This is corroborated by Murphy and Elwood who observe that children's learning out of school has important consequences for what they choose to do within school. It has an effect on performance, views of relevance, expectations, styles of expression and achievement. In her research, Lees' found that whereas academic girls expect careers, non-academic girls anticipate the need to combine unskilled and part-time employment with the responsibilities of housework and child care. Pro-school and academically or work-oriented girls were typically white females from middle class homes with strong parental support. Mirza comments that the Irish girls in her study saw their futures as home-makers, child-carers and part-time workers; whereas the black girls she interviewed anticipated a career.

Clearly the way in which women perform relative to men varies just as to class and ethnicity, as does the value of having or not having educational qualifications. Significantly, the mature women students interviewed by Pascall and Cox saw education as an escape route from a lifetime of domesticity and low-paid work. However, the gradual abolition of mandatory grants, the introduction of loans and the prospect of incurring high levels of debt have had a major impact on this group of students.

The range of social and economic reforms instigated by the Conservative governments of the 1980s and the New Labour policies of the 1990s have continued to support and foster a market philosophy. Pupils and students have been cast as educational clients, and parents have been recast as the consumers of education systems. Examination and assessment performance league tables, a more stringent school inspection process all serve as mechanisms to 'measure' standards, with an unprecedented emphasis on the phenomenon of the failing school. These new regimes have had a dramatic impact and Ball and Gewirtz note the accretive value of 'successful' girls in their study of contemporary school provision. Not only do they become 'a valuable and sought after resource' but 'their presence in school normally conveys positive impressions to parents about ethos and discipline'. It is important to note, however, that these assumptions operate differentially among girls: the 'good' girl is constructed across class lines. In a qualitative investigation drawing on data spanning nearly 20 years, Walkerdine found that none of the working class girls who succeeded in education trod a straightforward academic path, whereas only one middle class girl did not go on to university entrance. The educational trajectories of two girls, Patsy and Julie, who went to the same nursery, infant and junior schools, and whose parents did all the 'right things', may help to explain why. At 10, both girls were doing equally badly at junior school but whereas Patsy's performance was read as lack of ability by the teacher, Julie's performance was viewed as a problem of motivation. At 16, both girls got poor GCSE results and Patsy left school while Julie went on to university: 'at 21 Julie was back on track and was likely to become a graduate professional, while Patsy, painfully aware of her lack of qualifications, was equally likely to remain in relatively poorly paid, low-status work'.

In their history of postwar education and social change, Arnot argue that feminist campaigners were able to manipulate the concerns of the Conservative governments of the 1980s and 1990s by integrating equal opportunities work into debates about educational standards and performance and good schools. Sixteen-year old girls were already improving their results in the 1970s but 20 years on, the alarm at girls' successes in statutory assessments would bring different aspects of the patterns that form the kaleidoscope of gender, education and equality to the fore. Feminists might have been forgiven for thinking the dream of gender equality was nearer. And yet, it was the underachievement of boys which made hearts race, not the extraordinary success of schools and teachers in improving girls' academic performance. In the 1990s, the rise in female performance roused media reports obsessed with threats to male breadwinning, the collapse of family life and the crisis of fatherhood, and a spill over into an increase in problematic and anti-social behaviours, crime and deviance.

On the face of it, gendered reactions to the annual publication of the GCSE results developed a generalised narrative of female academic success and male failure. This received official legitimation in 1996, when Chris Woodhead, then Chief Inspector of Schools for England, wrote a column in The Times entitled 'Boys who learn to be losers: on the white male culture of failure'. In it he said that the apparent failure of white working class boys was 'one of the most disturbing problems we face within the whole education system'. Two years later, when the publication of new official statistics showed girls outperforming boys in terms of the proportion of pupils obtaining five A–C grades at GCSE in all but one local authority concern for boys' underachievement led then Schools

Standards Minister Stephen Byers to intervene. In a speech at the eleventh International Conference for School Effectiveness and Improvement, he argued that the 'laddish, anti-learning culture' was impeding boys' achievement. Henceforth each local authority was required to address the issue of male disadvantage in drawing up its Education Development Plan.

Others added their own recipes for change. In May 1997 the Professor of Education at Exeter University, Ted Wragg entered the public debate when he put forward a 10-point plan to help the boys. But the plan did not extend to girls, nor did it consider the interests of girls. Thus the old-fashioned problem of boys behaving badly was resolved by a recommendation that teachers appeal to boys' interests—humour, adventure and sport. Elsewhere some of the arguments underpinning the drive to recruit more male primary school teachers bear a striking similarity to the NAS backlash in the 1920s and 1930s. In addition, Arnot cites evidence from a 1995 sample that suggests the majority of new teachers are 'more supportive of class and ethnic equality than of gender equality'.

Such attitudes are likely to be reinforced by rhetoric about a generation of male losers and teaching strategies for the future that may lead to a further masculinisation of classroom environments. Anti-sexist work to raise achievement for all pupils might go further. Boys/men negotiate and take up a variety of masculinities and some of these confer power and prestige, while others are stigmatised and subordinate. We can relate this to the question of special educational needs. Young boys positioned as slow learners, poor at sport and lacking physical strength and skill, may resort to overtly challenging behaviour that may, in turn, make them liable to being classified as having special needs. Indeed, working class boys are found in greater numbers in 'less acceptable' categories of emotional and behavioural difficulties and moderate learning difficulties and middle class boys dominate the non-stigmatised category of specific learning difficulties.

But boys are not the only ones to suffer from a lack of insight into the effects of gender. Indeed not all boys are losing. To paraphrase David and Weiner we need to keep balance on the 'gender agenda'. Several factors have been glossed over amid the hysteria about the current positions of pupils in schools. First of all, boys and girls are both much more successful at school than they were 50 years ago, making the phenomenon one of relative rates of improvement for both sexes. Second, it is obvious that poverty plus factors of 'race' and ethnicity, remain crucial for both sexes. In the third place, when the attainment figures are checked carefully we see a tendency to confuse percentages and percentage points, and a tendency not to use proportionate figures. Consideration of the Welsh data and comparable English data for 1992–7 shows girls doing better at Key Stages 1 to 4 in English and Welsh, at Key Stage 4 in languages, some design subjects and humanities, no achievement gaps in mathematics and science, and gaps at other levels either static or declining.

On the basis of these research findings Gorard speculate that the educational phenomenon of the 'growing gender gap' does not actually exist. Fourth, comparative literacy rates have sparked panic about boys' achievement, even though girls have traditionally excelled at language-based subjects and despite empirical evidence to suggest boys' greater show of interest in film, computer and CD-ROMs may be a better preparation for changing world literacy than may often be the case for girls. Fifth, data from the Leverhulme Numeracy Research Programme, a study of teaching and learning in English primary schools between 1997 and 2002, shows girls do not match boys' performance in mathematics. At GCSE level, the tendency to play safe with examination entries of girls in mathematics means more girls than boys achieve grade C from the Intermediate tier, but mathematics departments in schools only encourage continuation with a B or C grade gained from the Higher tier. In August 2003 more boys got A* grades in GCSE mathematics, biology, chemistry and physics, and more boys took the elite single science subjects than the balanced science associated with state schools. Finally, it is deeply ironic that evidence once used to help explain the underachievement of girls is being used across time to signify different conclusions. Twenty years ago, perceptions of the differential abilities of boys and girls triggered a very different reaction to concerns about schoolgirl attainment in maths and science.

Consequently, as Mahony notes, 'it took a good deal of persuasion by feminists before policy makers would look beyond the innate capacities of girls themselves for explanations'. In contrast, the perception of boys as innately clever continues. Conversely, so does a tendency to imply that girls' academic attainment is the result of compliant hard work: even though the reduction of the coursework element at GCSE did not redress the balance in favour of boys. Female school performance has improved but there is plenty of evidence to support the argument that this is despite the continuing male dominance in the classroom, the playground, curriculum content and greater demands on teacher time and energy.

THE GAP, THE GRADIENT AND SOCIAL JUSTICE

The starting position of the Commission was that there is no inherent biological or "natural" explanation for the gross inequalities in health achievements we see between countries and within countries. There is no inherent biological reason why life expectancy for a girl born in Japan is 86 years, while for a girl born in Sierra Leone it is 43 years. Nor is there a biological explanation for why the maternal mortality ratio in Sierra Leone is 2,100 deaths per 100,000 live births while in Ireland the ratio is 1 maternal death per 100,000 live births. In the case of Malawi, Paul Farmer identifies the lack of sutures, sterile drapes, and anesthesia among the many reasons for the unacceptably high maternal mortality ratio. The Commission concerns itself with such lack of necessary medical supplies — as part of the conditions of daily living — and with the upstream causes of such conditions of daily living. Like Farmer, the Commission asks: how can these conditions be improved through social action? In its *Final Report*, the Commission presented evidence that the systematic differences in health achievements between countries and within countries across groups stratified by education, income, occupation, gender, ethnicity, race, and geographical area of residence are determined by social, political, and economic policies and practices. This evidence militates against analyses that focus narrowly on biological processes at the individual level in a contextual vacuum. One piece of compelling evidence can be found, for example, by examining under-five mortality against household wealth in developing countries. The difference in mortality levels within each country illustrates one detail of the scale of inequality in this indicator, with a substantial gap between the best and the worst off and, importantly, a step-wise gradient across the whole society.

The Commission argues that systematic differences in health achievements that are avoidable or preventable by reasonable means are unfair; they are health "inequities." To return to Paul Farmer's example, reducing maternal mortality through the provision of sutures certainly falls into the category of reasonable means in that it is both practically possible to provide sutures and providing sutures is neither morally offensive nor unreasonable. The same is true of many interventions that would make significant improvements in the conditions of daily living (the circumstances in which people are born, grow, live, work, and age). Indeed, a major source of the frustration driving the Commission's work to collect evidence was the recognition of how much health and health equity could be improved through reasonable means in contrast to the poor reasoning and complacency of many societies and international institutions.

Based on collected evidence and its analysis of the causation and distribution of ill health, the Commission adopted the view that taking action to reduce health inequities is a matter of social justice. The Commission states, "Achieving health equity within a generation is achievable, it is the right thing to do, and now is the right time to do it." This is not meant to be hollow rhetoric. Any meaningful understanding and commitment to the idea of social justice entails addressing manifest injustices, and such manifest injustices exist where reasonable means could be deployed to alleviate disproportionate ill health or prevent mortality. This social justice imperative applies to improving the health of those who suffer most egregiously as well as improving the health of those represented by the gradient, the remaining majority of the population. In light of the unprecedented intellectual and material resources that exist in the world today, the goal of social action, in principle, should be to flatten the social gradient in health by leveling up health outcomes across the social spectrum so that all are capable of achieving the health of the healthiest. This is what is meant by "closing the gap in a generation."

Generation Feasible

Numerous epidemiological studies have shown that gaps and gradients in health can vary significantly between countries and within countries over time, and there have been natural experiments that also provide valuable information. We know, therefore, that average measures of population health and the distribution of health are susceptible to social and political action. For example, with the deep political, social, and economic changes that followed the dissolution of the former USSR, average population health measures worsened, and the gradient in adult mortality by education steepened in Russia since the 1980s.

In New Zealand, "indigenous inequalities," that is, measurable health inequalities between mortality rates of the indigenous and non-indigenous populations, widened between the mid-1980s and the mid-1990s following a period when structural adjustment policies were introduced and social and income inequalities increased. These inequalities then narrowed following the introduction of pro-equity policies and health reforms in the late 1990s. Prevalence of certain chronic diseases is lower among low-income residents in the Canadian province of Quebec, which instigated an anti-poverty strategy in 2002, than in equivalent populations in other Canadian provinces that did not have such a policy.

Studies comparing Nordic countries with other developed countries associate generous and universal social welfare policies with lower levels of poverty and better outcomes for disadvantaged people. While these findings do not demonstrate direct causality, there is a plausible causal chain linking political decisions and social action to changes in the health of entire populations and lower socioeconomic groups. We have evidence that the absolute levels and social gradient of health achievements can rapidly worsen within a single generation. The Commission asserts that health and health equity could also improve dramatically in a single generation if and when appropriate social action is taken within and across countries.

SOCIAL CONDITIONS, HEALTH EQUITY AND HUMAN RIGHTS

Health equity is the concept underlying a commitment to reducing health inequalities — that is, systematic, plausibly avoidable differences in health, varying according to levels of social advantage, with worse health occurring among the disadvantaged.

This is a timely moment to re-examine the areas of convergence and divergence between human rights and health equity, given the relatively recent accumulation of a critical mass of knowledge about the health effects of social conditions (also known as the social determinants of health).

After briefly reviewing this knowledge base, the concept of health equity is examined. This is followed by a discussion of several human rights principles of particular relevance to health equity and, in many cases, to the link between social conditions and health. The final section explores the contributions that human rights and health equity can make to each other, particularly with respect to how each addresses the implications of the link between social conditions and health.

The term "human rights principles" is used throughout to refer both to those principles expressed as rights and other fundamental principles that are not generally referred to as rights in and of themselves but that, nevertheless, have major implications for the meaning of all rights.

"Health" refers to health status itself and is distinguished from medical care (often called "health care," a term not used here to avoid confusion with "health"), which, along with social conditions, is one of many important determinants of health. Several earlier discussions, including some by the author with Sofia Gruskin, JD, have focused on the relevance of human rights to health equity, and many authors have addressed the issue to varying extents in papers focused on other issues.

The World Health Organization has produced materials to educate health workers about human rights and raise awareness of the potential of human rights principles to enrich efforts to improve health and promote health equity. The goal of this paper is to revisit the links and distinctions between rights and equity with a particular focus on the theme of this issue of *Health and Human Rights* — the role of social conditions in health — and in light of the recent increase in awareness and accumulation of knowledge of the latter.

SOCIAL CONDITIONS SHAPE HEALTH AND HEALTH INEQUALITIES

Health-related behaviors (for example, smoking, alcohol intake, illicit drug use, physical activity, and diet) also would likely be mentioned, given the growing awareness of their health effects over the past few decades. For a long time, clean water, adequate sanitation, food safety, and protection from occupational and environmental physical hazards have been widely recognized as essential conditions for health (although often taken for granted, at least in settings where they are guaranteed). However, outside the development community or those who study or promote action on the social determinants of health, social and economic conditions in homes, neighborhoods, schools, and workplaces are generally less likely to be considered among the major influences on health.

Considerable evidence now indicates, however, that social and economic conditions — apart from access to and quality of medical care, which have undeniable importance — play a fundamental, powerful, and pervasive role in the health of populations in both resource-poor and resource-rich countries. The evidence includes, for example, widening social inequalities in health in the UK in the decades following the introduction of the National Health Service, which removed financial obstacles to medical care; the currently poor and progressively deteriorating US ranking on health internationally, despite higher medical care spending than any other nation; and increasing evidence and understanding of the health impact of social conditions. A large and rapidly growing literature documents strong and pervasive links between social and economic conditions and health in nations of all economic levels; although much remains unknown and contested, the biologic plausibility of many of those links has been documented by studies of pathways and physiologic mechanisms.

The term "social conditions" is used here — and often elsewhere — to refer to social, economic, and political conditions encompassing a wide range of modifiable factors that are outside the scope of medical care (the latter defined as preventive, curative, and rehabilitative services delivered by medical care personnel). Social conditions include potentially modifiable characteristics of both social and physical environments at the individual, household, and community levels — that is, features of homes, schools, workplaces, and neighbourhoods that could be shaped by policies (at least in theory, and given sufficient political will). Social conditions also include factors at the regional, national, and global levels that often shape conditions experienced locally. Examples of social conditions include poverty, quality of housing, homelessness, educational attainment and quality, unemployment, wage levels, lack of control over the organization of work, racial residential segregation, and other forms of discrimination.

Social Conditions and Health

The World Health Organization (WHO)'s Commission on the Social Determinants of Health released its final report in 2008, marking a watershed event in the history of public health and human development. The WHO Commission's report was ground-breaking in its unequivocal endorsement by the health sector of the importance of addressing inequalities in social conditions in order to address inequalities in health. Backed up by massive collections of evidence and examples of promising interventions in economically, politically, and culturally diverse settings, the WHO Commission report called for action, while also acknowledging the need for further investment in research to guide future action on the social determinants of health. Important advances in knowledge during the past 15 years include the growing understanding of biological mechanisms that may lead to cardiovascular disease and other chronic diseases (for example, through pathways involving chronic stress). These potential mechanisms may involve multiple physiologic systems, including neuroendocrine, autonomic, immune, and inflammatory processes. Evidence from animal studies demonstrates that chronically high levels of stress may lead to neuroendocrine dysregulation, which, in turn, may lead to physiologic processes responsible for premature aging and chronic disease through damage to multiple organs and systems. Further study among humans is needed in order to draw definitive conclusions, but many experts in the field believe that pathways involving psychological responses to social conditions are likely to be among the most important explanations of the social gradient in health in affluent countries.

Another important area of relatively recent discovery is that of early brain development. Studies reveal differences in brain development and cognitive function in response to social conditions that vary by social class. Studies also reveal tremendous developmental plasticity in early childhood, which offers opportunities to substantially ameliorate the adverse developmental effects of early social disadvantage through interventions such as high-quality early child care programs. The positive effects of early intervention also have ramifications for the future, given increasing scientific awareness of the links between social conditions experienced in early childhood and health in adulthood. An important pathway through which early childhood development is likely to influence health involves school readiness, which predicts school performance; the latter, in turn, predicts educational attainment, one of the most powerful predictors of economic resources (through employment opportunities), social influence and relative social standing in adulthood.

There also has been a marked increase in studies exploring how characteristics of neighbourhoods can affect the health of their residents, above and beyond the effects of characteristics of individual residents. Examples of neighborhood features that have been linked with health include the concentration of poor households in an area, levels of crime, accessibility to transportation and sources of employment, and degree of racial residential segregation. A growing body of literature suggests that the health effects of being poor in a neighbourhood with concentrated poverty may differ from those of being poor in a more affluent neighbourhood.

Mechanisms explaining improved health in better-off neighbourhoods may include more favourable social conditions in the wealthier neighbourhoods (for example, less crime, better housing quality, safer places to play or exercise, better access to nutritious foods, and/or more social cohesion and trust), which may mitigate the disadvantages of individual residents. One's perceptions of one's social status relative to others in one's immediate community also may have effects on health. Subjective social status and social cohesion are among the reasons that have been invoked to explain the findings observed in some studies demonstrating that members of groups residing in neighbourhoods where their numbers are more concentrated paradoxically appear to have better health, despite the higher concentrations of material disadvantage in those neighbourhoods.

This example illustrates the complexity of studying neighbourhood effects on health. Studying effects of communities on health is particularly challenging because characteristics of communities may influence health by shaping characteristics of households and individuals residing in them; if so, then estimating community effects while controlling for household/individual effects would entail adjusting for key mediators of the relationship between community characteristics and health; however, the existence of independent neighbourhood effects is always a question of interest.

The study of links between social factors and health is in its infancy. It is challenging, in part because of the complexity of the pathways involved, with the possibility of interactions with contextual and individual factors at each step, and in part because of the often long latent period between exposure and later manifestation in measurable health outcomes. While definitive knowledge of specific pathways and mechanisms is inadequate, sufficient knowledge has accumulated to establish that in resource-rich and resource-poor countries alike, social conditions are indeed powerful influences on health.

Conceptual Frameworks

For at least the past half century, a period during which medical technology has proliferated, prevailing ways of thinking about health often have tended to focus narrowly on medical care and/or on behaviors of individuals (for which individuals alone are held responsible). There has been little consideration of how social conditions — which could be modified by policies outside the reach of the medical care sector — might also be important to consider, including the role they can play in shaping individual behaviours. Against this background, it has been important to have conceptual frameworks to guide work on the nexus between social conditions and health; these frameworks provide important resources for thinking about both health equity and human rights, and hence for analytic work in both fields.

These advances in awareness of the impact of social conditions on health and health disparities led the Robert Wood Johnson Foundation to establish a national commission charged with recommending promising policy directions — *beyond the realm of medical care* — to improve health overall and reduce health inequalities in the United States. The commission, convened during 2008–2009, was composed of nationally prominent leaders, primarily from fields outside of health care such as education, economics, labour, community development, business, and journalism. The conceptual framework articulated in the Foundation's charge to the commission and rationale for the effort: that medical care and health-related behaviours are indeed important influences on health, but must be considered within the broader context of the social conditions that are more fundamental influences on health. While we as individuals need to behave responsibly and make healthy decisions, the societies in which we live must also act responsibly to create conditions that enable individuals to choose health. According to this framework, efforts to improve overall health and reduce health disparities in the United States must be directed beyond medical care and individual behaviour change to focus more broadly on social conditions — including the economic and social opportunities and resources that shape a person's opportunities to live, learn, work, and play in health-promoting environments. In the words of epidemiologist Geoffrey Rose, effective policies must focus at least to some extent on "the causes of the causes" rather than only on ameliorating the symptoms.

Understanding how Health Inequalities

The useful framework for understanding and addressing the links between social conditions and health. Developed by Finn Diderichsen, now at the University of Copenhagen, and based on current knowledge of the dynamics of health and health inequalities, this framework depicts how social inequalities in health are created, exacerbated, and perpetuated through effects of social stratification. Social stratification is defined as the sorting of individuals into groups with different relative positions in social hierarchies based on characteristics including social class, race or ethnicity, gender, disability, sexual orientation or other factors associated with different levels of social, economic and political opportunities and resources, and reflecting different levels of wealth, influence, acceptance, and/or prestige.

Diderichsen's diagram illustrates how social stratification leads to not only differential exposure to health-promoting or health-damaging experiences, but also to differential vulnerability to health damage among exposed individuals. For example, child mortality due to measles is generally confined to malnourished children who lack the immune defences of well-nourished children and succumb to bacterial super-infections that complicate their infection with the measles virus. Similarly, exposure to adverse peer group or advertising influences may have greater effects on the health-related behaviours of adolescents from socioeconomically disadvantaged families compared with their better-off counterparts. Social stratification also results in differential consequences at the same level of sickness or injury. For example, while a highly educated professional who becomes seriously physically disabled may not lose his or her ability to earn a living, a manual labourer suffering the same disability will certainly lose his or her livelihood as a result; similarly, a person with considerable accumulated wealth and adequate medical insurance is unlikely to become homeless when faced with loss of employment due to serious illness or injury, in contrast to someone with few financial assets facing the same illness and related expenses. These differential consequences of ill health lead to further social stratification and increasing health inequalities. The pathways linking social stratification and health can be interrupted by policies, however. Rather than accepting current levels or patterns of social stratification as inevitable, this perspective calls our attention to multiple points at which interventions can be considered to ameliorate the vicious cycle of disadvantage and health inequalities over lifetimes and generations.

HEALTH EQUITY AND HUMAN RIGHTS

Employing the Millennium Development Goals (MDGs) as a lens, he showed that, although the agenda and interests of the two communities overlap considerably, neither embraces cooperation with any enthusiasm or conviction. Much the same could be said about the character of the interaction between the health and human rights community and the social epidemiology and the social medicine communities. On the one side, work on the social determinants of health has rarely acknowledged the potential contributions of a human rights approach. On the other side, rights-based approaches to health, with some notable exceptions, have not engaged in a meaningful way with the growing body of research that demonstrates the significant impact of the social determinants of health and health inequalities on health status and population health.

The World Health Organization Commission on Social Determinants of Health (CSDH) is an important example of the first tendency. While the report, *Closing the gap in a generation: Health equity through action on the social determinants of health* (hereafter *Closing the gap*), addresses many of the same issues as does the health and human rights community, its authors seems reluctant to acknowledge this common ground. Even when the report uses rights-based terminology, it rarely cites relevant international human rights instruments or notes the potential contribution of United Nations human rights institutions. To offer examples, the report's first mention of the right to the highest attainable standard of health attributes the right to the Constitution of the World Health Organization and "numerous international treaties."

Despite the Commission's commitment to achieving universal health care, *Closing the gap* does not refer to Article 12 of the International Covenant on Economic, Social and Cultural Rights until page 158 of the 208-page report, and then only very briefly; nor does the CSDH acknowledge the role of the Special Rapporteur on the right of everyone to the enjoyment of the highest attainable standard of physical and mental health (hereafter the Special Rapporteur on the right to health) until page 173. The Committee on Economic, Social and Cultural Rights's seminal general comment on the right to "the highest attainable standard of health" warrants only a brief citation that is buried in the chapter on political empowerment and a listing as one of the proponents of health for all.

This reticence to recognize the shared agenda and potential contribution of the human rights paradigm is particularly surprising in view of the Commission secretariat's recommendation that the CSDH adopt a rights-based approach as an appropriate conceptual framework to advance towards health equity through action on the social determinants of health. The secretariat's framework document explains: Human rights offer more than a conceptual armature connecting health, social conditions and broad governance principles. . . . Rights concepts and standards provide an instrument for turning diffuse social demand into focused legal and political claims, as well as a set of criteria by which to evaluate the performance of political authorities in promoting people's wellbeing and creating conditions for equitable enjoyment of the fruits of development.

Others have also noted the conspicuous absence of human rights in the CSDH report. Paul Hunt, the former Special Rapporteur on the right to health, expressed disappointment that, despite "the multiple, dense connections between social determinants and human rights," the report's human rights comment, while not absent, is "underdeveloped and understated" and "disappointingly muted." Although he recognized the contributions of the report, he characterized the work of the CSDH as "a series of missed opportunities."

Closing the Gap in a Generation

The World Health Organization (WHO) launched the Commission on Social Determinants of Health (CSDH) in March 2005, with a mandate to marshal evidence on what can be done to promote health equity and to foster a global movement to achieve it. The multinational CSDH consisted of 20 commissioners chaired by Sir Michael Marmot, who is known for his pioneering work on the impact of social inequalities on health in the United Kingdom. Specifically, the CSDH was tasked with collecting, collating, and synthesizing global evidence on the social determinants of health and their impact on health inequity from countries at all levels of income and development, and with making recommendations on actions to address this inequity. To pursue its mandate, the Commission established a series of subject-matter working groups, termed "knowledge networks," on nine topics: globalization, early childhood development, employment conditions, women and gender equity, social exclusion, health systems, priority public health conditions, urban settings, and measurement and evidence. The resulting report, *Closing the gap,* builds upon and gives greater visibility to prior work in the field of social medicine. Its major contributions are the visibility it gives to the social determinants of health, its justice oriented trajectory, the extensive research it marshals, and its body of recommendations. Using language rarely, if ever, seen in a WHO document, the final report is unequivocal in condemning the disparities in life opportunities and health status between rich and poor countries and between the rich and poor "within countries":

Our children have dramatically different life chances depending on where they were born. In Japan or Sweden they can expect to live more than 80 years; in Brazil, 72 years; India, 63 years; and in one of several African countries, fewer than 50 years. And within countries, the differences in life chances are dramatic and are seen worldwide. The poorest of the poor have high levels of illness and premature mortality. But poor health is not confined to those worst off. In countries at all levels of income, health and illness follow a social gradient: the lower the socioeconomic position, the worse the health. It does not have to be this way and it is not right that it should be like this. Where systematic differences in health are judged to be avoidable by reasonable action they are, quite simply, unfair. . . . Putting right these inequities — the huge and remediable differences in health between and within countries — is a matter of social justice. . . . Social injustice is killing people on a grand scale.

The Commission ascribes these differentials to "a toxic combination of poor social policies and programmes, unfair economic arrangements, and bad politics." The report makes three overarching recommendations: 1) "improve the conditions of daily life — the circumstances in which people are born, grow, live, work, and age"; 2) "tackle the inequitable distribution of power, money, and resources" that serve as "the structural drivers of those conditions of daily life — globally, nationally, and locally"; and 3) "measure the problem, evaluate actions, expand the knowledge base" in order to understand the problem and assess the impact of action and "raise public awareness about the social determinants of health." As the title of its report attests, the Commission calls for closing the health gap in a generation (that is, within 30 years). While acknowledging that this is more likely an aspiration than a realistic goal, the CSDH expresses the belief that it is possible to achieve marked improvement in health equity within that time.

HEALTH EQUITY AND SOCIAL CONDITIONS

The human rights agreements referred to here include the Universal Declaration of Human Rights (UDHR), the International Covenant on Civil and Political Rights (ICCPR), the International Covenant on Economic, Social and Cultural Rights (ICESCR), and the officially recognized documents interpreting the ICESCR — the General Comments by the UN Committee on Economic, Social and Cultural Rights (CESCR), Limburg Principles on the Implementation of the ICESCR and the Maastricht Guidelines on Violations of Economic Social and Cultural Rights. Together the UDHR, ICCPR, and ICESCR are referred to as the International Bill of Human Rights. The International Convention on the Elimination of All Forms of Racial Discrimination (ICERD) is also cited in this paper.

The Right to Education

In countries of all levels of economic development, education — meaning general schooling, rather than health education — appears to be one of the most powerful social determinants of health. Education has appeared to be a stronger predictor of some health outcomes in some contexts than income or other measures of material resources; income or other material measures have, however, seemed more powerful predictors of other health outcomes, or in other contexts. It is difficult to disentangle education from material resources, given the importance of each in determining access to the latter.

The ICESCR expresses "the right of everyone to education . . . directed to the full development of the human personality." It notes that "education shall enable all persons to participate effectively in a free society." Sen's concept of basic capabilities has been influential in thinking about both human rights and health equity. In line with that concept, education, along with health, can be seen as a fundamental capability essential for fully achieving one's health potential as well as one's ability to function in society, including the capacity to earn a living and participate in the political process, concretely illustrating the interconnectedness of rights.

While the right to a standard of living adequate for health might not appear, in itself, necessarily to call for more than a minimum standard, consideration of the indivisibility of all human rights also would invoke the "right to the highest attainable standard of health." By extension, the human rights obligation would be to ensure to all citizens a standard of living required to achieve the highest attainable standard of health.

The "right to health" — or to the "highest attainable standard of health," as expressed in Article 12 of the ICESCR and other human rights agreements — has been criticized at times, however, for being vague or unrealistic, and therefore of limited use to guide policies. Despite the criticisms, there is evidence of its practical utility in the policy arena. Nevertheless, it is worth examining some of the shortcomings that have been articulated.

Some have pointed out that governments cannot be responsible for guaranteeing that everyone enjoys good health, let alone enjoys the highest possible levels of health. It is also reasonable to ask how one would monitor compliance with the right to health and how one would determine the highest attainable state of health for individuals or groups. Furthermore, without more rigorous definition, at least in theory, the right to the highest attainable standard of health could be used by some, in individual-level litigation, to justify unlimited expenditures on expensive medical technology for a few articulate, empowered individuals, to the detriment of investments in more equitable interventions with greater effectiveness in improving population health and reducing disparities. The CESCR's General Comment No. 14 on the right to the highest attainable standard of health as expressed in the ICESCR, however, explicitly emphasizes that, "[t]he right to health is not to be understood as a right to be *healthy*," because too many factors beyond a state's control influence health. Rather, it is "the right to a system of health protection which provides equality of opportunity to enjoy the highest attainable level of health."

Despite the fact that the indivisibility of rights implicitly links the right to health with the right to a standard of living adequate for health, the right to health has often been interpreted as applying only to medical care, and not as frequently used to argue for the need for greater equity in social conditions. CESCR General Comment No. 14, however, makes it clear that the right to health is not limited to medical care or traditional public health domains, stating, "On the contrary, the drafting history and the express wording [of the language of the right to health] acknowledge that the right to health embraces a wide range of socioeconomic factors that promote conditions in which people can lead a healthy life, and extends to the underlying determinants of health, such as food and nutrition, housing, access to safe and potable water and adequate sanitation, safe and healthy working conditions, and a healthy environment." A subsequent statement also notes, "The Committee interprets the right to health . . . as an inclusive right extending not only to timely and appropriate health care but also to the underlying determinants of health." Furthermore, UDHR Article 25.1, on the right to a standard of living adequate for health (discussed above), is explicit about the connection between social conditions and health. Alicia Ely Yamin has noted that "rights must be realized inherently within the social sphere," and that this "formulation immediately suggests that determinants of health and ill health are not purely biological or 'natural' but are also factors of societal relations."

The Indivisibility of all Human Rights

The principle of the *indivisibility, interdependence, and inter-relatedness of all human rights,* as expressed in the International Bill of Rights (UDHR, ICCPR, and the ICESCR), has great relevance to both health equity and the link between social conditions and health. According to this principle, all human rights — civil, political, economic, social, and cultural — are interdependent and indivisible from one another. For example, according to this principle, the inability to realize one's economic and social rights (for example, the right to a standard of living adequate for health; the right to education; and the right to the highest attainable standard of health) is recognized as an impediment to realizing one's civil and political rights (for example, freedom of speech and assembly; and the right to participate in the political process in one's society). Similarly, denial of civil and political rights can constitute a serious threat to health, as illustrated not only by examples of genocide and torture, but also by the health consequences of apartheid and other regimes in which particular population groups have been systematically disenfranchised.

The knowledge gained over the past decade or two on the social determinants of health and health equity can contribute to human rights discussions by providing an empiric illustration supporting the principle of the indivisibility of all human rights. The indivisibility of all human rights contributes to the concept of health equity in part by underscoring, for example, that failure to realize one's full health potential can have negative consequences for the ability to exercise one's civil and political rights, thereby strengthening arguments regarding a societal obligation to create conditions permitting everyone to achieve her or his health potential. It also can strengthen the arguments for the need to pursue equity in all the determinants of health, including living standards, education, and the ability to participate fully in society and the political process.

Article 25.1 of the UDHR explicitly acknowledges the link between living conditions and health: "Everyone has the right to a standard of living adequate for the health and well-being of himself and of his family" The right to a standard of living adequate for health is of clear, direct, and substantial relevance to health equity, in that health equity requires an equitable distribution not only of medical care, but also of the social and economic conditions necessary for health.

The right to "a standard of living adequate for health" does not entail an obligation to ensure equal standards of living, so long as a standard adequate for health is achieved. It seems reasonable that increases in living standards above a certain high level might not necessarily translate into increases in health; however, a US study including an unusually wide range of income levels showed incremental improvements in health (as reflected by functional limitations among the elderly) with income levels up to seven times the federal poverty level. In addition, income gradients in multiple child and adult health indicators in the US have been demonstrated in studies where the most affluent group had incomes at least four times the federal poverty level.

Non-discrimination

Another human rights principle with strong and pervasive links to core concepts of health equity and relevance to the role of social conditions in health is the cross-cutting principle of non-discrimination. Non-discrimination applies to all rights; the International Bill of Human Rights and multiple General Comments specify that everyone is entitled to all human rights without distinction based on "race, colour, sex, language, religion, political or other opinion, national or social origin, property, birth or other status." In ICESCR General Comment 20, the CESCR added "ethnic origin" to this list ("'race and colour,' which includes an individual's ethnic origin"), referring to all these categories as the "express grounds" for which discrimination is prohibited. It is worth noting that the language explicitly includes both socioeconomic resources and social position as prohibited bases for discrimination; the terms "social origin," "property," and "birth" refer unambiguously and explicitly to wealth and to the relative social and economic standing of the family into which an individual is born.

General Comment 20 also addresses the "other status" category of prohibited grounds for discrimination, stating that the "nature of discrimination varies according to context and evolves over time," therefore requiring a "flexible approach to interpreting 'other status.'" Referring to ICESCR Article 2, paragraph 2, the following paragraph subheadings within General Comment 20 (as a non-exhaustive list, given the fluid nature of discrimination) identified additional "implied grounds" for which discrimination is prohibited under the "other status" category: disability (paragraph 28), age (paragraph 29), nationality (paragraph 30), marital and family status (paragraph 31), sexual orientation and gender identity (paragraph 32), health status (paragraph 33), place of residence (paragraph 34), and economic and social situation (paragraph 35).

While the ICESCR itself does not state that priority attention should be given to disadvantaged groups, the UN Committee on Social, Economic and Cultural Rights, has made it unambiguously clear, both in their General Comments on the ICESCR, and in their comments on the reports that state parties are required to submit at regular intervals, that giving priority attention to vulnerable and marginalized groups is one of the Covenant's main intents, and a core obligation of states. Other official interpretations of the ICESCR supporting the obligation to prioritize vulnerable groups are stated in the Limburg Principles on the Implementation of the International Covenant on Economic, Social and Cultural Rights (1986), and The Maastricht Guidelines on Violations of Economic, Social and Cultural Rights (1997).

Affirmative action to preferentially promote the achievement of rights by groups who are vulnerable because they have historically experienced discrimination is justified, so long as the preference is not permanent, and is removed once a group is no longer vulnerable. The ICERD states: Special measures taken for the sole purpose of securing adequate advancement of certain racial or ethnic groups or individuals requiring such protection as may be necessary in order to ensure such groups or individuals equal enjoyment or exercise of human rights and fundamental freedoms shall not be deemed racial discrimination, provided, however, that such measures do not, as a consequence, lead to the maintenance of separate rights for different racial groups and that they shall not be continued after the objectives for which they were taken have been achieved.

Similarly, the CESCR stated the following in General Comment 16 (under "Temporary Special Measures"): The principles of equality and non-discrimination, by themselves, are not always sufficient to guarantee true equality. Temporary special measures may sometimes be needed in order to bring disadvantaged or marginalized persons or groups of persons to the same substantive level as others. Temporary special measures aim at realizing not only de jure or formal equality, but also de facto or substantive equality for men and women. However, the application of the principle of equality will sometimes require that States parties take measures in favour of women in order to attenuate or suppress conditions that perpetuate discrimination. As long as these measures are necessary to redress de facto discrimination, and are terminated when de facto equality is achieved, such differentiation is legitimate.

States have the responsibility not only to strive to end intentionally discriminatory actions and structures, but also to strive to end de facto discrimination, that is, structural or institutional patterns resulting in, exacerbating, or perpetuating inequality in obstacles to realizing rights, regardless of intent. The ICERD states: "Each State Party shall take effective measures to review governmental, national and local policies, and to amend, rescind or nullify any laws and regulations which have *the effect* of creating or perpetuating racial discrimination wherever it exists." Similarly, the CESCR's General Comment 20 defined discrimination as "any distinction, exclusion, restriction or preference or other differential treatment that is directly or indirectly based on the prohibited grounds of discrimination and which has the *intention or effect* of nullifying or impairing the recognition, enjoyment or exercise on an equal footing of [ICESCR] rights." Gillian MacNaughton has noted examples of reports from the International Committee for Civil and Political Rights in which the issues singled out as manifesting discriminatory patterns involve underlying social inequality between groups; for example, the disproportionate representation of African Americans among homeless people in the US.

Equality

The equality of all persons "in dignity and rights" can be seen as the basis for non-discrimination as well as for all human rights; this is paralleled by the basis for the concept of equity, which rests on valuing all persons equally. The operational definition of equality in the field of human rights — apart from equality before the law — has been much debated. The concept of equality has been no less contentious in the field of health equity. Equity and equality are seen by many as distinct, with equity potentially requiring inequality, that is, allocating more resources (including resources addressing social determinants as well as medical care) to those who need more. Two dimensions are often distinguished: horizontal equity, or equal resources for equal need, and vertical equity, or more resources for greater need; defining need can be challenging, however.

Furthermore, in situations where a particular group of persons — for example, women, or people of a lower caste — is especially disenfranchised, a clear call for equality rather than equity may be essential, because some definitions of equity may leave too much room for interpretation. For example, more enfranchised groups may argue that the treatment of a disenfranchised group is "equitable," given the latter's best interests and proper role in society. In any case, equity cannot be assessed without measuring equality and inequality: progress toward greater equity is measured by reductions in health inequalities.

Other Human Rights Principles

Human rights instruments acknowledge that governments, particularly in developing countries, often will be unable to immediately remove all obstacles to their populations' realization of all rights, particularly the economic and social rights, and therefore require states to show good faith efforts at progressively moving toward that goal. Governments are obligated to ensure the immediate fulfilment of some rights (generally those prohibiting active infringements on rights), and, at least, to progressively take steps toward ensuring that all persons can realize all of their rights. Governmental obligation lies not only in not violating (that is, respecting) the rights of their populations, but also in protecting these rights against violations by other parties, and actively promoting the realization of rights by all persons.

THE COMMISSION AND HUMAN RIGHTS

From the start, the Commission based its work on an awareness of human rights and the relationship between human rights and health. It also built on opportunities to discuss with human rights experts — including Paul Hunt, the former United Nations Rapporteur on the Right to Health — the possible role of international human rights law in the Commission's analysis and *Final Report*. While it was clear that human rights law would be an important part of implementing the Commission's recommendations, members of the Commission were not convinced that explicit consideration of the legal human right to health changed their final causal analysis. That is, to what extent can the violation of human rights — as defined by international statutes — explain the (social) causation and distribution of ill health and mortality? On the one hand, all the social determinants identified thus far in the causal chain of ill health and mortality could conceivably be recast as violations of human rights. Such recasting without providing the underlying epidemiological information and analysis would not in and of itself supply convincing evidence of causation. Further, providing epidemiological evidence with accompanying human rights legal analysis does not provide additional explanatory value. After epidemiological analysis, however, human rights law has immense value in guiding how societies must act in order to protect, promote, and fulfil the rights implicated in the social epidemiological analysis. The Commission said as much in the *Final Report* by stating that the right to health as set out by Paul Hunt's report presents a compelling case for action on the social determinants of health. On the other hand, it is not immediately clear how a human rights analysis of health can capture some of the central findings in social epidemiology, namely, the observations about the health of social groups and the broad social gradient in health within and across countries.

When evaluating the role of human rights in the Commission's analysis and recommendations, one also must bear in mind that the Commission was very aware that within the WHO and in the global health policy arena, the two dominant approaches to analyzing poor health and health inequalities focus on medical interventions/health systems or economic policy. The focus on disease prevalence and medical care/health systems aims to address ill health through the provision of medical interventions such as vertical programs or better functioning of health systems broadly conceived. And the perspective of economics, exemplified by the WHO Commission on Macroeconomics and Health, focuses on improving the cost-effectiveness of health systems in order to improve economic growth while also being mindful of the health needs of the "ultra" income-poor. The Commission championed an alternative framework of analysis that presented evidence of the full breadth of social determinants of health beyond that generally considered within the realm of medical interventions/health systems. The Commission also argued that all avoidable ill health and health inequalities must be addressed as a matter of social justice, not just those factors instrumental to economic growth.

Furthermore, the Commissioners were well aware that the social distribution of ill health and health achievements is a secondary concern in both the focus on controlling diseases and mortality through medical interventions and in investing in health for economic growth. It is quite conceivable that average indicators of health or economic growth targets could be reached through focusing on improving the health achievements of the more advantaged in societies. This is why equity and social justice are concerns that run throughout the Commission's analysis. Finally, but not least important, the Commission wanted to show that the health of individuals in both rich and poor countries could be evaluated within one framework of analysis, that the preventable deaths and suffering of the disadvantaged and the social gradient as it affects health in both rich and poor countries are the result of the way in which we organize our societies through economic, social, and political policies and practices. For these reasons and more, the Commission drew largely on the methods of social and natural sciences research in order to analyze the causes and distribution of ill health and mortality within and across countries.

IDEA OF HUMAN RIGHTS AND ENTITLEMENTS

Nevertheless, the idea of human rights and entitlements came to the fore throughout the Commission's discussions. Dr. Ricardo Lagos, former President of Chile and a member of the Commission, pointed out that Chile has introduced a system of social guarantees, or entitlements to health care, for a number of health conditions as rights of citizenship. Mirai Chatterjee, a Commission member from India, described how the Self Employed Women's Association campaigned and won legal rights for poor women in Ahmedabad to work as street market traders. So the ideas of human rights as well as rights and entitlements were present throughout the functioning of the Commission and appear in the *Final Report*. At the same time, the Commissioners and others would assert that human rights do not encompass the entirety of the idea of social justice. Advancing health and health equity as a matter of social justice will entail promoting, protecting, and fulfilling human rights, including the right to health, as well as taking additional social action. Moreover, in thinking about health and social justice, the Commission recognized an affinity between Amartya Sen's ethical arguments for seeing social justice as the expansion of freedoms and social epidemiological research on the effects on health of having control, autonomy, and ability to participate in social relationships. Indeed, Sen's thinking was influential in setting up the Commission and he served as one of the Commissioners. Expanding on Sen's line of reasoning, the Commission positioned the concept of empowerment for individuals, communities, and nations across three dimensions — material needs, psychosocial factors (having control over one's life), and political voice and participation in decision-making processes — as fundamental to making progress toward health equity.

In responding to the Commission's *Final Report*, some human rights advocates such as Paul Hunt and Mary Robinson have remarked that it should have granted a larger and far more central role to human rights. Received in the positive and constructive manner that Hunt and Robinson intended, these comments have been understood to mean that there is much more unexplored potential in bringing together human rights analysis and social epidemiology/social medicine. For example, the role of legal institutions, particularly those institutions that protect constitutional and international human rights, may have distinct contributions to make in addressing certain social determinants of health or for establishing social norms. Indeed, no modern approach to health and human rights would exist without the legal institutions that have established human rights law. Although the Commission has formally concluded its activities, as part of the follow-on activities, there have been efforts to think more concertedly on integrating social epidemiology/social medicine and human rights. In the next section, we present some of the initial analysis of the convergences and contrasts between social epidemiology/social medicine approaches and human rights-based approaches. While we identify a divergence at the point of causal analysis of health, we argue these approaches are not only convergent — in the sense that they both have common concern and push toward the same goal of greater health equity — but that they are also interdependent and must work together in order to advance health and health equity within and across countries. As concrete illustration of our reasoning about how social epidemiology/social medicine and human rights approaches can and should be integrated and jointly deployed to advance health and health equity, we have taken the liberty of focusing on Paul Farmer's rhetorical question in an earlier issue of this journal, "Should there be a right to sutures?"

Human Rights and Social Justice

In describing a visit to Malawi, Farmer reported the maternal mortality ratio in Malawi as being a shocking 1,800 per 100,000 live births. He described how the two obstetricians in a maternity hospital faced severe shortcomings in supplies, facilities, and personnel compared with the Harvard teaching hospitals where Farmer works part of the year. However, as a result of the efforts of the two Malawian obstetricians, the maternal mortality ratio within the hospital was reported to be 300 per 100,000 at the time of his visit. Given that this within-hospital maternal mortality ratio is still deplorably high, the fact that it could be seen as a consolation that it was one-sixth of the national ratio left Farmer speechless. Tarek Meguid, one of the obstetricians who showed Farmer around the hospital, described the lack of material resources — of supplies, facilities, and personnel — in terms of human rights abuses. Farmer, in turn, asked readers "Should there be a right to sutures? To sterile drapes? To anesthesia?"

Most readers would likely answer with a resounding "Yes, of course!" And yet, Farmer's questions raise one of the central conceptual problems in the health and human rights paradigm: how to frame a right to something that is not explicitly identified in human rights law? How to reconcile an understanding of the often dire health situation "on the ground" with the formal texts of human rights law is a dilemma for which even those deeply committed to the ideals of human rights often pursue remarkably different paths in order to advance global health and health equity. Even among human rights advocates, (putting aside the views of the skeptics and critics of human rights), if a particular right to something does not appear in the legal documents, then such a human right does not exist. But what if one believes, for example, that the provision of sutures is not only a reasonable and feasible means to prevent deaths but that it should be seen as a human right? In the following discussion, we frame this issue as one that may be addressed by pursuing three possible paths. Each path is a potential answer when faced with this not-so-uncommon situation, where the identification of the causal pathways to ill health and mortality on the ground is sought to be integrated with the idea and law of human rights.

The choice to continue to engage with international human rights law and with attempts to interpret the existing law via documentation, reporting, and various avenues of enforcement with the goal of addressing the missing cause or treatment, such as in the example of the provision of sutures. Path 2, rather than seeking formal engagement with human rights law, would seek to derive principles and values from human rights law and infuse them into health programs and interactions between individuals on the ground. Finally, Path 3 would in fact back away from the arena of human rights law and would instead attempt to bridge the analysis of the causes and distribution of ill health and mortality on the ground with ethical reasoning about social justice. Out of such ethical reasoning — informed by evidence of the causes, inequalities, and consequences of ill health — could arise arguments for advancing rights and other types of social action. The three paths are not mutually exclusive; all three could be effective to various degrees and could function in different arenas and at different institutional levels — international, national, community, and family.

The Commission followed the third path for some of the reasons outlined above. Nevertheless, because it appears that human rights are given a diminished role in Path 3 in comparison to the first two paths, it seems worthwhile to examine the intellectual and strategic motivations for pursuing each of the different ways of engaging with human rights to advance health and health equity.

On seeing the lack of medical supplies in Malawi as part of the causal chain of maternal mortality among poor women, Farmer was motivated to ask the questions in terms of "should there be a right?" because there are in fact, no enunciated human rights to sutures, to sterile drapes, or anesthesia. If there were indeed such human rights to sutures and other relevant medical supplies and services stated in the law, the concern would, understandably, be about enforcement and implementation of the legal rights. Indeed, a significant part — if not most — of the health and human rights scholarship over the past decade has concerned interpreting, implementing, or enforcing the right to health and other human rights related to health already existing in international law. But there is no such explicitly articulated legal right to sutures. Nevertheless, Farmer continues to press this example in terms of human rights law, calling attention to a broader definition of human rights that encompasses economic and social rights. Although no explicit human right to sutures is stated in either the Universal Declaration of Human Rights, the Covenant on Economic, Social and Cultural Rights, or in Right to Health General Comment No. 14, the existing language and rights in these legal human rights documents can be interpreted to provide individuals with a right to such essential health care supplies as sutures, sterile drapes, and anesthesia. Should effectively realizing this interpretation prove difficult, then it may still be possible to interpret rights to these supplies in the more recent conventions and declarations. For those who are disturbed about the unjustifiable lack of life-saving materials — that is, of medical neglect — such a search to make use of human rights law is motivated by both the fact that economic and social rights are intended to guarantee the material needs of human beings, and because human rights law is law; it has potential power — legal, political, and moral — to make governments and, increasingly, other actors, behave in particular ways to provide material goods and social conditions.

Farmer presents an additional line of reasoning for increased enforcement of economic and social rights, aside from the fact that they imply rights to various health care goods and services. He argues that more vigorous enforcement of economic and social rights would improve living conditions, leading to better health outcomes. To carry this point further, such improved health achievements would, in turn, also create more active citizens and democratic institutions. At the risk of being too simplistic, the reasoning for pursuing Path 1 would be to argue that where the causes of preventable morbidity and mortality are due to medical neglect and material privation, the enforcement of economic and social rights will provide health care, create conditions for better health and longevity, and create stronger social and political institutions. Farmer and many other individuals following this line of reasoning exhort practitioners of health and human rights and public health communities (and anyone else with the power to effect change) to fight against the entrenched orthodoxies in so many arenas, and to champion the enforcement and realization of economic and social rights. From this perspective, it is understandable, then, why human rights advocates express disappointment when analysis of health issues, especially on a global scale, is not explicitly framed in terms of existing human rights law, particularly an overarching right to health. It appears to be a wasted opportunity, one that fails both to recognize and make use of the entitlements identified in human rights law at the same time it fails to help support the efforts for greater enforcement and implementation of human rights law, particularly economic and social rights.

It is on this point — the recognition of the effects of economic and social conditions on the health of individuals and populations — that social medicine and human rights perspectives converge. The practice of social medicine has a long history and its practitioners have been centrally focused on the social conditions affecting the health of the worst off in societies. There has always been an overlap between those who are socially excluded from economic, political, and other resources and those who bear the highest burden of poor health. The causal relationship between poor health and social, economic, and political deprivations would understandably lead any medical professional working with the socially excluded to draw on concepts of protections and entitlements such as those enshrined in international human rights. Where it is clearly visible that the social structure — the social, economic, and political conditions and underlying ideologies — is allowing or, indeed, directly causing avoidable disease and deaths on a large scale, the idea and law of human rights appears to be the only available mechanism to fight back; one might envision human rights in such a setting acting as a safety net that empowers those who suffer most egregiously to claw back up the great chasm of inequality and deprivation. Moreover, in the present era of increasing globalization, international human rights law may be the best available instrument to address the ill health caused by transnational actors who are, in many cases, more powerful than some governments.

Before presenting points seen as critical of such rights-based approaches to health issues — especially as these paths reflect the perspectives of individuals whom we greatly admire — it seems appropriate and necessary to recall the words of Onora O'Neill, a notable philosopher who has written extensively on human rights. When asked by one of the authors of this article why she seems to be so critical of some arguments for human rights while also being so emphatically concerned with acute deprivations in the world, she replied that it is because we care so much about the idea of human rights that we must ensure that arguments to support them are unimpeachable. So, it is our hope that our evaluation of the first two approaches — increased enforcement of economic and social rights and infusing principles of human rights legislation into health programs and interactions between individuals on the ground—should not be misunderstood as being critical of the idea of human rights in our effort to share our reasoning for choosing the third path, which appears to diminish the role of human rights in comparison to the first two.

Idea of Human Rights Greatly

It is indeed because we care about the idea of human rights greatly that we are publicly presenting our reasoning. Sofia Gruskin, Editor of this journal for over a decade, expressed a similar concern when she wrote that "[g]reater clarity about the central paradigms of health and human rights is essential to make our work more effective, as well as to enable us to make counter-arguments that will be persuasive not only to the skeptics but to the public health community at large."

This idea that international human rights law taken as a whole offers both rights to health care and rights to the social and material conditions for good health was argued by Jonathan Mann and colleagues in the very first issue of this journal in 1994.21 Central to their "health and human rights framework" hypothesis was the notion that "the promotion and protection of human rights and promotion and protection of health are fundamentally linked."

It was evidently clear in the early 1990s, in light of the way HIV/AIDS was being dealt with in most countries, that public health programs can negatively affect human rights and that human rights violations can have negative health effects. Mann and colleagues transformed the conflict between a public health policy perspective and a human rights perspective into a hypothesis that a society that realizes the full breadth of human rights would produce healthier individuals and populations. Health programs, they argued, whether public health or clinical, that were in line with human rights would lead to better health outcomes, and the respect for all human rights would create conditions for individuals to be healthier. In fact it should be noted that the Commission has expressed a similar view in the *Final Report* that correctly designing the social processes in society to meet the needs or expand freedoms of its members will improve health and health equity. The Commission was able, rather than presenting it as a hypothesis, to make this argument as a conclusion drawn from empirical research.

One remarkable aspect of Mann's 1994 hypothesis is that it leads to conceptualizing human rights law as one component of a model of causation and distribution of health. This is illustrated in the discussion about possible ways to test the hypothesis, where Mann and his colleagues wrote, "For example, health professionals could consider using the International Bill of

Human Rights as a coherent guide for assessing health status of individuals or populations; the extent to which human rights are realized may represent a better and more comprehensive index of well-being than traditional health status indicators." While it was a groundbreaking contribution to overlay human rights law onto an analysis of the causes, distribution, and social responses to health issues, the consequent substitution of human rights law for the actual causes of ill health in a model of causation and distribution of health is problematic. As evident in our sutures example, for instance, the distinction between the lack of sutures and the lack of the right to sutures in explaining maternal mortality is profound in many respects and should not be minimized.

The observation that the lack of sutures plays a role in the causes of maternal mortality necessarily precedes reasoning that there should be a right to sutures. This epistemological priority or precedence of recognizing the causal role of the lack of sutures to the assertion that there should be a right to sutures is the source of consequent divergence between a social epidemiology/social medicine and a human rights approach to advancing health and health equity. Some human rights advocates would likely want to assert that it is the violation of the right to sutures that causes maternal mortality.

When it is asserted that the lack of a right to something is the cause of ill health and mortality, the distinction between the causal role and importance of that something and the right to that something collapses. Moreover, the collapsing of the two ideas creates confusion as to what is a human right. Human rights are not natural facts or objects, but ethical assertions about claims, privileges, liberties, immunities, and powers in relation to various human capabilities, including those capabilities expressed indirectly via material things.

Unnecessary and avoidable misunderstandings result from attempting to emphasize the importance of human rights by casting them as direct causal components of a model of causation and distribution of ill health and mortality. Moreover, such attempts undermine the important scientific analysis of causal pathways and distribution of ill health and open the analysis to the risk of being dismissed as conceptually incoherent. Last, such an analysis potentially alienates social and natural science researchers who can be valuable allies in the effort to advance health equity. The health and human rights framework can be very powerful indeed, if it supplements rather than attempts to substitute the analysis of the natural and social causes, distribution, and consequences of ill health and mortality. We suggest further below one possible way that epidemiology and human rights might be integrated.

But what about the case in which someone is advocating a right to sutures after recognizing the lack of sutures as a direct cause of maternal mortality? For the practitioner of social medicine, the primary aim is not to enforce economic and social rights, or any other rights, for their own sake. Rather, the preeminent goal is to address avoidable ill health and mortality, the curtailment of well-being.

Therefore, enforcement of economic and social rights is instrumental in order to address the needs for health care and other social conditions and material goods. The problem arises when the law is silent about some pressing concern, or when the law is insufficient, or, indeed, incoherent. Aside from being entangled in legal rubric, stretching the law to cover the causes, cures, and other necessary social interventions for some particular health deprivation may begin to look like "the tail is wagging the dog."

When there is no right to sutures, and yet the lack of sutures leads to the deaths of hundreds of thousands of women each year, it is understandable to seek a right to sutures somewhere in the law. Yet neither the existing economic and social rights nor any language in the current human rights corpus may be capable of doing all the work we want them to do.

At the same time, it would be unacceptable to conclude that the causes that are killing people are not human rights concerns simply because they are not explicitly identified in the existing law, and also unacceptable to opportunistically stretch the meaning of rights so much that the term "human rights" risks becoming an empty concept. Indeed, it is very helpful if some human rights exist in the law that have direct bearing on a health issue at hand, but human rights law should be recognized as being only one of many instruments of advancing health and health equity.

The large number of human rights advocacy organizations in the world testifies to the fact that the mere existence of human rights law does not mean that human rights are universally or even locally realized. Even at the domestic level, laws identifying certain rights do not mean that individuals, especially those that are socially marginalized, have their rights respected or fulfilled. To exhort that the full spectrum of legal rights must be respected because it says so in the law requires a respect for law, the means to enforce it, and mechanisms to hold individuals or institutions accountable for violations. While motivating respect for rights is difficult and requires constant vigilance and resources, it is nearly impossible to enforce a right to something that may not clearly exist in the law, especially in places where there is no respect for the law or a lack of institutions to enforce rights. It should not go unnoticed, however, that individuals and communities throughout the world recognize and respect various rights even when such rights are not specifically stated in the law. And if they are in the law, respecting such rights may not be primarily motivated by the fact they are enshrined in the law. Before the relatively recent establishment of international human rights law, advocates for the respect of human rights and for social change drew on arguments for why such things are good and "the right thing to do."

Public statements to provide such reasoning were often accompanied by large-scale social mobilization; indeed, this ethico-moral approach was often much more comprehensive than the method currently employed by rights activists, of pointing to what is explicitly stated in the law and playing language games. Realizing rights, whether economic and social or civil and political, by means of assertions that they must be respected simply because it says so in international law, is neither necessary nor sufficient for advancing health and health equity — unless and until international law has the power to command full adherence and there are institutional capacities and resources in all countries to (progressively) realize all human rights.

6

Human Rights Law

In an attempt partially to overcome many of the structural and conceptual problems in engaging with human rights law, Lynn Freedman has proposed an alternative approach to expand the reach and relevance of human rights "on the ground." Her strategy is innovative in that it seeks to supplement the dominant approach to human rights work that takes place within international institutions as academic and legal discussions, and instead focuses on holding governments accountable for upholding human rights. We suggest Freedman's approach as our Path 2. Freedman advocates a strategy that extracts various values and principles from existing human rights law and applies them to local contexts — the on-the-ground analysis of the causal chain of ill health and mortality. While Freedman focuses on addressing maternal mortality, and her approach fits nicely with our example of the right to sutures, this strategy could be applied to addressing any health issue.

Motivated by the understanding that human dignity is the core value of human rights law and is meant to inspire profound and fundamental change in everyday interactions, Freedman proposes communities identify a set of values and principles in human rights law and then articulate how they can help guide community-level programmes to address maternal mortality. Using the case of the right to sutures, following Freedman's path would mean that we do not look for a right to sutures in the law but that the values and principles of human rights law can help communities identify, analyze, and address maternal mortality. In fact, Freedman interprets the legal discourse on the human right to health as encompassing the right not to die an avoidable death in pregnancy and childbirth. This right then translates into a societal obligation to provide emergency obstetric care, which would entail the provision of sutures when needed. But even when dealing with nongovernmental actors and a concern not just about sutures but maternal mortality more broadly, Freedman argues that the two values of human dignity and non-discrimination (among others), which are central to human rights law, can and should guide the manner in which emergency obstetric care is provided to patients and families as well as how it impacts hospital staff. This strategy may be seen as expanding human rights work, perhaps even liberating human rights from the existing legal language and mechanisms of international law. Importantly, rather than making rights into causal components of health and well-being, Freedman suggests that human rights values and principles, when combined with other health-related disciplines such as epidemiology, medicine, and operations research, can provide a plan of action for communities and states — in other words, human rights discourse can become a community health planning tool.

Although it is an important and worthwhile strategy to apply human rights law to the reality of how individuals are living their daily lives, this path also suffers from insufficient power as a tool for motivation. It is unclear as to why the values and principles that Freedman uses to guide maternal mortality programmes should be convincing to others simply on the basis of their presence in human rights legislation. Indeed, is it not ethical reasoning that first produced the values that then became enshrined as various rights in human rights law? That is, why would individuals and communities change their views and behaviors from the status quo to be in line with these values because these values are derived from human rights law? Granted, there is an international consensus embodied in such laws, but how convincing is it that individuals need to work and interact or programmes are designed and operated in accordance with certain values and principles because they were derived from human rights law? Perhaps more persuasive would be an ethical or moral argument. Why not present these values and principles as being important in the analysis of health issues and require allegiance because it is the right thing to do, or is what is demanded by social justice? Dignity, non-discrimination, equality, and participation are all values than can be highlighted within the ethical reasoning concerning what to do about maternal mortality in communities throughout the world. Synthesizing scientific and empirical insights from fields such as epidemiology, medicine, operations research, and public health with ethical reasoning about social justice by communities should be just as motivating — if not more so — for taking action than arguing that certain value-motivated actions are required simply because the values can be found in human rights law.

The first path, in its best form, seeks to link the causal and distributional analysis of health issues with international human rights law. The second path seeks to craft and guide a social response by integrating various values with necessary and helpful insights from different fields while remaining grounded in human rights law. The third path can be seen as being a step farther away from either of the first two, as it seeks to derive values from ethical reasoning that takes place at community-level, national, regional, and global spheres. The initial conclusion of that ethical reasoning, which took place within the Commission and is now ongoing and open to all, was to classify ill health and health inequalities that are avoidable through reasonable means as inequities. Furthermore, the Commission determined that such manifest inequities must be addressed as a matter of social justice. In addition to this ethical argument — that if one can reasonably prevent ill health and death, one should do so — is the argument that one must act to address social determinants of ill health and health inequalities on the basis of the duties to protect, promote, and fulfil relevant human rights.

There is broad convergence between research and action on rights-based approaches and social determinants of health when existing international agreements about human rights encompass actions to address the relevant social determinants. Indeed, perhaps it can be argued that enunciated rights and values implicit in human rights law cover the entire gamut of the social determinants of ill health and mortality. However, social epidemiology has more explanatory potential than human rights approaches because the objects of research are not themselves ethical assertions, nor is the scope of social epidemiology limited by what is written in the law. Yet human rights law has the power to bridge social epidemiology with social action. The power of human rights lies in its prescriptive power to guide prospective social action through identifying legal obligations as well as underlying moral obligations of societies to act in particular ways. However, local and global discussions that link social epidemiological analysis with ethical reasoning about social justice would involve more actors and allow for a broader scope of social action, more expansive rights and responsibilities, and easier social acceptance. It is necessary to find a way to integrate these two approaches.

Perhaps one method that avoids the conflation of causal factors and human rights is to incorporate rights as distal factors in the chain of causation. A social environment that does not protect, promote, or fulfil the rights to food, clothing, shelter, or civil and political liberties can be understood to have a role in the chain of causation and distribution of ill health without being a direct causal factor. It would also make understandable the assertion that if individuals have a right to health, then they should also have a right to the determinants of health. In this way, integrating epidemiology and human rights — or constitutional rights for that matter — would illuminate the role of the lack of rights in the causal chain of ill health and mortality, while also avoiding having to show that every violation of a human right is bad for health. Such an integrated framework could move forward the agenda to improve health and health equity by harnessing the power of both human rights and epidemiology.

Health Equity and Social Conditions

The human rights agreements referred to here include the Universal Declaration of Human Rights (UDHR), the International Covenant on Civil and Political Rights (ICCPR), the International Covenant on Economic, Social and Cultural Rights (ICESCR), and the officially recognized documents interpreting the ICESCR — the General Comments by the UN Committee on Economic, Social and Cultural Rights (CESCR), Limburg Principles on the Implementation of the ICESCR and the Maastricht Guidelines on Violations of Economic Social and Cultural Rights. Together the UDHR, ICCPR, and ICESCR are referred to as the International Bill of Human Rights. The International Convention on the Elimination of All Forms of Racial Discrimination (ICERD) is also cited in this chapter.

HUMAN RIGHTS DEVELOPMENT

The human rights community possesses an elaborate set of principles and norms that relate to the practice of development. The intellectual and operational focus of the human rights community, however, has rested almost exclusive upon a sub-set of civil and political rights in isolation from their economic context and broader struggles of social and economic change. No major human rights watchdog organizations exist for economic, social, and cultural rights, which are generally relegated to obscure UN sub-committees whose work never becomes newspaper headlines. Beyond routine declarations about the indivisibility of all rights, for all intents and purposes, most economic, social and cultural rights have not been part of human rights practice for most of the last half century.

Why were these rights so neglected? It seems there are two major reasons. The first is political: the economic rights agenda is more deeply connected to interventionist, non-liberal, and possibly even anti-individualist approaches to social change. This approach was, and remains uncomfortable to many powerful people and governments in the West (Scott 1999: 644). This tension was reinforced by the Cold War politics, when ESC rights –and *all* human rights, really—became deeply politicized. Economic, social and cultural rights were championed by communist and many Third World countries, who used them as weapons in the fight for a New International Economic Order and against US/Western hegemony. Western countries, in the meantime, focused exclusively on civil and political rights. For many politicians in the West, the entire body of law related to economic rights and the "right to development" was synonymous with cynical attempts to wiggle out of civil and political human rights obligations and destroy free markets worldwide. The end of the Cold

War profoundly changed the nature of the competing blocs and the strength of their ideological discourses, and as a result this vehemently partisan and partial interpretation of human rights has lost its sway. Indeed, the "universality, indivisibility, interdependence and interrelationship of all human rights" –in the language of the 1993 Vienna declaration— are now only rarely explicitly challenged, except by a handful of Asian countries. Yet, another major barrier against the mainstreaming of ESC rights remains.

There is a sense within the human rights community that the very nature of economic, social and cultural rights is fundamentally different from, and more difficult to implement than, civil and political rights.

The latter, it was argued, are "negative" rights, meaning that governments need to abstain from certain behaviors (arbitrary imprisonment, torture, etc.), whereas the former are "positive" rights, often involving costly action. As such, many organizations have found it easier to push for the former. At the conceptual level, this separation has been broken down over the last two decades, and human rights declarations nowadays always refer to the indivisibility and complementariness of the two categories of human rights if not to their mutually reinforcing nature. In practice, however, the separation is still deeply alive.

The reason for this separation may be that it is not immediately clear what the Convention on Economic, Social and Cultural Rights obliges signatories to do. As article 2 states: "Each party undertakes to *take steps* individually and through international assistance and cooperation, especially economic and technical, *to the maximum of its available resources*, with a view to *achieving progressively* the full realization of rights recognized in the covenant, by all *appropriate means*, including particularly the adoption of legislative measures."

With rights so vague and full of escape clauses, who could not forgive human rights advocates for their focus on monitoring and exposing the much clearer civil and political rights?

It is only in 1994 that the Committee on Economic, Social and Cultural Rights finally clarified these vague terms more stringently, giving them some intellectual and practical bite.

According to the so-called Maastricht principles, the "maximum of available resources" clause, which had been interpreted as removing pressures from Third World countries on the grounds of their general state of poverty and budgetary limitations, has been interpreted to mean that a *minimum core obligation* exists to ensure the satisfaction of the minimum essential levels of rights, and that states must demonstrate that every effort has been made to use the resources at their disposition in an effort to satisfy, as a matter of priority, these minimum obligations. Similarly, the "achieve progressively" wording, usually interpreted so to allow indefinite postponement of state obligations, has been defined to mean a) that states must move as expeditiously as possible; and b) that retrogressive measures are not permissible, not even if justified by progress on the realization of other rights (CESR 1994). Note also that the Convention on ESC rights contains two rights whose obligations are unconditional, *i.e.*, not subject to progressive realization. These are the right to primary education and the freedom to establish trade unions (de Feyter 2001: 264).

In addition, the human rights community has come to define the nature of state obligations regarding economic, social and cultural rights along a continuum that blurs the distinction between commission and omission. These include the obligation to *respect* (i.e., states ought not take any measures that deprive people from a right they already enjoy); the obligation to *protect* (i.e., states must provide protection against deprivation by a third party); and the obligation to *provide* or *fulfill* (i.e., states have to progressively ensure that everyone on their territory enjoys the full rights). These three categories then, as applied to each individual right, can be the basis of a human rights analysis and for the development of subsequent strategies to address concrete rights issues. The categories can also provide the means to develop indicators, measure outcomes, and develop strategies – the kind of stuff development actors desperately need.

THE RIGHT TO DEVELOPMENT

Development as a concept first entered the human rights edifice through the debate on the "right to development." The idea was launched by the Senegalese jurist M'Baye in 1972, during a period of radical reform for the New International Economic Order (NIEO) and the Charter on the Economic Rights and Duties of States. This was a period, beginning in late 1972, during which many Third World countries used their numerical majority in the UN to negotiate reforms in the global political economy of trade, finance, investment, aid, and information flows.

This effort was led by well-known nationalist Third World statesmen, who were emboldened by the success of the OPEC embargo, which was widely perceived to have been a victory of the Third World over rich countries, and which many thought reshuffled the world's economic cards. The notion of a right to development fitted well within this struggle, providing a legal and ethical authority to the Third World's request for international resource re-distribution.

In addition, it acted as a counter-argument against rich countries' exclusive insistence on enforcement of political and civil human rights, with the argument essentially resting on the maxim that 'there are other rights that for the people of the Third World are more of a priority than Western civil rights, and you all ought to contribute to their realization rather than continuing to bother us about civil and political rights' (Rosas 1995: 248-5; Development gap paper 340). Acrimonious discussions about the NIEO persisted for years, but led to no concrete results, apart from the signing of a few international commodity agreements. By the early 1980s, these negotiations, and any thought of a new international economic order, were unceremoniously terminated after the election of Ronald Reagan, Margaret Thatcher, and Helmut Kohl and the simultaneous weakening of OPEC and the outbreak of the Third World debt crisis. The intellectual and political pendulum swung dramatically rightwards, and structural adjustment replaced international reform.

Surprisingly, though, the notion of a right to development did not die altogether – partly because the developing countries learned that, in the words of Ian Brownlie, "it had become evident that the political futures market was in the area of human rights and it was therefore prudent to pursue policy goals under that banner." After much legal wrangling, in 1986 the right to development was finally adopted as a UNGA resolution, stating that "the right to development is an inalienable human right by virtue of which every human person and all peoples are entitled to participate in, contribute to, and enjoy economic, social, cultural and political development, in which all human rights and fundamental freedoms can be fully realized." This was the kind of rhetorical victory that diplomats cherish: the Third World got its right to development, while the First World ensured that the right could never be interpreted as more of a priority than political and civil rights, and that it carried no resource transfer obligations. On a less cynical level, the declaration does present a holistic approach, forcefully affirming the indivisibility of all human rights, putting the economic, social, and cultural rights on par with the civil and political ones – an important step in the development of the human rights edifice.

Demonstrating the extent to which rich countries found even this non-binding and emasculated compromise unacceptable, the U.S. voted against the resolution while 10 or so other OECD member states abstained. Hence, even in its watered-down form, the right to development amounted to a rich country vs. poor country debate, as it had been from the beginning. In addition, according to most legal scholars, it was bad law: vague, internally contradictory, duplicative of other already clear codified rights, and devoid of identifiable parties bearing clear obligations. What it really said is that all rights are important – period. Article 6 of the resolution, for example, states "All human rights and fundamental freedoms are indivisible and interdependent; equal attention and urgent consideration should be given to the implementation, promotion and protection of civil, political, economic, social and cultural rights." While conceptually correct in affirming the indivisibility of human rights, the new supposed right to development does not provide any means for implementation. As law, it remains soft, declaratory, and deliberately emasculated.

Human rights, once set down on paper, never die, even though no one may care much about their survival. Rather, they mutate into working groups, commissions, and expert panels, each of which produces reports that are occasionally the subject of discussions in low-level meetings. Sometimes, however, out of this patient work, contested or marginal rights obtain a second lease on life, which is what happened to the right to development. At the 1993 World Conference on Human Rights in Vienna, the right to development was re-adopted, this time with unanimity, as part of the broader Vienna Declaration and Program of Action. The relevant article 10 reads:

"The World Conference on human rights reaffirms the right to development, as established in the Declaration on the Right to Development, as a universal and inalienable right and an integral part of fundamental human rights. ... While development facilitates the enjoyment of all human rights, the lack of development may not be invoked to justify the abridgment of internationally recognized human rights."

Note that, as in the General Assembly Declaration on the Right to Development, the latter sentence was inserted at the insistence of the Western countries. Still, the Vienna Declaration was adopted with unanimity, and it can thus be claimed that the right to development now reflects a global legal consensus, and as such represents a significant victory for its advocates, Pyrrhic as it may be.

Following this promotion, in 1997 the right to development was honored with its very own "independent expert," whose mandate was (barely) renewed by the UN Human Rights Commission in late 2000. The expert has by now produced four annual reports, followed by annual discussions in the appropriate sub-Committee of the Human Rights Commission.

In retrospect, the right to development remains contested, and has had little if any impact. If, on the one hand, one believes that it affirms a claim by people to a form of economic growth that is distributed fairly over the inhabitants of a country and supported by international resource transfers, then one has to confront the opposition of most rich countries and the apathy of most poor countries –as well as the fact that there is nothing in international law generally that would even remotely support such a claim. If, on the other hand, one believes it affirms that all people have the right to development, which consists of, and is realized through, the realization of every existing category of human rights, and which all people, states, and organizations ought to respect, then one essentially is in the presence of a correct, beautifully worded, operationally meaningless, and duplicative assertion. The latter is clearly what the right to development amounts to, and the kind of meaningless statements it leads to are nicely exemplified in the following quote form the UN Working Group on the Right to Development, describing the right as being "multidimensional, integrated, dynamic and progressive. Its realization observes the full observance of economic, social, cultural, civil, and political rights. It further embraces the different concepts of development of all development sectors, namely sustainable development, human development, and the concept of indivisibility, interdependence, and universality of all human rights".

Perhaps recognizing the difficulty of defining the right in abstract legal terms, the Independent Expert, Arjun Sengupta, has tried to better define the concrete substance of a right to development. Given the fact that, ultimately, very few people care what he does with his mandate, he has been able to go remarkably far in this work, thinking rather interestingly about a number of the conceptual issues related to development, to which we will come back later.

Some of these points go far beyond the right to development, but relate to what can be called the international law of development. In this work, he oscillates between a very strong defense of the liberal mantra –no development without free markets, free trade, free flows of investment, and free elections – and an equally strong acceptance of a deep interventionist role for national and international governments in the promotion of development.

In short, his policy prescriptions are inconsistent, contradictory, vague, and economically weak. These words may sound like a mean-spirited attack on the personality or competency of Mr. Sengupta, but they are truly not meant to convey that. He is a lawyer, after all, and has sure done more of an effort to get a grasp of his economics than most economists ever do with the law. More importantly, he works in a field of total absence of criteria or structures for judging effectiveness: as said above, as good as nobody cares about what he writes n any case, and the human rights edifice hardly provides him with a tool to challenge the dominance of economic thinking as the sole way of thinking about development. Hence, he must improvise, stumbling on, like a person in the dark, hands stretched out, trying to break nothing too expensive and still get somewhere...

THE USEFULNESS OF THE HUMAN RIGHTS FRAMEWORK

States that sign human rights treaties and agreements commit themselves to cooperate with other states, to the maximum of their capacity, to secure economic and social rights. Many references can be found in international human rights law to such commitments, although human rights law is not very specific about what the commitment implies. It does not make clear when, and how much, states should act abroad to promote economic and social rights. In human rights law, the primary obligation to protect rights undoubtedly falls on national governments. Other states have a duty to act when the national state is unwilling or unable to fulfil its obligations. This might be described as the "do good" dimension of international obligation.

States equally have an obligation not to violate the rights of others abroad, and to act to prevent violations when it is in their power to do so. This is relevant in many areas of policy-wherever, for example, the policies or behaviour of (richer) countries create conditions that obstruct the ability of people living in developing countries from achieving their social and economic rights. This might be described as the "do no harm" dimension of international obligation.

Responsibility for violations of rights can often be clearly attributed. But this is not always the case, of course. Frequently, there is no simple or objective way to judge whether or when the policies of one country cause rights to be violated in another country; the chain of causality may be too complex or too indirect. (Consider, for example, the difficulties of assessing the impact of debt policy on health or education provision.)

Nevertheless, the human rights framework does provide a foundation for making judgements. In addition, because it offers legal precision and justiciability, it has the potential to develop more precise tools for assessing government responsibilities and helping officials and other actors to reach transparent and objective judgements about the level and appropriateness of international action to protect economic and social rights and promote development.In considering the application of human rights principles to international policies, particularly with respect to economic and social rights, it will no doubt be helpful to distinguish categories of problem; and do so in relation both to actions that need to be taken, and the responsibility of institutions to act. In some cases, a state or other actor is knowingly responsible for a violation. In others, the responsibility may be indirect or unknowing. In many cases, no particular actor can plausibly be held responsible. (While many people are impoverished because of human action, for example, it is not reasonable to presume that all poverty is due directly or immediately to human agency.) In some cases, finally, outside actors accept that they should take action even though they have no responsibility for the problem concerned. (International support to deal with natural disasters is an obvious example in this category).

Obligation has Increased with Capacity

It can also be said that, relative to the postwar era when the main international standards were approved and certainly relative to earlier periods of history, governments today have a greater responsibility to act internationally because they have more capacity to do so.

- They are much better informed, in real time, about events in other countries and the impact of their policies;
- They are much richer, and dispose of vastly greater resources;
- Technical and scientific knowledge and expertise have enormously increased: richer societies are in a position to resolve problems that could not be resolved earlier and their power to do so will continue to increase;
- Industrialized societies have far greater administrative and organizational capacity-though the weaknesses of international governance remain probably the greatest constraint on competent and prompt decision-making on international matters.

Taken together, these factors suggest that states now have a much stronger duty to act, and a duty to do more, than was the case when the human rights standards were drafted.

THE CONCEPT OF GLOBAL ADMINISTRATIVE LAW

The concept of global administrative law begins from the twin ideas that much global governance can be understood as administration, and that such administration is often organized and shaped by principles of an administrative law character. With the expansion of global governance, many administrative and regulatory functions are now performed in a global rather than national context, yet through a great number of different forms, ranging from binding decisions of international organizations to nonbinding agreements in intergovernmental networks and to domestic administrative action in the context of global regimes. Examples include UN Security Council decisions on individual sanctions; World Bank rule-making for developing countries; the setting of standards on money laundering by the Financial Action Task Force; or domestic administrative decisions on market access of foreign products as part of the WTO regime.

Many regulatory functions in global governance are also performed outside such formally public, governmental structures, namely by hybrid private-public or purely private institutions, such as ICANN, the Internet Corporation for Assigned Names and Numbers, or the International Organization for Standardization (ISO).

Despite these widely varying forms and institutions, we can observe in all these examples the exercise of recognizably administrative and regulatory functions: the setting and application of rules by bodies that are not legislative or primarily adjudicative in character. If similar actions were performed by a state agency, there would be little doubt as to their administrative character (except, perhaps, for the examples of private regulation). Classically, however, regarding them as administrative would have been difficult because of their international nature; the term 'administration' was closely tied to the state framework and could, at most, point to the domestic implementation of international norms.

This categorical distinction, however, has today become problematic: too interwoven are the domestic and the international elements in these processes of regulation. This is most obvious for government networks in which domestic officials are engaged in both the rule-making on a global scale and the implementation on the domestic level, often without any intervening act. Likewise, when the UNHCR conducts status determination for individual refugees, the posited distinction of an international level for relations between states, and a domestic level for relations between states and individuals breaks down. And WTO dispute settlement can in many cases be regarded as another layer of judicial review of domestic administrative action.

It is this interwovenness of the different spheres that leads us to regard the conglomerate of regulatory forms as part of one very variegated but recognizably 'global' administrative space. The enmeshment of the domestic and international in governance also has important repercussions for the mechanisms through which administrative actions can be held to account. Under the classical distinction between the domestic and the international realms, international norms were agreed upon on the international level, but the state remained free to adopt them or not, as their obligatory character and effect depended on domestic ratification and implementation. Because of this freedom, domestic accountability mechanisms were thought to be (reasonably) effective: parliamentary process and administrative procedures could have a meaningful impact.

The more the domestic and international processes are interwoven, however, the more this freedom breaks down, and with it the effectiveness of classical accountability mechanisms. Decisions in an intergovernmental network such as the Basel Committee for Banking Supervision, though not formally binding, commit the participating domestic officials to implementation and will thus have a strong impact on any later domestic administrative procedure. UNHCR findings on refugee status directly determine the fate of the individual refugee. And WTO dispute settlement decisions are in most cases factually decisive for domestic administrative action; the costs of noncompliance would simply be too high to allow domestic administrative processes real freedom to deviate from a WTO decision.

In the global administrative space, the classical distribution of labour between the different levels has largely broken down when it comes to ensuring regulatory participation and accountability. The resulting accountability and participation problems are beginning to be addressed, in part because of an interest of global regulatory institutions and actors in bolstering their legitimacy in the face of growing political challenges. In many areas of global governance, and in highly variegated forms, mechanisms are emerging that seek to enhance participate the accountability of global regulatory decision-making. The structural similarities between many of these disparate phenomena are striking: they testify to a growing trend of building mechanisms analogous to domestic administrative law systems to the global level; transparency, participation, and review are central among them.

This trend is reflected, for instance, in the Inspection Panel set up by the World Bank to ensure its compliance with internal policies; in notice-and-comment procedures adopted by international standard-setters such as the the OECD; in the inclusion of NGOs in regulatory bodies like the Codex Alimentarius Commission; or in rules about foreign participation in domestic administrative procedures as set out in the Aarhus Convention. We argue that this is a general trend of practice towards a global administrative law.

Whether pursuit of accountability, participation and transparency is desirable in particular cases involves far-reaching issues. Accountability can dissipate effectiveness, participation can result in captire by special interests, transparency can mean populism triumphs over justice. Institutional design is important: there may be robust accountability but to the wrong people or on the wrong topics. Bracketing such issues in descriptive terms global administrative law as we understand it encompasses the legal mechanisms, principles and practices, along with supporting social understandings, that promote or otherwise affect the accountability of global administrative bodies, in particular by ensuring these bodies meet adequate standards of transparency, consultation, participation, rationality and legality, and by providing effective review of the rules and decisions these bodies make.

We describe this field of law as 'global' rather than 'international' to reflect the enmeshment of domestic and international regulation, the inclusion of a large array of informal institutional arrangements (many involving prominent roles for non-state actors), and the foundation of the field in normative practices, and normative sources, that are not fully encompassed within standard conceptions of international law.

THE NORMATIVE POTENTIAL AND PROBLEMS OF GLOBAL ADMINISTRATIVE LAW

The papers in this symposium approach the idea of global administrative law from widely varying perspectives, but they all shed light on a number of core normative issues. Does global administrative law produce normatively positive outcomes, and for whom? What are the normative grounds for deciding whether the pursuit of global administrative law approaches to global governance is desirable or undesirable in particular cases? Is it desirable to pursue global administrative law as an integrated agenda, an abstraction calculated to spill over and make unpredictable connections between one case or place and another apparently quite different case or place? And is the administrative law model adequate in the circumstances of global politics and society? It is beyond our capacities at this stage to give confident general answers; the contributions to this issue all contribute to a response, but they paint a complex picture.

Enhancing the Accountability of Global Governance

Several papers regard the rise of global administrative law mechanisms as generally furthering important normative goals, especially enhancing the accountability of global governance. In their paper on the Basel Committee on Banking Supervision, Michael Barr and Geoff Miller take an essentially utilitarian stance in assessing the work of the Committee.

In their view, the coordination of national banking regulation is necessary to avert crises in the highly integrated global financial system; this coordination cannot realistically be undertaken other than by negotiation among the leading national regulators; and the Basel process for achieving this has been improved by the gradual adoption in it of global administrative law mechanisms.

They acknowledge problems, but argue that the general effect of these mechanisms has been the formulation of better banking standards, and the blocking or modification of some normatively undesirable initiatives. For instance, they note that national and international notice-and-comment processes have led to the modification of proposals for the Basel II Accord on capital adequacy that might have damaged lending to small businesses; and they document the functional efficiency in many countries of the arrangements for variable applicability ultimately built into the Accord. Barr and Miller also see the increased information and participation in the Basel Committee as inherently valuable in bolstering accountability and legitimacy, and they point in particular to the beneficial effects of interlocking accountability mechanisms on the domestic and international planes.

Yet they recognize that broadening participation as such might not lead to sufficient inclusiveness: as regards developing countries, more than mere notice-and-comment procedures might be called for, especially given that Basel standards have a particularly strong impact on these countries as compliance with them is often a requirement for lending by the international financial institutions.

Errol Meidinger also sees a broadly positive result of the use of global administrative law in his study of forestry standard-setting and certification. He traces an iterative process in the development of this decentralized regulatory regime, involving NGO campaigns and consumer boycotts, a multiplicity of private standard-setting initiatives by groupings with a spectrum of orientations from industrialist to environmentalist, pulls exerted in these different directions on state regulators and professional forestry experts, then some convergence as the groups realise they need to align more closely with each other's work.

He notes also a slow striking of balances, between globally-framed standards that work for global markets but may not be responsive to different local forest and social conditions, and firm-level or national-level standards that may allow too much play to opportunism and local power dynamics. Noticeand- comment procedures in rule-making as well as contestation of particular instances of certification have contributed to a stronger inclusiveness of the regulatory regime complex, and Meidinger's normative assessment in terms of accountability has a generally positive tendency. But actual responsiveness to a broad range of interests is in large part due to the competition between different regimes rather than formalized participation procedures, highlighting the complex political circumstances for making global administrative law effective.

A broader and more explicitly normative and theoretical defence of building a global administrative law can be found in the paper by Terry Macdonald and Kate Macdonald who see it as part of a solution to the problems of democratic accountability where electoral mechanisms are not available. They identify a need for accountability wherever a responsible power-wielder has such an impact on the autonomy and equality of individuals in the affected population that democratic regulation is warranted.

Such accountability cannot be electoral if the power-wielder is neither directly elected nor delegated by an elected actor with whom it shares the same public constituency. They propose two core requirements for non-electoral democratic accountability: public transparency, by which they mean mechanisms enabling relevant publics to know what is being done with public power; and the capacity of the affected public to disempower political agents, by sanctions where necessary. They use these criteria both to interpret existing practices in the garment industry (focused particularly on workers in Nicaragua in factories owned by Taiwan businesses selling to US brand retailers), and to propose ways in which accountability might be reshaped and further developed.

They point out that any such accountability depends both on a clear specification of roles and responsibilities and on industry-specific modalities, and that the disempowerment of commercial agents of public power in this industry faces serious hurdles, including gaps between NGO-led sanctions campaigns in the US and the knowledge and interests of current or prospective workers and unions in Nicaragua. Thus, Macdonald and Macdonald see the development of non-electoral accountability as normatively desirable, and the non-electoral accountability mechanisms they propose might be adaptable to a broad range of institutional settings; but they point also to the great challenges to its realization in the specific context of the export garment industry.

The Boundaries of Global Administrative Law

The paper by Macdonald and Macdonald also raises serious questions about the boundaries of global administrative law. On the one hand, it asks whether any distinction between administrative law and public law in general is warranted in a context in which the distinction between government (based directly on electoral legitimacy) and administrative actors (resting on a more indirect basis of legitimacy) has broken down. But more broadly, the paper suggests that it might be useful to look to private law rather than public law for inspiration.

Private law might have stronger resources for holding decentralized private actors accountable – actors who should be held accountable because, on the global plane, they exercise 'public power'. This brings up the question whether any distinction between public and private law should be maintained in the global order, recalling similar debates in domestic legal orders.

Gus Van Harten and Martin Loughlin, in their paper on investment arbitration as global administrative law, insist on the distinction. They express doubt that 'the rule-making powers or regulatory practices of international organizations possess such authority as to constitute a distinct system of administrative law', but they see value in describing in public law terms international mechanisms that check state administrative action.

Having developed rapidly since the 1990s, investment arbitration appears as a powerful tool to constrain domestic regulation, in particular because it allows individuals to initiate review of state action without a need to exhaust local remedies and with the possibility to claim damages and directly enforce awards in national courts. It is also distinct from international commercial arbitration in that it is aimed at the exercise of the state's public authority rather than merely a state's acts of a private character.

For Van Harten and Loughlin, using the lens of administrative law highlights the commonalities of investment arbitration with domestic mechanisms of judicial review, and it brings out significant tensions in the structure of arbitral procedures with an origin in private, commercial contexts; for example, it raises doubts as to the adequacy of a system relying on arbitrators with few safeguards of independence and impartiality.

The administrative law lens also allows foregrounding genuinely public law questions, especially those relating to the justification of review and the constitution of the quasi-judicial bodies involved, but also the role of public concerns in judicial processes. Van Harten and Loughlin do not take a stance as to the desirability of administrative law mechanisms in global governance, but their approach points to potential insights from adopting a distinct administrative law perspective on it.

Limits to Universality

A number of contributions to this symposium regard the growth of global administrative law with considerable caution and are particularly guarded as to the universal applicability of some of its elements. Christopher McCrudden and Stuart Gross, for example, see considerable complexity in the case they study, of the interplay of WTO government procurement rules and local dynamics in Malaysia. The global administrative law demand for transparency in government procurement, and for mechanisms by which unsuccessful foreign bidders could challenge a contract award in local courts or administrative proceedings, has been resisted by the Malaysian government, which sees such demands as a threat to its bumiputera policy that overtly favours ethnic Malays in government contracting.

This policy has been part of a social bargain in which ethnic Chinese Malaysians have retained a significant economic position, but have not enjoyed full political equality. Whether the government contracting practices have in fact been beneficial to most Malays, or to the country, are not questions for which there is an agreed metric on which to base an answer.

Such contracting has been a major part of the political patronage system, and has been associated with corruption and gross inefficiency; but peninsula Malaysia has also enjoyed substantial prosperity, a general if uneven rise in most socio-economic indicators, and no major recurrence of the terrifying race riots of the late 1960s. Whether the gains to Malaysia from embracing transparency and review would outweigh the possible losses is a high-stakes question with no obvious answer.

The Malaysian government insists that the decision rests with the domestic political system, but, as McCrudden and Gross point out, international pressure on countries to change their procurement practices is strong. It is now very difficult for a state to join the WTO as a new member without also being required to join the 'voluntary' plurilateral WTO Government Procurement Agreement, and Malaysia lobbied hard against negotiation even of a 'Transparency in Government Procurement' Agreement in the WTO, for fear of a package deal requiring adherence to it.

The case is complex but it attests that there might be good reasons for rejecting such principles as transparency and review in particular circumstances, and that global administrative law can at most make a very attenuated claim to universal reach. Carol Harlow takes the exploration of the potential reach of global administrative law a step further and seeks to uncover the sources and traditions underlying it. She identifies four potential sources: procedural principles as they have emerged in national administrative law systems; rule of law values as promoted by proponents of free trade and economic liberalism; good governance values as pursued by the Bretton Woods institutions; and human rights values, in particular due process. Given the divergent emphases in these different strands as well as among national traditions, she finds it difficult to identify a sufficiently general set of administrative law principles that could form the heart of a global administrative law.

Moreover, she points out, administrative law in its modern form is essentially a Western construct, dependent on particular constitutional backgrounds, and extending it to the universal level – though perhaps feasible – risks not only neglecting other value systems but also benefiting particular economically powerful actors rather than the citizenry as a whole. Especially in the socio-economic situation of developing countries, rights to seek review of government action may eventually benefit only those who can afford the 'skilful in-house lawyers' necessary to use them.

Leaving Space for Politics

Harlow's paper also raises another fundamental concern about global administrative law, namely that it might shrink the space for politics in favour of juridified mechanisms, limiting democracy and establishing a juristocracy instead. A related point returns in Bronwen Morgan's paper on transnational water services regulation. Morgan sees regulation in this area as shaped by an iterative process of interaction between protest or politics (which she describes as informal) and the legal sphere (which she describes as formal).

She emphasizes that multinational water services companies can be targets or utilizers of this formal law and of its interactions with politics; equally, water consumers and their organizations mix formal and informal strategies for participation and voice. Global water companies may prefer administrative fora in which their own participation far surpasses that of consumer groups, such as bilateral investment treaty arbitrations, ISO standard-setting, or regulatory-negotiation arrangements with national government regulators.

By contrast, consumer groups have greater difficulty in switching between domestic and international levels; they may prefer economic and social rights processes, and collective legal actions such as *amparo* proceedings, which may tip the balance their way. Forms of administrative law have unequal effects. And as she notes: 'global administrative law is increasingly about challenging or routinizing the power to have the last word on setting the rules of the game'. Yet this implies that disruption rather than routinization might often be necessary to achieve normatively important goals, and that the orderly processes of administrative law alone may not produce satisfactory outcomes, even if results achieved by disruption eventually need to be embedded in legal forms in order to be stabilized.

She argues that is the unsettled landscape of global regulatory governance, and in particular from the perspective of citizens of developing countries all too often marginalized in its fora, leaving space for unruly politics rather than fixed procedures might remain essential.

Krisch sees the shape of accountability mechanisms in global governance centrally determined by a contest of different constituencies – national, international and cosmopolitan – over who should be entitled to control regulatory outcomes. This contest results in a pluralism of procedures and regimes that seek to establish accountability through mutual challenge, but do not constitute an overarching, hierarchically ordered scheme as in domestic administrative law systems; instead, none of the constituencies fully controls regulatory outcomes, but each can equally contest them. Krisch traces the operation of such a pluralist model in the governance of international trade in genetically modified organisms, examining the interplay between the dynamics and rules of the World Trade Organization, the Cartagena Protocol on Biosafety and European Union law.

He argues that a pluralist, heterarchical model might be more adequate to the context of global governance than frameworks of a more constitutionalist character, as it can refrain from deciding important questions of principle (who should have ultimate authority?) and instead focus on practical accommodation and approximation between different competing constituencies and their visions. In this approach, too, space is kept open and procedures are not fully institutionalized in order to reflect the openness and fluidity of hierarchy and authority in current global politics; in contrast, further constitutionalization would appear likely to stabilize and legitimize an order which is socially far from settled and in which continuous transformation remains a central task.

Accountability mechanisms modelled on domestic administrative law may have an uneasy place in these more fluid settings, and in building a global administrative law, we might have to have recourse to alternative forms.

THE SCOPE OF INTERNATIONAL HUMAN RIGHTS LAW

The concept of human rights developed largely from Western political theory of the rights of the individual to autonomy and freedom. International human rights law evolved in order to protect those individual rights from limitations that might be imposed on them by states. States are bound by international law to respect the individual rights of each and every person and are thus accountable for abuses of those rights. The aim of the human rights movement is to enforce states' obligations in this regard by denouncing violations of their duties under international law.The exclusive focus on the behaviour of states confines the operation of international human rights law entirely within the public sphere.

Gender-Neutral Law

Gender Biased Application International human rights law is facially gender-neutral. The rights embodied in the Universal Declaration of Human Rights are defined as be-longing to "all human beings," not just to men."All the major human rights instruments include sex as one of the grounds upon which states may not discriminate in enforcing the rights set forth. Although international law is gender neutral in theory, in practice it interacts with gender biased domestic laws and social structures that relegate women and men to separate spheres of existence: private and public. Men exist as public, legal entities in all countries, and, barring an overt abuse by the state, participate in public life and enjoy the full extent of whatever civil and political rights exist. Women, however, are in every country socially and economically disadvantaged in practice and in fact and in many places by law. Therefore, their capacity to participate in public life is routinely circumscribed.

This gender bias, if unchallenged, becomes so embedded in the social structure that it often assumes the form of a social or cultural norm seemingly beyond the purview of the state's responsibility, rather than a violation of women's human rights for which the state is accountable. In some cases, even civil and political rights violations committed directly by state actors have been shrugged off as acceptable. For example, in 1986 a Peruvian prosecutor told an Amnesty International delegation visiting the state of Ayacucho that rape of civilian women by soldiers "was to be expected" when troops were conducting counter-insurgency operations.

When gender-neutral international human rights law is applied in these genders biased social contexts, those making the application-both governments and nongovernmental organizations-do not necessarily challenge the gender bias embedded in the social structure or in the state's determination of its responsibilities.

In past human rights practice, organizations often have not challenged the relegation of women and what happens to them to the private sphere, whether in law or in practice, and have allowed social or cultural justifications to deter them from denouncing restrictions on women's capacity to participate in public life. Even where abuses against women have occurred in realms they traditionally monitor, such as police custody, they have not consistently reported them. For example, only very recently have human rights organizations begun to report on rape of women prisoners as a form of torture. Thus, in the absence of a challenge to states' consistent relegation of women to the private sphere, application of inter-national law can have the effect of reinforcing, and to some extent replicating, the exclusion of women's rights abuses from the public sphere and therefore from the state's international obligations. In a very real sense, gender-specific abuses-even those directly attributable to states-have until recently been "privatized" internationally and either go unchallenged or are left out of human rights practice altogether. Nowhere is the effect on international human rights practice of the public/private split more evident than in the case of domestic violence-which literally happens "in private." States dismiss blatant and frequent crimes, including murder, rape, and physical abuse of women in the home, as private, family matters, upon which they routinely take no action. More-over, the state's failure to prosecute violence against women equally with other similar crimes or to guarantee women the fundamental civil and political right to equal protection of the law without regard to sex have largely escaped international condemnation.

At least four interrelated factors have caused the exclusion of domestic violence in particular from international human rights practice:

1. Traditional concepts of state responsibility under international law and practice;
2. Misconceptions about the nature and extent of domestic violence and states` responses to it;
3. The neglect of equality before and equal protection of the law without regard to sex as a governing human rights principle; and
4. The failure of states to recognize their affirmative obligation to provide remedies for domestic violence crimes. These factors, independently and in relationship to one another, are beginning to change and, with them, so is the treatment of domestic violence under international law. The following parts attempt to trace the course and direction of this emerging change.

The Concept of State Responsibility

The concept of state responsibility defines the limits of a government's accountability for human rights abuses under international law. Of course, all acts are done by real people, individually or with others, and not by the fictive "person" of the state. Therefore, responsibility is generally understood to arise only when an act by a real person or persons can be imputed to the state.

Traditionally, the idea of vicarious responsibility for acts is a perfectly acceptable one: such responsibility flows from the authorized acts of agents of the state, or persons acting with the apparent authority or condonation of the state. In traditional human rights practice states are held accountable only for what they do directly or through an agent, rendering acts of purely private individuals-such as domestic violence crimes-outside the scope of state responsibility.

More recently, however, the concept of state responsibility has expanded to include not only actions directly committed by states, but also states' systematic failure to prosecute acts committed either by low-level or para state agents or by private actors. In these situations, although the state does not actually commit the primary abuse, its failure to prosecute the abuse amounts to complicity in it. For instance, in three significant cases, Velasquez, Godiriez and Fairen, and Solis, decided by the Inter-American Court on Human Rights in 1988-1989, the tribunal found that the government of Honduras was responsible for a series of forced disappearances carried out between 1981 and

1984 by members of the Honduran military who were acting as private individuals.

The test of the state's responsibility for an act differs depending upon whether the actor is the state or a private individual.

To hold a state ac-countable for the actions of state actors, one of two things must be shown:

1. The state explicitly authorized the act (*i.e.*, a senior official committed or authorized it); or
2. The state systematically failed to prosecute abuses com-mitted by its agents, whether or not these acts were ordered by senior officials. In the latter case, one must usually show a pattern of non prosecution of acts that violate human rights, and that the state has agreed to enforce those human rights. For example, the state is responsible if it fails systematically to prohibit or prosecute torture, because the right to be free from torture is guaranteed under international law. Governments have agreed not to torture people themselves, and have undertaken to ensure that no one else in the state tortures. If the state failed to prosecute torturers, it would violate its international obligations. The test is different when the actors are private. For example, systematic non enforcement of laws against armed robbery by private actors alone is not a human rights problem; it merely indicates a serious common crime problem.

Non prosecution of the crimes of private individuals becomes a human rights issue (assuming no state action or direct complicity) only if the reason for the state's failure to prosecute can be shown to be rooted in discrimination along prohibited lines, such as those set forth in Article 26 of the Covenant on Civil and Political Rights. There are rights to bodily integrity in international human rights law which armed robbery appears to violate. However, these are rights against the state, not rights that states must enforce against all other persons. States cannot be held directly accountable for violent acts of all private individuals because all violent crime would then constitute a human rights abuse for which states could be held directly accountable under international law. The state's international obligation with regard to the acts of private individuals is to ensure that where it does protect people's lives, liberty, and security against private depredations, it must do so without discrimination on prohibited grounds. Therefore, there would have to be systematic, discriminatory none enforcement of the domestic criminal law against murder or assault for domestic violence to constitute a human rights issue, not merely a showing that the victims' lives ended or their bodies were harmed. The expansion of state responsibility to include accountability for some acts of private individuals is one of the factors necessary to permit analysis of domestic violence as a human rights violation. However, in many cases it is also necessary to show a pattern of discriminatory non-prosecution which amounts to a failure to guarantee equal protection of the law to women victims. The following part is an overview of new information about the vast extent of violence experienced by women and the frequency of its non- or discriminatory prosecution, which was revealed as a general characteristic, not merely a rare anomaly of domestic criminal law.

Widespread Violence and a Pattern of Non-Prosecution

As noted, domestic violence generally has been understood as a "private" matter in which governments should not interfere and for which they are not accountable. Traditionally the home has been idealized as a place of safety and security, a sanctuary from duty, responsibility, and work. The relationships between members of the family were also idealized as respectful and supportive. The reality is quite different, "modern studies suggest... and that much of this violence is directed at the female members of the family." New information on domestic violence has surfaced as a result of a long international campaign by women's rights groups to raise consciousness about women's issues.

After successfully pushing for the inclusion of a commitment to equal rights for women in the UN Charter and Universal Declaration of Human Rights, women's organizations worked for the establishment of the UN Commission on the Status of Women and other formal mechanisms for the advancement of women's status. The Commission and affiliated nongovernmental organizations (NGOs) drafted a variety of conventions to combat discrimination against women internationally and pressed for the General Assembly to declare a Decade for Women programme. It was the international resurgence of women's activism in the 1960s and 1970s, and the pressure generated by women's organizations internationally, that made the UN Decade for Women (1975-1985) a reality.

As the Decade unfolded, women's rights activists coordinated international efforts to study the position of women in all societies and the reasons for their subordinate status. In 1985, the participants at the Final Conference of the Decade for Women in Nairobi, Kenya, reached a consensus, that violence against women exists in various forms in everyday life in all societies. Women are beaten, mutilated, burned, sexually abused and raped. Such violence is a major obstacle to the achievement of peace and other objectives of the Decade and should be given special attention.... National machinery should be established in order to deal with the question of violence against women within the family and society.

In 1989, the UN Commission on the Status of Women in Vienna compiled a mass of domestic violence statistics and analyses by women's rights activists and academics, and published its report, Violence Against Women in the Family. The report's author reviewed over 250 Articles, books, and studies of various aspects of domestic violence, of which only ten had been published earlier than 1971. Furthermore, the report is only a small sample of the huge amount of new material being published about this old problem.

The report concluded: Women have been revealed as seriously deprived of basic human rights. Not only are women denied equality with the balance of the world's population, men, but also they are often denied liberty and dignity, and in many situations suffer direct violations of their physical and mental autonomy. Domestic violence has been revealed as widespread and gender-specific.

For example, in the United States a 1984 National Crime Survey found that women were victims of family violence at a rate three times that of men, and that of all spousal violence crimes, 91 per cent were victimizations of women by their husbands or ex-husbands. In Colombia during 1982 and 1983, the Forensic Institute of Bogota found that out of 1,170 cases of bodily injury, 20 per cent were due to marital violence against women. The Forensic Institute also determined that 94 per cent of persons hospitalized in bodily injury cases were battered women. In Thailand, a study in Bangkok revealed that more than 50 per cent of married women were beaten regularly by their husbands. And the reported number of women killed in dowry disputes in India almost doubled between 1985 and 1987, rising from 999 reports to 1,786 reports per year.

The Underlying Right to Equal Protection of the Law

The inclusion within the limits of state responsibility of failure to prosecute human rights abusers, whether by state agents or private individuals, is not-in and of itself-enough to position domestic violence within the human rights framework. Evidence of a state's failure to prosecute is not sufficient unless a pattern can be shown that reveals the failure to be gender discriminatory and thereby a violation of the internationally guar-anteed right to equal protection of the law. However, even though increased research into and understanding of domestic violence indicated that states were discriminating against women in the enforcement of criminal laws; gender-discrimination under international law was not a central human rights concern.

Until recently, sex discrimination has been visibly absent from the agendas of most governmental and nongovernmental bodies concerned with human rights, with the exception of the Committee on the Elimination of All Forms of

Discrimination Against Women, the UN body which monitors state conduct under the Convention on the Elimination of All Forms of Discrimination Against Women. The Committee and the other women's rights bodies located in Vienna have undertaken landmark work in holding governments accountable for discrimination on the basis of sex, whether by commission or omission. These organizations have made notable progress despite insufficient resources and limited enforcement mechanisms in the instruments they oversee.

However, and more importantly for the purposes of this chapter, the mainstream Geneva-based human rights bodies, which oversee instruments that have stronger protective mechanisms, have used the existence of this separate women's human rights regime as an excuse to marginalize sex discrimination and most other women's human rights violations, which nonetheless fall clearly within their own mandates. Within the cumulative human rights practice of governments and governmental bodies, sex discrimination has been de-emphasized and placed outside the rubric of central human rights concerns. International nongovernmental human rights organizations, including the two largest groups, Amnesty International and Human Rights Watch, have until recently reflected and perpetuated this trend.

7

Human Rights, Justice and Jurisdiction of the Court

HUMAN RIGHTS AND JUSTICE

Granted that oppression, suffering and dependence involve violations of justice and rights, how is this to be explained? Three ways of thinking about justice and rights are to be considered: (a) that developed in liberation theology; (b) the theories of justice and rights developed in our culture, within the liberal tradition; and (c) the conceptions of justice and rights within the social teaching of the Church. A critical comparison of these three approaches will show the key importance of the cultural factor in our understanding of justice and rights.

Liberation Theology

It is somewhat surprising to a reader from the "first world" that the literature on liberation theology makes infrequent appeal to the rights language which has become the typical language of protest in Western culture, and only relatively rarely appeals to the doctrine on human rights of official Roman Catholic social teaching. In Boff's account the experience of contrast provokes "ethical indignation." Such indignation or protest presupposes some positive awareness of the values being violated, otherwise it would be impossible for one to experience contrast. At this point, where one would anticipate some reference to the values of justice, no such reference is made. Though justice is mentioned quite frequently, it is usually in a rather general sense. Thus, for example, Boff explains how, in contact with the exploited social class of the poor, a person experiences a genuine encounter with the Lord and makes a commitment to justice, identified as the prime characteristic of the Kingdom of God. The epistemology of "this new discourse on faith," as Boff describes it, is concerned with the correct articulation of connections between faith and social conflicts, or salvation and historical liberation. It is noteworthy that the connection is to be made immediately between faith and social conflict. There does not seem to be any need, in this discourse, for an ethical analysis in terms of justice and rights, which might mediate between faith and social reality.

In Gustavo Gutierrez's major work, no particular importance is attached to detailed analyses of justice and rights. When the word "justice" is used, it has the broad meaning of "righteousness" or is given more specific content drawn from the Scriptures—for example, not keeping back the wages of the poor, not oppressing the alien, the orphan and the widow. The basic ethical issue is identified as one of conflict arising out of oppression and the striving for liberation; the fundamental issue is control and dependency. What was wrong with the developmental proposals of the past was that they were to be achieved within the existing structures of power without challenging them. What is called for is a break with the status quo, that is, a profound change of the private property system, access to power by the exploited class, and a social revolution that would break the structure of dependence and thus allow for the change to a new society. Together with this goes a tragic and conflictual picture of reality which, Gutiérrez argues, is not sufficiently acknowledged in such official Church documents as *Gaudium et Spes* and *Populorum Progressio*.

In his *Ethics and the Theology of Liberation*, Enrique Dussel bases his analysis on dependence, domination or exclusion from the centre, by which is meant the centre of power. In his later work, this author again focuses on the realities of dependence and oppression. He poses the question whether it is even possible to philosophize in a dependent culture. The answer might seem to be negative, since a dominating culture is one in which the ideology of the dominator has been adopted by the dominated, that is the colonized. However, there is another possibility, namely, that philosophical discourse take another point of departure, specifically from the opposition, the contrast or, as Dussel expresses it, the dissymetry between the polarities of centre/periphery, dominator/dominated, totality/exteriority. From this starting point he maps out a pattern of thinking in which politics introduces ethics, which then introduces philosophy. But, he does not find it necessary or appropriate to articulate the ethics in terms of justice or rights.

The notion of justice receives explicit treatment in José Míguez Bonino's *Towards a Christian Political Ethics*. However, Bonino is concerned first of all with what he calls a "theological determination of priorities." He criticizes Christian tradition with having given first place to order, or more precisely peace considered as order, in preference to justice. In Bonino's view, the requirements of justice must take priority over social and political order. Justice means "the right of the poor." Thus, the criterion of right government is the rights of the poor. This interpretation of justice is justified by direct appeal to the Scriptures and to some of the early Fathers. The notion of justice here would seem to have a close affinity with "the preferential option for the poor" which is fundamental to liberation theology. However, I think it is still true to say that where one would expect to find a developed ethics of justice and rights, these are absent. I will now examine two traditions which might be called upon to fill this gap.

Rights in the Liberal Tradition

The notion of rights has been developed in relationship with freedom. According to Wilhelm Weber, the idea of freedom which emerged from the Renaissance, the Enlightenment and the French Revolution began as an abstract idea of equal rights for all. As this proved too general, it could not be made operational and there arose two clearly divergent responses; on the one hand, that to advocate equal rights for all without changing the social and economic order was to promote a mere abstraction, and therefore what was required was precisely a change in the social and economic order; on the other, that any proposal to organize such a change of the social and economic order would be a threat to the rights of individuals which were held paramount. There thus emerged two profoundly different ideologies of freedom in the politics of the 19th and 20th centuries which have continued to the present. One is concerned with the generality, with the freedom of the totality. The other is concerned with the freedom of the individual and resistant to any notion of subsuming the individual under the totality.

From this historical division have emerged three basic conceptions. One takes its stand on the freedom of the individual and has as its central affirmation civil and political rights. This is the tradition of liberal democracy and the Western cultural tradition. The second affirms the centrality of social and economic rights, and has an affinity with the Marxist position. Christian social ethics, at least as articulated by some representatives from the first world, has proposed a "third way," in which civic and political rights are upheld, together with social and economic rights. The social teaching of the (Roman Catholic) Church has proposed its own version of such a third way.

In the Marxist view the rights claimed in the liberal tradition are those of the dominant members of a bourgeois civil society: they are those of egoistic persons separated from others and from the community. It is a question of preserving the liberty of the ego regarded as an isolated monad withdrawn into oneself. Thus, eagerness to preserve human rights is simply a mask for the love of money, property and bourgeois dominance. Only the communist society can guarantee the rights of man, namely, the rights to produce, to technical education which aids human mastery over human destiny, and to participate in the building of a new society. These are set forth as goals and guides for the State and for State bureaucratic authorities. The individual has rights only as a member of the socialist society, controlled in principle by the working class. This, in turn, guides the actions of the state and requires of the state active protection of all social rights. The individual has proper claims against bureaucratic structures when the structures prevent full participation in the socialist civil society.

It might be suggested, then, that the reticence in using the language of justice and rights is part and parcel of the assumption of Marxist categories by liberation theology. Such an answer would be an oversimplification. I would suggest that an examination of representative theories of justice and rights in the liberal tradition manifests the source of difficulty.

In John Rawls's theory of justice, for example, individual liberty has priority. Rawls's second principle, however, states that social and economic equalities are to be arranged so that they are both to the greatest benefit of the least advantaged and attached to offices and positions open to all under conditions of fair opportunity. Rawls's theory thus includes what might be called a type of "preference for the poor."

A trade off between individual liberty and other social goods would be permissible in certain social conditions, if it is necessary to raise the level of civilization to the point where basic needs have been generally met. If an actual historical situation were such that the conditions did not allow the effective realization of equal liberties, then Rawls's theory could rationally justify restrictions on liberty. But this would seem to be of little help when what is required is a radical transformation of the social conditions distorted by oppressive power structures. What is needed is not an abstract theory, but a conception of justice which can guide the transformation in actual historical circumstances.

The proprietarian theory of Robert Nozick is summed up in the slogan "From each as they choose, to each as they are chosen." His position could sanction a system in which the wealthy and their successors could maintain economic and legal privileges indefinitely and in which the less well off are caught in an endless cycle of relative deprivation. Other authors, such as Alan Gewirth develop a theory of rights by a closely reasoned analysis of the necessary conditions of human action, but do not seem to consider situations where actions, in concrete history, may be suppressed by distorted power relationships. It would seem clear that such theories of rights and justice are culture bound and inadequate to interpret the oppression and dependence of Central America or of Latin America as a whole.

The Social Teaching of the Church

The official statements of Church teaching in this area strongly defend a wide range of fundamental human rights. It is not being suggested that liberation theologians would ignore these rights. However, there are differences which may account for the absence of extensive reference to the social teaching of the Church in the work of liberation theologians. For some, at least, there is a dichotomy between liberation theology and the social teaching of the Church. The "Instruction on Certain Aspects of the 'Theology of Liberation'," for example, presumes that there are sharp differences.

The relationship between liberation theology and the social teachings of the Church calls for a more thorough treatment than I can provide here. However, there are reasons for thinking that one source of difficulty is cultural. A number of authors, among which Marie Dominique Chenu is one of the most forthright, have challenged the social teaching of the Church as having an ideological character. If so, the theologies of liberation would not be constructed on the basis of this social doctrine. Josef Ratzinger, in an earlier article, also criticized an ideological element in Catholic social doctrine. More recently Werner Kroh objected to its three level model where theological doctrine stands on the top, a separate and distinct social teaching structured in terms of the "natural law" on the next level, and practical implementation on a third. It is argued that the "natural law" component contains particular cultural features drawn in the main from Europe, which are given the status of the "natural" and thus assume a fixed, ideological character. Insofar as these alien but absolutized cultural elements are included within the natural law component of this teaching, theologians of liberation would justifiably have reservations about its applicability to their situation. Furthermore, the assumption of basic order and harmony and the consequent hesitation to accept the conflictual character of human reality, which has marked such teaching, might well be seen as not appropriate to a situation calling for the radical change of power relationships. There is reason then to suggest that both the rights theories from the liberal tradition and the social teaching of the Church contain elements which make it difficult for them to deal with a situation of distorted power relationships, such as that of Central America.

Granted these real shortcomings in the available theories of rights and justice, I would argue nevertheless that there is need for a more explicitly developed theory of justice within liberation theology as it has been developed in Latin America. For example, we need to be able to say explicitly why the increasing gap between rich and poor and why a condition of imposed dependency is wrong. Unless these points can be explained, moral norms cannot be formed for the action required to change the situation. Such a change, most would agree, is precisely what ought to be sought in Central America.

HUMAN RIGHTS AND GENDER JUSTICE IN INDIA

Gender injustice is a problem that is seen all over the world. But unless there are certain attitudinal changes, women will continue to get a raw deal. They need to be educated. Educated mothers take care of their children irrespective of the boys or girls. It is well known fact that the education of a girl is the education of family continuing its impact on the future generations while the education of a boy is the education of a single person. Women has to be treated as equal partners in decision-making and implementation rather than as beneficiaries. The development of a nation depends upon GDI that is, Gender Development Index and HDI that is Human Development Index. Our country ranks 98 for the former and 127 for latter.

In these days of globalization, the global picture of women is most ignoble and inequitable. Women constitute 50 per cent of the world's population, and account for 66 per cent of the work done, but they have only a share of 10 per cent in the world's income and own one per cent of the world's property.

Gender equity: Engendering all areas of public policy, elimination of adverse sex ratio, and provision of support services to working women, taking into account the multiple burden on a woman's day to day life. The psychology of industries in India weighs heavily against women. One of the reasons is that women in industry are to be given preferential welfare and social facilities and benefits. To avoid this, in the post-independence era, industries have preferred to reduce the number of women employees. Rajasthan and Madhya Pradesh bar people with more than two children from contesting the panchayat elections. Apart from being unconstitutional, in terms of gender implications, Health Watch (1999) pointed out, 'Do we really believe that the male would-be elected official, hungry for a seat, would not consider casting aside his current wife who has borne him more than the allowed number of children in favour of a new one with none or fewer?...The only people likely to be affected by an electoral restriction would in this case be the cast-off wife and the woman who cannot stand for office because it would mean abandoning her children.'

Further, it discriminates against women from backward areas, where the average total fertility rates (TFR) is above two and concentrated among the poorest and most disenfranchised of the Indian people, from staking their claim to elected bodies through the 33% reservations for women in the Panchayati Raj institutions. The TFR for Muslims, scheduled castes and tribes according to the latest NFHS-2 Survey is 3.6, 3.2, and 3.1 respectively.

In 1995, the UNDP introduced methods of calculating a gender-related development index (GDI) and a gender empowerment measure (GEM). In the Human Development Report 1997, a methodology was introduced for calculating a Human Poverty Index (HPI) based on deprivations in basic human needs. The Human Development Report 2001 has introduced indicators for measuring Technology Achievement (TAI). In HDI, GDI, GEM, HPI and TAI, India occupies a deplorably low position, although some marginal improvement has been noted in HDI in recent years. The major contribution of the human development reports is in sensitising nations on the need to accord greater priority to basic needs like nutrition, education, health, sustainable livelihoods and gender and social equity. As a result, political leaders in developing countries are now aspiring to work for a better rank for their countries in HDI. In India, this has resulted in Rajasthan, Madhya Pradesh and Tamil Nadu developing State level human development reports. To this extent, measurement and ranking are exerting a beneficial impact on priorities in public policies and investment. The development of a nation depends upon GDI that is, Gender Development Index and HDI that is Human Development Index. Our country ranks 98 for the former and 127 for latter.

There are many causes that add to gender in-justice, and almost each and every cause is the creation of human being. Whose main task is the protection of human rights of each and every human around him/her-all the humans present on this mother planet the Earth. The two main causes regarding the same are:

In different parts of the world, male chauvinism in different degrees has led to gender injustice. In some developed countries too, women were accorded the right to vote very late. They had to launch a determined struggle to secure the right of adult franchise. Even when women secured the right to vote, initially they did not receive in the legislatures the recognition they deserved on the basis of their merit and ability. If the social-reform programme is to be pursued vigorously, certain attitudinal changes are urgently called for. These comprise change of context, change of relations and change of values. Without such a comprehensive change in the existing value judgments of the present consumerist culture, the battle for gender justice cannot be won.

In India, with a highly utilitarian approach, poor parents do not aspire for a female child for two selfish reasons. Firstly, because of the fabulous dowry to be paid on the daughter's marriage, parents consider a daughter as a "financial liability". And, secondly, because the daughter has to leave the parents' house after marriage, she is no longer considered useful as an earning member of the family.

The instinctive urge, particularly of poor parents, is to prevent the birth of a female child. The most astounding statistics reveal that in a prominent hospital in Mumbai, the pre-sex determination tests revealed that during 1978-1982, nearly 8,000 pregnant women were expected to give birth to a female child. But to prevent this, 7,999 of them underwent abortions.

Article 21 of India's Constitution on "Protection of life and personal liberty" states: "No person shall be deprived of his life or personal liberty except according to procedure established by law." In the case of female children in the womb of expectant mothers, they are not only denied the right to live, but are robbed of their right even to be born, as revealed by the statistics mentioned earlier. This is the travesty of gender justice!

Human Deprivations In India or in other developing countries are largely due to the neglect of women. Human distresses in these countries could be minimized if adequate attention is paid to the empowerment of women , that nearly one quarter of our population is still below poverty line and about one fifth of the people are undernourished. There were 39% adult illiterates in 2003.

The commitment to gender equity is well entrenched at the highest policy making level-the constitution of India. A few important provisions for women are:

- Article 14 – equal rights and opportunities in political economics and social spheres.
- Article 15 – prohibits determination on grounds of sex.
- Article 15(3) – enables affirmative discrimination in favour of women.
- Article 39- equal means of livelihood and equal pay for equal work.
- Article 42 - just and humane conditions of work and maternity relief.
- Article 51(A)(e)-fundamental duty to renounce practices, derogatory to the dignity of women.

Apart from the above mentioned provisions, the legislation has also made certain policies such as National Policy for empowerment of women 2001etc. In various five year plans such as-Seventh plan, Eighth plan(1992-97), Ninth plan(1997-2002) and the Tenth plan, various schemes and policies were introduced. The battle for gender justice has been a long-drawn struggle.

The sustained efforts of several social reformers, even in the face of resistance from social orthodoxy, have given impetus to the cause of gender justice. Constitutional provisions, various laws, and judgements of courts have made their own contribution to the cause of gender justice. However, more fundamental is the work and role of social reformers who sought to change the mind-set of orthodox tradition-bound society and usher in women's reforms in the social, economic and educational fields.

Despite resistance from orthodoxy, women's education gradually acquired greater acceptance. In the old orthodox society the Sati system of widows mounting the funeral pyre of their husbands was an atrocious practice.

If this practice was gradually discarded, it was not only because of the Sati Prohibition Act in Bengal in 1829 at the behest of Bentinck, Governor-General, but mainly due to the social reform movement against the Sati system carried on by the eminent social reformer Raja Rammohan Roy.

Though the Sati system is banned under law, in isolated cases it is still implemented in a clandestine way due both to remnants of orthodox beliefs, and to machinations by the relatives of the widow to garner her wealth and property by forcing her to mount the funeral pyre of her dead husband.

Still, there are efforts to continue to build a halo of sanctity around the Sati system. This only amounts to a glorification of gender injustice and has to be resisted through an awakened public opinion.

Gender injustice is a problem that is seen all over the world. What ever the causes may be, it is our that, is the duty of humans to protect the human rights of those who are victims.

Even though the government is trying to take care of this natural right by formulating various policies, enacting and formulating laws. This is not a one man's job – entire humanity will have to join hands. As already mentioned above that development of a nation depends upon Human Development Index, how will we Indians be able to live in a developed nation? As again and again said by our Hon'ble President A.P.J. Abdul Kalam that India must be a developed nation by 2020. How will the statistics improve if we do not take care about it. Education is a need because the children of educated mothers improve their capabilities and thereby enlarge their choices enjoying long and healthy life, educated environment and having access to better educated qualifications.

CRIMES WITHIN THE JURISDICTION OF THE COURT

Article 5 of the Rome Statute grants the court jurisdiction over four groups of crimes, which it refers to as the "most serious crimes of concern to the international community as a whole": the crime of genocide, crimes against humanity, war crimes, and the crime of aggression. The statute defines each of these crimes except for aggression: it provides that the court will not exercise its jurisdiction over the crime of aggression until such time as the states parties agree on a definition of the crime and set out the conditions under which it may be prosecuted. In June 2010, the ICC's first review conference in Kampala, Uganda adopted amendments defining "crimes of aggression" and expanding the ICC's jurisdiction over them. The ICC will not be allowed to prosecute for this crime until at least 2017. Furthermore, it expanded the term of war crimes for the use of certain weapons in an armed conflict not of an international character.

Many states wanted to add terrorism There is no universally agreed, legally binding, criminal law definition of terrorism.Common definitions of terrorism refer only to those violent acts which are intended to create fear (terror), are perpetrated for a religious, political or ideological goal, deliberately target or disregard the safety of non-combatants (civilians), and are committed by non-government agencies. Some definitions also include acts of unlawful violence and war. The use of similar tactics by criminal organizations for protection rackets or to enforce a code of silence is usually not labeled terrorism though these same actions may be labeled terrorism when done by a politically motivated group.

The word "terrorism" is politically and emotionally charged,and this greatly compounds the difficulty of providing a precise definition. Studies have found over 100 definitions of "terrorism". The concept of terrorism may itself be controversial as it is often used by state authorities to delegitimize political or other opponents, and potentially legitimize the state's own use of armed force against opponents (such use of force may itself be described as "terror" by opponents of the state). Terrorism has been practiced by a broad array of political organizations for furthering their objectives. It has been practiced by both right-wing and left-wing political parties, nationalistic groups, religious groups, revolutionaries, and ruling governments.An abiding characteristic is the indiscriminate use of violence against noncombatants for the purpose of gaining publicity for a group, cause, or individual.) and drug trafficking to the list of crimes covered by the Rome Statute; however, the states were unable to agree on a definition for terrorism and it was decided not to include drug trafficking as this might overwhelm the court's limited resources.

India lobbied to have the use of nuclear weapons A nuclear weapon is an explosive device that derives its destructive force from nuclear reactions, either fission or a combination of fission and fusion. Both reactions release vast quantities of energy from relatively small amounts of matter. The first fission ("atomic") bomb test released the same amount of energy as approximately 20,000 tons of TNT. The first thermonuclear ("hydrogen") bomb test released the same amount of energy as approximately 10,000,000 tons of TNT.

A modern thermonuclear weapon weighing little more than 2,400 pounds (1,100 kg) can produce an explosive force comparable to the detonation of more than 1.2 million tons (1.1 million metric tons) of TNT. Thus, even a small nuclear device no larger than traditional bombs can devastate an entire city by blast, fire and radiation. Nuclear weapons are considered weapons of mass destruction, and their use and control has been a major focus of international relations policy since their debut.

Only two nuclear weapons have been used in the course of warfare, both by the United States near the end of World War II. On 6 August 1945, a uranium gun-type device code-named "Little Boy" was detonated over the Japanese city of Hiroshima. Three days later, on 9 August, a plutonium implosion-type device code-named "Fat Man" was exploded over Nagasaki, Japan. These two bombings resulted in the deaths of approximately 200,000 Japanese people—mostly civilians—from acute injuries sustained from the explosions. The role of the bombings in Japan's surrender, and their ethical status, remain the subject of scholarly and popular debate. Since the bombings of Hiroshima and Nagasaki, nuclear weapons have been detonated on over two thousand occasions for testing purposes and demonstrations.

Only a few nations possess such weapons or are suspected of seeking them. The only countries known to have detonated nuclear weapons—and that acknowledge possessing such weapons—are (chronologically by date of first test) the United States, the Soviet Union (succeeded as a nuclear power by Russia), the United Kingdom, France, the People's Republic of China, India, Pakistan, and North Korea. In addition, Israel is also widely believed to possess nuclear weapons, though it does not acknowledge having them.

One state, South Africa, has admitted to having previous fabricated nuclear weapons in the past, but has since disassembled their arsenal and submitted to international safeguards.) and other weapons of mass destruction(A weapon of mass destruction (WMD) is a weapon that can kill and bring significant harm to a large number of humans (and other life forms) and/or cause great damage to man-made structures (*e.g.* buildings), natural structures (*e.g.* mountains), or the biosphere in general. The scope and application of the term has evolved and been disputed, often signifying more politically than technically.

Coined in reference to aerial bombing with chemical explosives, it has come to distinguish large-scale weaponry of other technologies, such as chemical, biological, radiological, or nuclear. This differentiates the term from more technical ones such as chemical, biological, radiological, and nuclear weapons (CBRN).) included as war crimes but this move was also defeated. India has expressed concern that "the Statute of the ICC lays down, by clear implication, that the use of weapons of mass destruction is not a war crime.

This is an extraordinary message to send to the international community." Some commentators have argued that the Rome Statute defines crimes too broadly or too vaguely. For example, China has argued that the definition of 'war crimes' goes beyond that accepted under customary international law. Customary international law are those aspects of international law that derive from custom. Along with general principles of law and treaties, custom is considered by the International Court of Justice, jurists, the United Nations, and its member states to be among the primary sources of international law.

For example, laws of war were long a matter of customary law before they were codified in the Hague Conventions of 1899 and 1907, Geneva Conventions, and other treaties. The vast majority of the world's governments accept in principle the existence of customary international law, although there are many differing opinions as to what rules are contained in it.

The Statute of the International Court of Justice acknowledges the existence of customary international law in Article 38(1)(b), incorporated into the United Nations Charter by Article 92: "The Court, whose function is to decide in accordance with international law such disputes as are submitted to it, shall apply...international custom, as evidence of a general practice accepted as law."

Customary international law "... consists of rules of law derived from the consistent conduct of States acting out of the belief that the law required them to act that way." It follows that customary international law can be discerned by a "widespread repetition by States of similar international acts over time (State practice); Acts must occur out of sense of obligation (opinio juris); Acts must be taken by a significant number of States and not be rejected by a significant number of States." A marker of customary international law is consensus among states exhibited both by widespread conduct and a discernible sense of obligation.

A peremptory norm (also called jus cogens, Latin for "compelling law") is a fundamental principle of international law which is accepted by the international community of states as a norm from which no derogation is ever permitted.

Examples include various international crimes; a state which carries out or permits slavery, torture, genocide, war of aggression, or crimes against humanity is always violating customary international law. Other examples accepted or claimed as customary international law include the principle of non-refoulement, immunity of visiting foreign heads of state, and the right to humanitarian intervention.)

Territorial jurisdiction

During the negotiations that led to the Rome Statute, a large number of states argued that the court should be allowed to exercise universal jurisdiction

Universal jurisdiction or universality principle is a principle in public international law (as opposed to private international law) whereby states claim criminal jurisdiction over persons whose alleged crimes were committed outside the boundaries of the prosecuting state, regardless of nationality, country of residence, or any other relation with the prosecuting country. The state backs its claim on the grounds that the crime committed is considered a crime against all, which any state is authorized to punish, as it is too serious to tolerate jurisdictional arbitrage.

The concept of universal jurisdiction is therefore closely linked to the idea that certain international norms are erga omnes, or owed to the entire world community, as well as the concept of jus cogens–that certain international law obligations are binding on all states and cannot be modified by treaty.

According to critics, the principle justifies a unilateral act of wanton disregard of the sovereignty of a nation or the freedom of an individual concomitant to the pursuit of a vendetta or other ulterior motives, with the obvious assumption that the person or state thus disenfranchised is not in a position to bring retaliation to the state applying this principle.

The concept received a great deal of prominence with Belgium's 1993 "law of universal jurisdiction", which was amended in 2003 in order to reduce its scope following a case before the International Court of Justice regarding an arrest warrant issued under the law, entitled Case Concerning the Arrest Warrant of 11 April 2000 (Democratic Republic of the Congo v.

Belgium). The creation of the International Criminal Court (ICC) in 2002 reduced the perceived need to create universal jurisdiction laws, although the ICC is not entitled to judge crimes committed before 2002. According to Amnesty International, a proponent of universal jurisdiction, certain crimes pose so serious a threat to the international community as a whole, that states have a logical and moral duty to prosecute an individual responsible for it; no place should be a safe haven for those who have committed genocide, crimes against humanity, extrajudicial executions, war crimes, torture and forced disappearances.

Opponents, such as Henry Kissinger, argue that universal jurisdiction is a breach on each state's sovereignty: all states being equal in sovereignty, as affirmed by the United Nations Charter, "Widespread agreement that human rights violations and crimes against humanity must be prosecuted has hindered active consideration of the proper role of international courts. Universal jurisdiction risks creating universal tyranny—that of judges." According to Kissinger, as a practical matter, since any number of states could set up such universal jurisdiction tribunals, the process could quickly degenerate into politically-driven show trials to attempt to place a quasi-judicial stamp on a state's enemies or opponents.

The United Nations Security Council Resolution 1674, adopted by the United Nations Security Council on April 28, 2006, "Reaffirmed the provisions of paragraphs 138 and 139 of the 2005 World Summit Outcome Document regarding the responsibility to protect populations from genocide, war crimes, ethnic cleansing and crimes against humanity" and commits the Security Council to action to protect civilians in armed conflict.) However, this proposal was defeated due in large part to opposition from the United States.

A compromise was reached, allowing the court to exercise jurisdiction only under the following limited circumstances:

- Where the person accused of committing a crime is a national of a state party (or where the person's state has accepted the jurisdiction of the court);
- Where the alleged crime was committed on the territory of a state party (or where the state on whose territory the crime was committed has accepted the jurisdiction of the court); or
- Where a situation is referred to the court by the UN Security Council.

Temporal jurisdiction

The court's jurisdiction does not apply retroactively: it can only prosecute crimes committed on or after 1 July 2002 (the date on which the Rome Statute entered into force). Where a state becomes party to the Rome Statute after that date, the court can exercise jurisdiction automatically with respect to crimes committed after the statute enters into force for that state.

Complementarity

The ICC is intended as a court of last resort, investigating and prosecuting only where national courts have failed.

Article 17 of the Statute provides that a case is inadmissible if:

- The case is being investigated or prosecuted by a State which has jurisdiction over it, unless the State is unwilling or unable genuinely to carry out the investigation or prosecution;
- The case has been investigated by a State which has jurisdiction over it and the State has decided not to prosecute the person concerned, unless the decision resulted from the unwillingness or inability of the State genuinely to prosecute;
- The person concerned has already been tried for conduct which is the subject of the complaint, and a trial by the Court is not permitted under article 20, paragraph 3;

- The case is not of sufficient gravity to justify further action by the Court."

Article 20, paragraph 3, specifies that, if a person has already been tried by another court, the ICC cannot try them again for the same conduct unless the proceedings in the other court:

- Were for the purpose of shielding the person concerned from criminal responsibility for crimes within the jurisdiction of the Court; or
- Otherwise were not conducted independently or impartially in accordance with the norms of due process recognized by international law and were conducted in a manner which, in the circumstances, was inconsistent with an intent to bring the person concerned to justice."

JUDICIAL DIVISIONS

The Judicial Divisions consist of the 18 judges of the court, organized into three divisions—the Pre-Trial Division, Trial Division and Appeals Division—which carry out the judicial functions of the court. Judges are elected to the court by the Assembly of States Parties. They serve nine-year terms and are not generally eligible for re-election. All judges must be nationals of states parties to the Rome Statute, and no two judges may be nationals of the same state. They must be "persons of high moral character, impartiality and integrity who possess the qualifications required in their respective States for appointment to the highest judicial offices".

The Prosecutor or any person being investigated or prosecuted may request the disqualification of a judge from "any case in which his or her impartiality might reasonably be doubted on any ground". Any request for the disqualification of a judge from a particular case is decided by an absolute majority of the other judges. A judge may be removed from office if he or she "is found to have committed serious misconduct or a serious breach of his or her duties" or is unable to exercise his or her functions. The removal of a judge requires both a two-thirds majority of the other judges and a two-thirds majority of the states parties.

Office of the Prosecutor

The Office of the Prosecutor is responsible for conducting investigations and prosecutions. It is headed by the Prosecutor, who is assisted by two Deputy Prosecutors.

The Rome Statute provides that the Office of the Prosecutor shall act independently; as such, no member of the Office may seek or act on instructions from any external source, such as states, international organisations, An international organization (or organisation) is an organization with an international membership, scope, or presence.

There are two main types:

1. *International Nongovernmental Organizations (INGOs):* Non-governmental organizations (NGOs) that operate internationally. These may be either:
   - International non-profit organizations. Examples include the International Olympic Committee, World Organization of the Scout Movement, International Committee of the Red Cross and Medecins Sans Frontieres.
   - International corporations, referred to as multinational corporations. Examples include The Coca-Cola Company, Sony, Nintendo, McDonalds, and Toyota.
2. *Intergovernmental Organizations, Also Known as international Governmental Organizations (IGOs):* The type of organization most closely associated with the term 'international organization', these are organizations that are made up primarily of sovereign states referred to as member states). Notable examples include the United Nations (UN), Organization for Security and Co-operation in Europe (OSCE), Council of Europe (CoE), European Union (EU; which is a prime example of a supranational organization), European Patent Organisation and World Trade Organization (WTO). The UN has used the term "intergovernmental organization" instead of "international organization" for clarity.

In addition, Global Public Policy Networks (GPPNs) may be considered a third category. These take various forms and may be made up of states and non-state actors.

Non-state actors involved in GPPNs may include: intergovernmental organizations, states, state agencies, regional or municipal governments, in partnerships with non-governmental organizations, private companies, etc.) non-governmental organisations.

A non-governmental organization (NGO) is a legally constituted organization created by natural or legal persons that operates independently from any government and a term usually used by governments to refer to entities that have no government status. In the cases in which NGOs are funded totally or partially by governments, the NGO maintains its non-governmental status by excluding government representatives from membership in the organization. The term is usually applied only to organizations that pursue some wider social aim that has political aspects, but that are not overtly political organizations such as political parties. Unlike the term "intergovernmental organization", the term "non-governmental organization" has no generally agreed legal definition. In many jurisdictions, these types of organization are called "civil society organizations" or referred to by other names.

The number of internationally operating NGOs is estimated at 40,000. National numbers are even higher: Russia has 277,000 NGOs; India is estimated to have around 3.3 million NGOs.) or individuals.

The Prosecutor may open an investigation under three circumstances:

- When a situation is referred to him by a state party;

When a situation is referred to him by the United Nations Security Council The United Nations Security Council (UNSC) is one of the principal organs of the United Nations and is charged with the maintenance of international peace and security. Its powers, outlined in the United Nations Charter, include the establishment of peacekeeping operations, the establishment of international sanctions, and the authorization of military action. Its powers are exercised through United Nations Security Council resolutions. The Security Council held its first session on 17 January 1946 at Church House, London. Since its first meeting, the Council, which exists in continuous session, has travelled widely, holding meetings in many cities, such as Paris and Addis Ababa, as well as at its current permanent home at the United Nations Headquarters in New York City.

There are 15 members of the Security Council, consisting of five veto-wielding permanent members (China, France, Russia, the United Kingdom, and the United States) and 10 elected non-permanent members with two-year terms. This basic structure is set out in Chapter V of the UN Charter. Security Council members must always be present at UN headquarters in New York so that the Security Council can meet at any time. This requirement of the United Nations Charter was adopted to address a weakness of the League of Nations since that organization was often unable to respond quickly to a crisis.) acting to address a threat to international peace and security; or

- When the Pre-Trial Chamber authorises him to open an investigation on the basis of information received from other sources, such as individuals or non-governmental organisations.

Any person being investigated or prosecuted may request the disqualification of a prosecutor from any case "in which their impartiality might reasonably be doubted on any ground". Requests for the disqualification of prosecutors are decided by the Appeals Division.A prosecutor may be removed from office by an absolute majority of the states parties if he or she "is found to have committed serious misconduct or a serious breach of his or her duties" or is unable to exercise his or her functions.

However, critics of the court argue that there are "insufficient checks and balances on the authority of the ICC prosecutor and judges" and "insufficient protection against politicized prosecutions or other abuses". Henry Kissinger says the checks and balances are so weak that the prosecutor "has virtually unlimited discretion in practice". As of 16 June 2003, the Prosecutor has been Luis Moreno Ocampo of Argentina, who was elected by the Assembly of States Parties on 21 April 2003 for a term of nine years.

Registry

The Registry is responsible for the non-judicial aspects of the administration and servicing of the court. This includes, among other things, "the administration of legal aid matters, court management, victims and witnesses matters, defence counsel, detention unit, and the traditional services provided by administrations in international organisations, such as finance, translation, building management, procurement and personnel".

The Registry is headed by the Registrar, who is elected by the judges to a five-year term. The current Registrar is Silvana Arbia, who was elected on 28 February 2009.

Headquarters, offices and detention unit

The official seat of the court is in The Hague, Netherlands, but its proceedings may take place anywhere. The court is currently housed in interim premises on the eastern edge of The Hague.

The court intends to construct permanent premises in the Alexanderkazerne, to the north of The Hague.

The ICC also maintains a liaison office in New York and field offices in places where it conducts its activities. As of 18 October 2007, the court had field offices in Kampala, Kinshasa, Bunia, Abeche and Bangui. The ICC's detention centre The ICC currently has twelve detention cells in a Dutch prison in Scheveningen, The Hague.Suspects held by the International Criminal Tribunal for the former Yugoslavia are held in the same prison and share some facilities, like the fitness room, but have no contact with suspects held by the ICC.

The ICC registrar is responsible for managing the detention centre.The rules governing detainment are contained in Chapter 6 of the Regulations of the Court and Chapter 5 of the Regulations of the Registry. The International Committee of the Red Cross (ICRC) has unrestricted access to the detention centre.

Facilities

Each individual has his own toilet and washing area. They have access to a small gym and are offered training with a physical education instructor. Detainees are provided with meals, but they may also cook for themselves, purchase food from the prison shop, and have ingredients ordered in. However, Charles Taylor's lawyers have complained that "the food which is served is completely eurocentric and not palatable to the African palate".

Each detainee has a personal computer in his cell, on which he can view material related to their case. They are offered computer training, if required,and language courses.)comprises twelve cells on the premises of the Scheveningen branch of the Haaglanden Penal Institution, The Hague.Suspects held by the International Criminal Tribunal for the former Yugoslavia The International Tribunal for the Prosecution of Persons Responsible for Serious Violations of International Humanitarian Law Committed in the Territory of the Former Yugoslavia since 1991, more commonly referred to as the International Criminal Tribunal for the former Yugoslavia or ICTY, is a body of the United Nations established to prosecute serious crimes committed during the wars in the former Yugoslavia, and to try their perpetrators. The tribunal is an ad hoc court which is located in The Hague, the Netherlands.

The Court was established by Resolution 827 of the United Nations Security Council, which was passed on 25 May 1993. It has jurisdiction over four clusters of crime committed on the territory of the former Yugoslavia since 1991: grave breaches of the Geneva Conventions, violations of the laws or customs of war, genocide, and crime against humanity. The maximum sentence it can impose is life imprisonment. Various countries have signed agreements with the UN to carry out custodial sentences. The last indictment was issued 15 March 2004. The Tribunal aims to complete all trials by the middle of 2011 and all appeals by 2013, with the exception of Radovan Karadžiæ whose trial is expected to end in 2012 and the appeal to be heard by February 2014. Ratko Mladiæ and Goran Hadaia have been charged, however are still at large and thus do not fall within the court's completion strategy.

The International Criminal Tribunal for the former Yugoslavia should not be confused with the International Criminal Court and the International Court of Justice; both courts are also based in The Hague, but have a permanent status and different jurisdictions) are held in the same prison and share some facilities, like the fitness room, but have no contact with suspects held by the ICC.The detention unit is close to the ICC's future headquarters in the Alexanderkazerne.

As of February 2011, the detention centre houses six suspects: Thomas Lubanga, Germain Katanga, Mathieu Ngudjolo Chui, Jean-Pierre Bemba, Callixte Mbarushimana and also former Liberian President Charles Taylor. Taylor is being tried under the mandate and auspices of the Special Court for Sierra Leone, but his trial is being held at the ICC's facilities in The Hague because of political and security concerns about holding the trial in Freetown. The ICC does not have its own witness protection programme, but rather must rely on national programmes to keep witnesses safe.

DEVELOPMENT OF THE CONSTITUTION

The Constitution of the Indian Republic is the product not of a political revolution out of the research and deliberations of a body of eminent representative of the people (who sought to improve upon then existing system of administration). This very fact makes a retrospect of the constitutional development indispensible for a proper understanding of this Constitution.

Government of India Act; 1858

The British Crown assumed sovereignty over India in 1858 and Parliament enacted the first salute for the governance of India under the direct rule of the British Government. By this Act, the powers of Crown were to be exercised by the Secretary of State for India assisted by a Council of fifteen members. The Secretary of State, who was responsible to the British Parliament, governed India through the Governor–General, assisted by an Executive Council.

Indian council Act 1861

The Indian Council Act of 1861 introduced a grain of popular element as it provided that the Governor General's Executive Council should include certain additional non-official members. The Act transact legislative business as Legislative Council. But this Council was neither representative nor deliberative in any sense.

Indian Council Act 1892

The Indian Council Act 1892 introduced two improvement namely (a) that the non-official members of the Indian Legislative Council were henceforth to be nominated by the Bengal chamber of Commerce and the Provincial Council were to be nominated by certain local bodies such as universities, district boards, municipalities; (b) the Councils were to have the power the discussing the annual statement of revenue and expenditure, *i.e.*, the Budged and of addressing questions to the Executive, But the Act retained the majority of official members.

Morley–Minto Reforms

The first attempt of introducing a representative and popular element was made by Morley-Minto Reforms which were implemented by the Indian Council Act, 1909. The size of Provincial Legislative councils was enlarged by including elected non-official members so then the -member of official majority had gone up. An element of election was also introduced in the Legislative Council at the Centre but the official majority was maintained.

The deliberative functions of the Legislative Councils were also increased by giving them the opportunity of influencing the policy of administration and on any matter of public interest except certain specified subjects, such as the Armed Forces, Foreign Affairs and the Indian States. The positive vice of th Act of 1909 was that it provided for the first time for separate representation of Muslim Community and thus sowed the seeds of separatism.

Indian Council's Act of 1919

The next landmark in the Constitutional development of India is the Montagu–Chelmsford Report which led to the enactment of Government of India Act, 1919.

The Indian National Congress became more active during the first World War and started its campaign for self-government. In response to this popular demand the British Government made a declaration on August 20, 1917 that the policy of British Government was that of increasing association of Indians in every branch of administration and the gradual development of self governing institutions.

The then Secretary of State for India (Montagu) and the Governor – General (Chelmsford) entrusted the task and gave a legal shape to their recommendations as Government of India Act 1919.

The main features of the system introduced by this Act were as follows:

Dyarchy in the Provinces

Responsible government in the Provinces was sought to be introduced for the administration of the Province, by resorting to device known as 'Dyarchy' or dual government. The subjects of administration were to be divided into two categories-Central and Provincial. The Central subjects were those which were exclusively kept under the control of the Central Government. The Provincial subjects were subdivided into 'transferred' and 'reserved' subjects. The transferred subjects were to be administered by the Governor with the aid of Ministers responsible to legislative Council. The reserved subjects were to be administered by the Governor and his Executive council without any responsibility to the legislature.

Relaxation of Central control over the Provinces

Broadly speaking subjects, of all India importance were brought under the category of 'Central control over the provinces not only in administrative but also in legislative and financial matters. This devolution of power to the provinces should not be mistaken for a federal distribution of powers. But provinces got power by way of delegation from the Centre.

The Indian Legislature was made more Representative

The Indian Legislature was made more representative and for the first time, bi-cameral. It was to consist of an Upper House, named the Council of State, composed of 60 members of whom 34 were elected, about 144 members of whom 104 were elected.

But there were also certain shortcomings of the 1919 Act. Firstly the structure still remained unitary and centralized 'with the governor-general in Council as the keystone of the whole constitutional edifice; and it is through the governor-general in Council that the Secretary of State and ultimately, Parliament discharged their responsibilities for peace, order and good government of India. Secondly the great dissatisfaction was the working of Dyarchy in the provincial sphere. The Governor came to dominate ministerial policy by means of his overriding financial powers and control over the official block in the Legislature. The main defect of the system from the Indian standpoint was the control of the purse.

Bibliography

Anaya, S. James: *Indigenous Peoples in International Law*. Oxford: Oxford University Press, 1996.

Arat, Zehra F.: *Democracy and Human Rights in Developing Countries*. Boulder, Colorado: Lynne Rienner Publishers, 1991.

Asha, K. : *Globalization, Democracy and Culture : Situating Gandhian Alternatives,* Jaipur, Pointer, 2002.

Azmi, Majaz : *Muslim Wife,* Idara Ishaat-e-Diniyat Pvt. Ltd, New Delhi, 1991.

Bell, Daniel A.: *East meets West. Human rights and democracy in East Asia,* Princeton, Princeton University Press, 2000.

Brems, Eva: *Human Rights: Universality and Diversity*. The Hague: Martinus Nijhoff Publishers, 2001.

Brems, Eva: *Human Rights: Universality and Diversity*. The Hague: Martinus Nijhoff Publishers, 2001.

Bronstein, P. A.: *Teaching a Psychology of People,* Washington, American Psychological Association, 1988.

Calman, J.: *Toward Empowerment: Women and Politics in India,* Colorado, Westview Press, 1992.

Cassese, Antonio: *Human Rights in a Changing World*. Philadelphia: Temple University Press, 1991.

Chung, Him. *Indian Rural Market Development in the Reform Era.* Aldershot, Hants, England; Burlington, VT: Ashgate, 2004.

David P.: *Human Rights and World Politics*. Second Edition. Lincoln: University of Nebraska Press, 1989.

Davis, Michael C.: *Chinese Values and Human Rights,* Hong Kong: Oxford University Press, 1995.

Edward, Mortimer : *Faith and Power, the Politics of Islam,* Oxford, New York, 2002.

El-Hinnawi, E.: *Environmental Refugees.* Nairobi: United Nations Environment Programme, 1985.

Fine, M.: *Women with Disabilities: Essays in Psychology, Culture, and Politics*, Philadelphia, Temple University Press, 1988.

Forsythe, David P.: *Human Rights and World Politics*. Second Edition. Lincoln: University of Nebraska Press, 1989.

Gilligan, C.: *In a Different Voice: Psychological Theory and Women's Development,*Cambridge, Harvard University Press, 1993.

Hannum, Hurst: *Autonomy, Sovereignty, and Self - Determination: The Accommodation of Conflicting Rights*. Philadelphia: University of Pennsylvania Press, 1990.

Hausman, D. M.: *The Inexact and Separate Science of Economics*, Cambridge, Cambridge University Press, 1992.

Jacobson, David : *Rights Across Borders: Immigration and the Decline of Citizenship*. Baltimore and London: The Johns Hopkins University Press, 1997.

Kegan, R.: *In Over our Heads: The Mental Demands of Modern Life,* Cambridge, Harvard University Press, 1994.

Khan, M A : *Social Work and Social Policy, Concepts and Methods*, Book Enclave, Delhi, 2007.

Kimlycka, Will: *The Rights of Minority Cultures*. Oxford and New York: Oxford University Press, 1995.

Matsumodo, D.: *People: Psychology from a Cultural Perspective*, Pacific Grove, Brooks/ Cole, 1994.

Mayer, Ann E.: *Islam and Human Rights: Tradition and Politics*. Oxford and Boulder: Westview Press, 1999.

Medawar, J.: *The History of Family Planning in Britain*, England, Penguin, 1971.

Monshipouri, Mahmood: *Democratization, Liberalization, and Human Rights in the Third World*, Boulder, Colorado: Lynne Reinner Publishers, 1995.

Musgrave, Thomas D.: *Self-Determination and National Minorities*. Oxford: Clarendon Press, 1997.

Pennings, J. M.: *Decision Making, An Organizational Behaviour Approach,* New York, Markus Wiener Publishing, 1983.

Peter R.: *Human Rights: Chinese and Dutch Perspectives,* The Hague: Kluwer Law International, 1996.

Prasad, Kiran : *Women, Globalization and Mass Media : International Facets of Emancipation*, The Women Press, Delhi, 2006.

Reynard, A.: *Human Rights in Prisons,* Strasbourg: Council of Europe, 1986.

Ross, J.A.: *Family Planning and Child Survival Programs as Assessed in 1991*, New York, Population Council, 1992.

Stephen C.: *Human Rights and Chinese Thought: A Cross-Cultural Inquiry,* New York: Cambridge University Press, 2002.

Ware, H.: *Prepared for the Expert Group Meeting on Population and Women*, Gaborone, Botswana, 1992.

Weber, M.: *The Theory of Social and Economic Organizations*, New York, Oxford University Press, 1947.

Weber, Max: *Citizenship in Ancient and Medieval Cities*. Minneapolis, MN: The University of Minnesota, 1998.

Whelder, B.: *The Psychology of the Child,* New York, Basic Books, 1964.

Zehra F.: *Democracy and Human Rights in Developing Countries*. Boulder, Colorado: Lynne Rienner Publishers, 1991.

Index

❑❑❑